THE WORLD
THAT WAS OURS
The Story of the Rivonia Trial

Hilda Bernstein

SAWriters

London

Published by SAWriters
an imprint of Robert Vicat Ltd
25A Greencroft Gardens, London NW6 3LN

ISBN 1 872086 01 2 (cased)
ISBN 1 872086 00 4 (paperback)

Set in 10/12 pt ITC Garamond by Robert Vicat Ltd, London
Printed and bound in Great Britain by
Richard Clay Ltd., Bungay, Suffolk

This book is dedicated to the men of Rivonia:

Nelson Rolinhlala Mandela
Walter Max Ulyate Sisulu
Ahmed Mohamed Kathrada
Denis Theodore Goldberg
Govan Archibald Mbeki
Raymond Mhlaba
Elias Motsoaledi
Andrew Mlangeni
Lionel Bernstein

And to their counsel:

Abram Fischer

Note on the 'Special Branch'

The political arm of the South African police was originally established during the Second World War, and called the 'Special Branch'. Some years later, it was renamed the 'Security Police'. Because we had become so accustomed to the term 'Special Branch', I have used both these terms in the book; and sometimes 'SBs', which is simply our generic title for the same thing.

Acknowledgement

Permission to include the verse from Laurence Binyon's poem 'The Burning of Leaves' has been granted by The Society of Authors as the literary representative of the Estate of Laurence Binyon.

Contents

Now is the time for stripping the spirit bare
Time for the burning of days ended and done,
Idle solace of things that have gone before;
Rootless hope and fruitless desire are there.
Let them go to the fire, with never a look behind.
The world that was ours is a world that is no more.

Laurence Binyon

FOREWORD

There came a time when it seemed as though the ground was no longer firm beneath our feet; as though the world had tilted and we were uncertain about each step.

But this was not only a personal concern. The same sense of disorientation existed in the organizations within which we worked. It was not so much a loss of direction; there was no doubt about what we believed, what we were working for; no hesitation in political aims. The uncertainty arose from the blows we had received, as though we were concussed by the widespread arrests, the jailings and bannings, the loss of those who had escaped across the borders to safer countries; the iron clamps placed on speech, publications, activities, even social associations.

The personal/domestic and the public/political, two facets of our lives that had existed side by side for so long, were now fused together, sand grains coalesced into a solid lump of glass.

We had long been accustomed to the intrusions into our house; the permanent tapping of our phones, the listening devices, the watch kept on our home and all who entered; to the limitations on our social life, the prohibitions against seeing old friends, against going to even the most unpolitical of gatherings — a concert, a parents' meeting at a school; the periodic raids, the violations of privacy, the reading of personal letters, the poking around in drawers and cupboards; the vacuuming away of books, written material, typewriters.

But the changes that were now taking place were qualitative, lives not privately invaded but publicly revealed, our faces familiar not just to the members of the Special Branch but to anyone who picked up a newspaper; our children no longer protected but victims in a war the younger ones could scarcely comprehend.

And the disorientation we felt was the experience and outcome of the Rivonia Trial that was dealing blows to the liberation movement as a whole.

I wrote this book about the last two years of our life in South Africa because I thought it would be easier for people outside our country to understand the total situation through the impact of events on one family. It is, therefore, a personal and subjective story.

The heart of the book is the Rivonia Trial, the trial at which Nelson Mandela and seven others were sentenced to life imprisonment.

But wasn't that twenty-five years ago?

Yes it was, and between then and now lie dozens, hundreds of political trials with more lurid evidence than that given at the time of Rivonia; of dramatic confrontations between freedom fighters and police, including shoot-outs and murders. And sentences — fifteen, twenty, thirty years; life. Yet these are the fortunate ones; so many sentenced to death, so many hanged. As many as fifty at a time on death row, awaiting execution for offences arising out of political protest; the world's busiest hangman with his multiple method of despatch — a row of nooses and the drop. Does this not diminish the importance of the Rivonia Trial? Locked away for twenty-five years, six of them still there, who remembers the men of Rivonia?

The world remembers. The silenced prisoners have become world heroes, their organization, the African National Congress, still illegal in its own country has risen to become the most powerful political representative, both inside and outside South Africa, of the struggle to overthrow apartheid. The number one accused, Nelson Mandela, silenced, shut away, is the world's most famous political prisoner with honours heaped on him from universities, governments, civic authorities, in hundreds of places. In a remote part of Spain you will see a bridge across a road with huge letters: FREE MANDELA. Arrive at a road junction outside a small town in France: there is a special plinth with a sculpture and plaque commemorating Mandela. At a railway station in a small town a portrait with the message: Mandela — Free Citizen of this Town. Libraries, parks, streets, buildings, are named after him, not just in the big cities but in the country and distant villages. Mandela has become the symbol of those struggling for a free and just South Africa; and to the world, a symbol of the necessity to eradicate racialism.

The Rivonia Trial became the platform from which, for the first time, the black-out of state censorship and of press self-censorship was broken; and for the first time since the State of Emergency of 1960 and the banning of the ANC, the whole story of black oppression and black struggle and aspirations was told through the testimony of Mandela and his fellow accused.

It was the first important political trial in which the primary purpose was not to prove the guilt or innocence of the defendants, but in which the trial itself became a forum for expounding their beliefs, the justification of actions considered treasonable by the State, but which they were not prepared to deny. Yes, said the accused, we helped form Umkhonto we Sizwe, and this is why we did it, these are the reasons why, after forty-eight years of peaceful protest, our organization decided to launch a campaign of sabotage.

It was the first trial that exposed the erosion of justice in South African courts through laws that abrogated the rule of law, and through the rise and dominance of the secret police who, in the end, were the only ones who had jurisdiction over the incarceration or the freedom of those arrested.

Twenty-five years ago, a time of seeming defeat for those opposing apartheid, was the turning point, the beginning of a new, more militant movement, on which was to be built new generations of protest bursting out as the years went by — while the Rivonia men remained in jail — in mass strikes in the 1970s; the uprising of students and school children in 1976; and the continuing resistance in the towns and countryside in the 1980s under a permanent State of Emergency.

To understand the present we need to know about the past. In the contemporary history of South Africa Rivonia is a giant episode, not just for South Africa, but for people worldwide. It is an essential part of our comprehension of the nature of racial discrimination that poisons our country and exists in various forms almost everywhere.

Our world had tilted; we walked uneasily in those days. But not for long. We had gained a new balance. How fortunate we were to have been part of that great catalyst of change, the trial of those arrested at Rivonia.

*   *   *

In preparing this book, which appeared in an earlier form in 1967, I have had the advantage of adding a great deal of material about the Rivonia Trial through the generosity of the instructing attorney in the trial, Joel Joffe. He has allowed me to draw on his own unpublished account of the trial and the details and observations he recorded. His manuscript is, in its own right, a valuable record.

I have used actual names except where it was necessary to protect people from possible repercussions. For this reason, too, I could not mention friends whose loyalty and assistance can never be forgotten; they will understand.

The assistance given in the form of encouragement and critical advice from the following is truly appreciated: Babette Brown (who made me write in the first place); Phyllis Altman; Bill Pomeroy; and my husband who patiently helped to construct the book and to edit the manuscript.

What I have written is the truth as I saw it, but the whole truth will not be written for many years to come.

Prologue

11 July 1963

There was a sense of unease all afternoon. It was true there had been many such days and nights; and the premonition is only recalled in its full oppressiveness after disaster has been realised; many, many such times; the precise cause, the months and even the years of them have silently blurred, lost consequence.

But not this one.

He had to be home by half-past six every evening. He had to be within confines of house and garden by six-thirty, not being permitted to leave again until six-thirty the next morning. There was even something of a secure feeling about this twelve-hour house arrest, because the children knew their father would always be home in the evening. Whatever I might be doing, however many times I was out, Dad would always be there now. He had been under the restrictions of house arrest for nine months.

He had to report to police headquarters — Marshall Square — in the centre of Johannesburg every day between the hours of twelve and two, except on Sundays and holidays when he was not permitted to leave our house at all.

This was a routine without any comforting overtones. We had never discussed it, Rusty and I, but we both had the feeling that one day he would walk into Marshall Square in the usual way to report, and not come out again. He only told me long afterwards that the daily reporting had become a nerve-racking ordeal, that he had to take a deep breath before entering those dark-red brick walls every day to sign his name in the special book kept by the Sergeant in charge of those under house arrest.

It had been a big new book at the end of the previous year. The Sergeant had carefully headed the pages with the many names, several pages for each person. But one by one others had gone — some into jail, some into hiding, some out of the country. The Sergeant flipped over more and more unused pages as the numbers dwindled, until now there were only two still left to sign — Rusty and Helen Joseph.

1

It was a Thursday in July, which is midwinter in Johannesburg. Rusty had left home at midday. He said: 'I'm going in to report. Then I have to deliver some drawings. And this afternoon I'll be busy — I'll be home late.'

'Late' meant some time around six in the evening. 'Busy' was undefined because it was not necessary, we understood each other. Our activities had become so circumscribed, we were both under so many bans and restrictions imposed by the apartheid regime, that for us all political activity had become illegal. The first bans had been issued ten years before, when we had been prohibited from membership of a long list of organizations, and from attending any 'gatherings'. A 'gathering' had been defined as two or more people coming together for a common purpose.

To comply with such restrictions would have required us to abandon all active opposition to apartheid. We were incapable of such renunciation and never even considered it. We had continued to work, each in the spheres that interested us most and suited our capabilities best. But it had become axiomatic that the less you knew the safer you were. You had to know only what immediately concerned you, nothing more; danger in knowledge, even in so intimate a relationship as that of husband and wife. Rusty and I were aware in a general way of what the other did, but we sought no particulars. This was mutual protection, not lack of trust.

When he said he would be busy that afternoon I knew he did not refer to his architectural practice; if it had been that it would have been more clearly stated: 'I'm going to Brenthurst' — the clinic for which he was designing a new wing; or, 'to the Municipal office to look up some plans'. Since the State of Emergency in 1960 following the Sharpeville shootings, when we had both been in jail for some months, he had abandoned his office in town. Our house was now his office, and our bedroom the room where he worked. His drawing-table was placed under the full width of the wall-long windows, and it was there he did most of his work, whistling softly through closed teeth as he moved T-square, set-square and rulers across architectural plans and drawings.

'This afternoon I'll be busy.' The tension began from that

2

moment. I said, 'Take care of yourself ... be careful.' I wanted to say, 'Don't go! It has become too dangerous.' I did not, partly because of the years of discipline in refraining from interference, and partly because I did not think it would make any difference. He was as acutely aware of the dangers as I. It was calculated risk.

He backed out of the drive in our big black Chevrolet, a car we had bought for long-distance holiday trips, big enough for four children, clothes, tents, and camping gear. In it we had enjoyed such marvellous expeditions in the past, to the Natal and Cape coast, to the Game Reserve and the forests of the Northern Transvaal. Past now, because Rusty was confined to the magisterial district of Johannesburg. I could still go away with the children if I wished, without him; there would not be much pleasure in that.

A few minutes later he returned, drove in along the driveway, went into the garage, came out again, called goodbye once more and was gone.

Perhaps I began watching for his return before I could have expected him. It was five or half-past. The winter day was over. In less than half an hour the light would alter from full daylight to complete dark, from the sun and cloudless blue sky and clarity of the dry, highveld winter to the crisp dark, and the brilliance of a million stars.

Every evening that winter I had watched the phenomenon of the evening sky from the kitchen window as I prepared supper. Just as light faded and the blue became pale and colourless, before it was dark, the whole sky would be diffused with a purple-red glow, crimson, indigo, deep violet. They said it was caused by volcanic ash reflecting the light of the setting sun.

And I watched it that evening also while apprehension increased with the fading light, as though my fear, which was related to such real and tangible things, had less palpable origins rising from the blindness of the night.

Come home, I urged him in my heart. Come! Come! Come!

Only two or three times before had he arrived back after six. He knew he had to allow time for the odd mischance, traffic hold-ups, car trouble, something like that. These could be cited in mitigation of sentence, but they would not affect the basic

3

offence — breach of the conditions of house arrest, for which he could go to jail for anything up to three years. We took risks where it was necessary, we broke restrictions when it had to be done. But not in a way that invited sanctions.

Ten minutes past six. Quarter past. Once only had he come home at twenty minutes past six. Before, when he had come home late, I had been in the kitchen cooking the evening meal and listening for the sound of car wheels on the gravel of our driveway. Then the slam of the car door, Rusty's footsteps into the house, his voice greeting the children in the front room, his progress to the kitchen to say 'Hello!' and kiss me. And each time I had said, 'You cut it a bit fine tonight, didn't you,' a statement, not a question, reproof for the anxiety which could not be completely repressed.

'Tons of time,' he would say, 'ten minutes at least.' On that Thursday evening, at twenty minutes past six, I thought, I will hear the car, hear the slam of the door, he will come into the kitchen and once more I will say, 'You cut it a bit fine tonight, didn't you?'

At the precise moment, as I heard myself saying those words in my mind, I knew he would not come. Knew it with absolute and final certainty. Knew I would not hear the sound of the car door slamming, knew he would not again walk into the kitchen to the words of my mild reproof. I had not been told, but I guessed where he had gone, and with whom; thus the full significance of his failure to arrive was clear to me, the enormity of the consequences, the shape of the long ordeal that lay ahead. I felt a pain so strong it seemed to have physical origins, and I knew.

I knew he was not coming home that night, nor any night in the weeks and months and probably years ahead.

*   *   *

In all such times of disaster the children became both an added burden and a steadying anchor. There was always the difficulty of presenting some explanation for what could not yet be understood and was in any case barely explained. There was the burden of imposed domestic duties at times of crisis when to be

4

free to come and go without accounting for actions, to stay away from the house for long periods if necessary without having to think about children, meals, school routines and all the rest, would have given greater ease of action. Yet this imposed routine was also a steadying factor.

More than anything else, a veneer of normal behaviour had to be kept so that the children did not become the victims of *our* involvement in a dangerous and complicated world of illegal activity — at any rate not more than was unavoidable.

At the most difficult times they also prevented descent into any emotional morass, thereby denying me the questionable pleasure of 'letting go'.

Toni, nineteen, and studying to become a nursery-school teacher, was adult and experienced enough in our way of life to guess at situations without questions. She was self-centred and touchy in normal times; calm, controlled and with abilities to cope magnificently whenever there was a crisis. Patrick, a handsome, moody and introverted adolescent, was away on a camping trip. How much he understood of what we were doing, how much he accepted, how much he resented or hated could not be judged. He had become incapable of communication and was wrapped in his own world of groping and dissatisfaction. Frances was eleven, questioning and perceptive, but still a child in all her relationships. Keith was six, our 'treason-trial baby' — he had been born two days before Rusty was arrested for treason in 1956 — good-natured, loving and on that particular July evening in bed with a septic throat.

I longed to share the awful knowledge of what had happened, to discuss with someone what course of action to take. But the most important thing was to keep fear and the suspicion of disaster away from the two younger children. They would have enough to face when the time came.

My own behaviour had to appear normal and rational to the police, whose watch on our home, telephone-tapping and perhaps listening devices within the house itself, would keep them informed of anything unusual, suspicious.

*   *   *

I had an appointment (political) for later in the evening to meet a young lawyer friend, Bob Hepple. He was to pick me up at half past seven near a suburban hotel, and we were to go together in his car to meet others.

I suspected that Bob must also have been with Rusty in the afternoon. If Bob did not come that evening it would confirm my worst fears of what had happened. If he did, then the situation might not be as bad as I imagined. I *had* to go to meet Bob. But I could not leave the house. The police might come and raid. I *had* to be there.

In the front room Toni sat on a low wooden table in front of a blazing fire. She said, 'Daddy's late' — it was an unanswered question. We had supper, Toni, Frances and I, then Frances went next door to a friend. Toni and Claud, the African from Zimbabwe who had worked for us for fourteen years, were filled with unspoken anxiety. It was as though they both watched every movement I made and silently asked *What's happened?* and in my mind I was giving them the answer — *For us, disaster.* Claud washed the supper things, and I asked Toni to sit with Keith while I went out for a little while.

I went to Ivan Schermbrucker, whose home was within walking distance. I walked in as he was eating supper. He left the table to talk to me on the back veranda of his house, away from telephones and listening bugs.

I said, 'Rusty didn't come home tonight.'

'What time must he be in?'

'Half-past six.'

'Where did he go?'

'He didn't tell me, but I can guess.'

I asked him if he would go to meet Bob Hepple. I warned him it might not be safe. He agreed to go. 'Don't wait too long if he doesn't come,' I told him.

I went back to the house and waited.

Keith had a temperature and dozed restlessly, waking to ask why Rusty was not home yet. Toni and I sat stiff-backed on the table in front of the fire and waited.

Some time after eight I walked out into the garden to see if Ivan was coming. A torchlight flickered among trailing winter creepers and a breathless young voice in the darkness

6

exclaimed, 'Oh, you gave me such a fright!' It was Ivan's child, braving the darkness to bring a note. It said simply: '*I waited nearly half an hour. He did not come.*'

* * *

There is a long night ahead. We are unable to read. We listen all the time, listen for the sound of a car in anticipation that the police will come. If he is in the hands of the police, surely they will bring him to the house to search; they always raid after an arrest. We, Toni and I, have made a quick check to see there is nothing lying around that we don't want them to find. It is not easy to be sure.

We sit and listen. Twice the phone rings and Toni runs to answer it. Someone asks to speak to Rusty. 'What shall I say?' she whispers with her hand over the receiver. 'Tell them he's busy you'll ask him to call them back.' An engineer phones to speak to him about a building job. People often phone in the evening because they know he is always at home. But we dare not say 'He's not here'. Perhaps he is not yet in the hands of the police; and as they listen on our phone they will know that he has broken the conditions of his house arrest.

I think — he should not have gone. The risk was too great. But it was risks all the time, there is no way of doing anything without risk; complete safety lies in complete immobility. The decision has constantly to be made between what is courageous and what is foolhardy; what is caution and what is cowardice. Sometimes the difference between courage and foolhardiness lies in whether or not you are caught.

The fire burns down, we rake away the grey ash and put on more coal. We make ourselves coffee and go to Keith when he wakes and calls and murmurs, 'What time is it?' and, 'Hasn't Daddy come home yet?' Time is blurred in his mind but he feels it is late; it has been dark for long now, and Rusty is always home before it gets dark.

We wait for them to come. Sometime during this night, we are sure, they will come.

We have some more coffee, and some time near one o'clock in the morning I say, 'We might as well go to bed.' 'I suppose so,' Toni replies. Neither of us can read or do anything at all. We may as well wait horizontally in the dark instead of shivering before the embers of the fire, embedded now in a mess of grey ash.

Keith's feverish throat trouble wakes him often enough to ensure that I am completely wakeful. If I doze a little he brings me back to full consciousness with his need for a drink of water and a word of comfort. I have put him in Rusty's bed next to mine, so that I don't have to get up so often to go to him.

At two in the morning, at half-past two, when it is quietest and seems darker than ever before during the night, that is the time to expect them. Now our suburb is still, all Johannesburg is sleeping. Moonlight has given delicate mystery to the yellow and white mine dumps around the city; the sounds you hear are carried from far off, the lonely shunting of a train is from the other side of town, faint and clear. Trains in the night are always sad and nostalgic and full of longing, echoing journeys, distance, change . . . escape. We hear them without listening. It is not the sound of trains but the sound of cars that alerts us. The car sounds, too, are distant and rare, beyond the street, beyond the hill …

At three in the morning even these sounds ebb away, life itself seems to ebb away, you are left with nothing. Then, the afflictions that apartheid has brought oppress us; it is as though our ability to acknowledge what is happening to a whole nation is like the possession of some fundamental truth that others refuse to recognize. We feel like Mrs Moore in *A Passage to India*, who has visited the caves and holds the knowledge of truth and evil. The truth is clear; it is heard all the time in the terrible, sad boom of the caves, echoing inside our ears, reverberating within the hard-boned skull, full of foreboding. The reverberations, if you succumb to them, can bring madness or death.

At four in the morning the night has exhausted itself. A bird stirs and is still again, the sky is old, faded, resentful of light; in the townships Africans are preparing to get up, in the suburbs the white people are still lost in sleep.

At five it is still dark, but light will come soon and swiftly. At six I fall asleep at last. And then it is morning and the police have not come.

Before seven every morning, Claud takes a basket and goes to

8

the shops on the corner to collect our milk and buy the *Rand Daily Mail*. I wait for him next to the newly-lit fire in the kitchen, where the floor is already washed and the table set for breakfast.

When he brings the paper I search the front page — nothing there; glance through it rapidly; then again more carefully. Not a word.

What can I do now?

I decide to go into town to Innes Chambers where all the barristers have offices. I will see if Bob Hepple is in his office. If he is not, perhaps a discussion with one of the lawyers I know might help.

On each floor of the building there is a reception desk which you cannot pass without the permission of the typist sitting there. I ask for Mr Hepple. 'He hasn't come in this morning,' the receptionist says.

'Are you expecting him?'

'He should have been here. We are waiting for him.'

I turn to go and find myself face to face with J.D., a lawyer who is an acquaintance. 'What are you doing here?' he asks.

'I wanted to see Bob Hepple, but he isn't in yet.' Then I decide to speak to him. 'J., I'm in trouble.'

'Come down to my office. We can't talk here.'

In his office, I tell him what has happened — what I believe and fear has happened; and that so far there has been a curtain of silence; no police, no news in the paper. We sit opposite each other in the comfortable armchairs with which the lawyers equip their offices. I am uneasy at being away from home, I am still convinced the police will come, and that they may be there now.

'I must go home,' I tell J., 'and I want to go quickly.' He says, 'I will give you a lift.'

As we leave his office, we meet Harold Wolpe. Harold is also a lawyer, as well as a political colleague.

'Harold, I'm afraid Rusty's been arrested, and probably a whole lot of other people as well. I think they've taken a whole group of leading people ... he didn't come home last night ...'

Harold looks at me in amazement and says, 'But don't you know what happened?'

9

'What?'

'It's in *Die Transvaler* — splashed all over the front page. Rusty has been arrested — and Walter, and Kathy and Govan, and a whole lot of others, at Arthur Goldreich's house in Rivonia; Arthur and Hazel have also been arrested. They're all being held under ninety days.'

'When?'

'Yesterday afternoon. Didn't the police come?,

'No — but I'm sure they'll be there now. Oh J., please take me home, I must get home quickly.'

When the rush of morning traffic has subsided, as it has now, it takes less than fifteen minutes from the centre of town to our house in the suburbs. We drive without a word. I feel perfectly calm, and do not think that I am suffering from shock. Only the weight of some physical impediment seems to be pressing down within me, so that from time to time I must draw in air like a sigh in order to breathe properly.

Only once I say to him, 'You must understand, it's not just because of Rusty that it's so terrible. Honestly, that's not the main reason that it's so terrible for me —'

And he replies, 'I know; I understand.'

He thinks it better that he should not drive right up to our house. He drops me a block away in a street parallel with ours, and I run in through a neighbour's gate to enter our home over the back fence, at the bottom of the garden. I run all the way, gasping with a breathlessness not caused only by physical effort. Down the long green slope at the back of our neighbour's garden, up a compost heap to the corner of a fence, down over a wall into the garden of the house next door to ours; across this garden and through a gate made in the hedge to our own back garden.

The last thing I do before reaching our garden is to stop just for a moment and empty the contents of my handbag — a notebook, a diary and some personal letters — into the long dry grass near the hedge.

PART I
NORMAL LIVES

1
Divided City

The route through the back garden was a familiar one, the dilapidated wire-mesh fence overgrown with the dried stalks of rambling flowers, bean plants, and a prickly creeper that bore unnamed, edible berries, had been pressed down in one corner and a small pile of stones erected.

It was all trees. The pines and wattle in the Scout Hall grounds at the end of the garden seemed to enlarge it and spread its half-acre beyond the almost invisible wire fence. Most of our garden was here at the back of the house; but in front there was a large area of lawn and a drive leading to the garage, lined with six great jacaranda trees.

The jacarandas, with their strong high shoots, smooth grey branches and *mille-feuilles*, held the winter sunlight away from our front room, made the whole house colder and darker; on to the lawn minute leaves swept down silently all winter when a breeze blew. After them, the twigs dropped and then came the clatter of round hard seedpods on the corrugated iron roof of our home; until spring and the massive glory of the flowers dropping their bugles until the whole lawn was a mauve carpet, and flowers bursting with tiny explosions when the car wheels pressed them into the gravel of the drive. Under the jacarandas was the colder blue of stiff-spined agapanthus whose stalks bled with sticky milk when they were cut to stand in a big vase. Trees, trees. A lemon tree stood outside our bedroom window, bearing fruit the whole year round; beyond it, prunus with its marvellous dark leaves and delicate pink blossom; fig trees, apricots, orange-flowered wattle, almonds and vines.

Trees seemed to grow overnight, thin, tall and brittle in the light, high air. We chopped huge branches off the jacarandas to let more light into our front room; in a season they had sent up new grey shoots, long and smooth and higher than before.

In the back garden, there was everything you could want in a

13

highveld summer, a cycle of figs, early plums, peaches, apricots, apples, quinces, late plums, and last of all, the little black catawba grapes, which heralded the end of summer. The path under the vine was stained with them and smelt like a wine cellar. There were two crops of figs each year, targets for the birds that squabbled noisily as their beaks slashed the green casing, releasing the sweet red fruit that later fermented and rotted on the ground. Under the fig trees close to the kitchen, I had established a herb garden with obstinate, slow-starting chives that spread into great clumps and were split to provide plants for my friends; thyme sprawled untidily along the edge; the rosemary bush with spiky, fragrant leaves, parsley and basil. In our climate, even the annuals protected from winter frosts by the trees behaved like perennials and renewed themselves unattended.

The almond trees blossomed every spring, but bore a crop of fruit only in alternate years. The maize grew beyond man height. Popcorn hung yellow and drying on a string outside the kitchen door.

The house was living, all summer long it breathed and murmured with people and sound; all doors were open, it was as though there were no doors, just squares of light through which people passed from one activity to another. Summer lasted from the end of one winter until the beginning of the next. Even in winter, the front door was not locked, only closed on colder days. Sometimes we forgot to lock it at night. Frances practising the piano, Patrick fiddling with his guitar, the radio, the record-player, the typewriter, the kitchen sounds, the drum of the washing machine; and most of all, people — people coming to swim, to talk, to borrow books; the children's friends at all ages and stages; people who never rang the bell or knocked, but called a greeting as they came in.

Our house in Regent Street, Observatory, Johannesburg, had been altered to suit our needs fourteen years before when we moved in — before the Nationalists had come to power when circumstances had not yet made us aware that political conditions could dictate architectural needs.

What the house really needed now was a high surrounding wall and a locked and solid gate; windows with sills above head level, none overlooking the entrance area; an entrance hall completely detached from the house; and an incinerator.

Our house had only one of these essentials: a slow-combustion stove in the kitchen which burned all the year round to heat our water. I was to come to depend on this ugly, old-fashioned, soot-depositing stove for the conditions in which to continue my work.

But in all other respects, everything betrayed us. The gates did not fit and never closed; through them there was a clear view of the whole house straight into the main room through the floor-to-ceiling window. The front door and sidelights were glazed with ribbed glass through which forms could be seen and even identified; it opened directly into our living-room without the intervention of a passage or hall — we had removed the wall between.

For the visitor on the stoep outside our front door, the big window was on the right; immediately on the left were the windows of our bedroom, also opening on to the stoep. What could not be seen could be heard. You had no time — from almost the moment you heard a car door slam at night or footsteps disturb a loose stone on the path, they were at the window and everything within, movement or sound, was blatantly exposed.

Through the open gate and the exposed driveway, our lives were watched much of the time by a man, who had been posted by the police behind a stone wall across the road.

*   *   *

The purely physical conditions of our lives became ever more difficult. The year 1960 was a watershed, when Rusty and I were both arrested and scooped off to jail during the State of Emergency following the Sharpeville shootings. By then open opposition to apartheid had almost come to an end. Persecution of individuals had increased enormously. The law had become an instrument of political oppression.

I think it was when I came home from prison in 1960 that I knew our house no longer responded to our needs. For even with the bans and restrictions we had lived under for so long, the many constraints on activity, the troublesome years of the Treason Trial, which started in 1956, the raids and closing-down

15

of organizations and periodicals and the closing-in of fascist-like laws — yes, even with the State of Emergency and the never back-to-normal of its aftermath, we had not screened off our lives. They were wide open as our doors were open, as our home had been for so long.

It was coming to an end. They were to scatter our friends and empty our garden; they would succeed, bit by bit, in sealing us off and drying up our home. They would impose silence, loneliness; and force us to close our front door, and keep it closed and locked.

Even the inanimate things bore the influence of changes imposed by political circumstance.

The hi-fi record-player in the front room was a result of the bans placed on us many years ago which prohibited us from attending meetings. When we had to spend so many evenings at home it seemed a justified expense. The drawing-table in our bedroom and cupboards fitted into other rooms, which held blueprints, plans and rolls of drawing paper, recorded the passage of the Treason Trial, which ultimately forced Rusty to close down his office in town and transfer his practice to the house.

The garden, too, bore small signs of change. There were various places where papers were hidden overnight for safekeeping; there were the sweet peas, planted each winter, now sited along our front veranda to form a brightly-coloured barrier screening the front door from the road.

At the bottom of the garden even a bath recorded, in its own passive way, something of the change in our lives. It had been dumped down there when a new one was installed in the house; the children used it for games. Best of all they liked to light a fire in the bath, which we allowed because the flames could not spread, and cook themselves pasta or mealies in a battered blackened pot. But now we too were lighting fires in the bath, at first only to burn banned periodicals sent to us from the socialist countries. Then magazines which had been legal for years were suddenly declared illegal — retrospectively illegal — and the possession of just a page from one might send you to jail.

And finally, although this was only at the end, there were great quantities of books and pamphlets which we had put into storage fifteen years before to save them being taken in police raids; and now they were all banned, or by authors who were banned, and could not be put in the dustbin or given away, but had to be burned. So we became book-burners. Books resist burning, their pages curl and singe and the fire goes out; it is necessary to *work* at the burning to destroy them successfully. Perhaps that bath, packed solid with black brittle ashes of books and papers, had become the most striking symbol of the evil and destructive times to which we had come.

Our lives adapted to new routines which in turn would become normal, a set of disciplines set by necessity, changing into habit. Watch the rear-view mirror of the car when driving away from the house to check who may be following. Never say anything of consequence on the telephone — telephones are always dangerous; unplug them or bury them beneath blankets and cushions when talking politics. They can be used to pick up and transmit conversations even when the receiver is down; so turn up the radio or keep a record playing during a meeting to baffle the tape-recorder.

The disciplines are never completely obliterated so that, in future, in any country, telephones are reserved for trivialities and the sound of music remains a compulsive background for political discussion.

The disciplines extend, become more imperative. No word may be carelessly spoken in front of the children, children may repeat things unintentionally that may lead to trouble! No document may be handled carelessly; raids are more frequent. Every appointment must be closely kept; waiting at meeting places beyond the specified time is dangerous.

Sometimes I was consumed with a desire to conform to middle-class normality, to be unknown, obscure, unwatched; to bake cakes and take children to the dentist, embroider cushion covers and discuss only literature or modern art when friends came to dinner; to go on holidays and be just ordinary people like all the others, caravanning by the sea; to join an art class and be just a housewife fiddling with paints.

Whenever I tried, something would happen to strip the screen of normality and reveal our difference. Holiday friends at the camping site would say something intolerably insulting about

17

Africans; to remain silent was to be a party to their attitudes. We spoke, and were immediately set apart from all others. A new ban or another police raid would take place and we would be publicized in the Press, which tore aside anonymity. One way or another there was never a topic of conversation which did not, inevitably, become related to the realities of our lives: racism, the police state.

I had been elected to and served three years on the Johannesburg City Council. They were the tumultuous post-war years. The war had brought a halt to building, and industrialization brought a flood of people to the city and its locations. In the South African context, the word 'location' has a special meaning; it is a place attached to a town where Africans live. It is not a town on its own, but a sort of fungus-growth. The locations filled beyond capacity. In a phrase they themselves used, the African people 'overflowed' and set up squatters camps, shacks of cardboard and hessian, on the edges of the locations.

As a councillor I could go to the locations and the shanty-towns. I went to places forbidden to all outsiders: the compounds where African municipal employees lived, the lowest-paid of all workers; saw how they slept on concrete shelves in dark holes; how they queued to wash in cold water, after they had washed the mules that pulled the Council's carts — hot water for the mules, cold for the men. I served on a Slums Court and went to unknown back-yards in the heart of Johannesburg.

This might have been an impersonal way of seeing the many divisions of my city. For both Rusty and myself there was a more intimate way, through our own friends. We had friends in the suburbs and friends in the locations. Compounds and shanty-towns were sealed off from all but municipal authorities; but for many years it was possible to visit the locations with few difficulties.

The locations turn the people into outcasts.

The physical separation makes them outcasts from the society that only flourishes through their unremitting labour. These years I am writing about finally entrenched the imposed divisions.

Gradually all Africans were being moved to Soweto so that the original location, Orlando, became only part of the huge Soweto complex, little brick boxes spreading and sprawling for miles and miles, row after row of tiny houses divided into localities: Orlando, White City, Jabavu, Moroka, Pefu, Mximkulu, Phomaleng. But the streets are unnamed, only the houses numbered in each locality, the numbers rising to thousands and tens of thousands. The boxes are like cancerous cells, spreading outwards in all directions, endlessly repeating themselves over the treeless slopes of the high veld. The people are divided along ethnic lines, the tribal barriers that dissolved in the towns are recreated by authority among the matchbox houses of Soweto.

We accepted the challenge of physical separation and surmounted those physical barriers, and this in itself required positive effort. But in addition we had been prohibited from any gatherings for more than ten years; legally we could no longer enter the location, legally we could not sit together with any group of people for a 'common purpose'.

Yet the locations remained. We lived double lives. We had the large house and garden brilliant with flowers and fruit, but were outcasts from most of white society whose principles we rejected completely, even though we lived and moved among them. Could there have been another way? We were not permitted by law to live in the location.

As restrictions and bans confined us more and more, we fought to hold on to even a single thread of contact between the suburb and the location, lest we too should become guilty of complicity in imposing the ghetto life of segregation on our fellow-men. The locations were part of our lives.

Everything in South Africa is like a mirror with two sides. One side reflects what you know best; the other is a dark pool into which you must peer constantly to realize the strange and changing scenes it reflects.

The house in Regent Street, Observatory, shines brightly at us from one side of the mirror; on the other are the homes and lives of our friends and comrades in the locations.

* * *

In 1961 the fruits of several decades of work and struggle disappeared from the South African scene and a new, harsher era arrived.

19

The marathon Treason Trial, in which Rusty had been one of the accused, came to an end after trundling its way through the courts for more than four years. It had begun in December 1956 with a great flourish of headlines and middle-of-the-night arrests of 156 leading political people of all races; the charge high treason. For a time it had been the focus of attention both inside South Africa and outside, the inspiration for political action, the meeting point for committees and organizations. It was awful, wonderful, inspiring and boring beyond words. For years, attending the treason court was a way of life for those involved. Yet when it ended, it had lost all significance on the political scene. It was a played-out drama bearing little relation to the surroundings in which it was enacted.

The Treason Trialists had been accused of planning the violent overthrow of the Government; the element of violence was essential for the charge to succeed. Four years' evidence had shown conclusively that there had been no intention of violent overthrow, but even more, police witnesses for the State repeatedly testified to the fact that the African National Congress leaders constantly held their followers to such a policy of non-violence.

Yet even as this evidence unfolded month after month, year after year, and inside the courtroom political events marked time, outside the land was changing. New laws, new situations, new policies were overtaking the snail-pace of the trial. Already, by 1961, the arguments, the evidence and the pleas had become remote, as though it had all happened a long time ago in another era. There was an air of unreality, for the men and women facing the charge of high treason were being tried for policies which they had already outlived.

On 21 March 1960, eight days before the verdict of 'not guilty', a crowd of about 2,000 gathered in peaceful protest against the pass laws at the small town of Sharpeville. Seventy-five police fired about 700 shots into the crowd (described by journalists as 'perfectly amiable'). Sixty-nine were killed, 180 injured. Most were shot in the back as they turned to run away.

As protests mounted, internally and world-wide, the African National Congress, after forty-eight years of peaceful, legal work, was declared (together with the Pan-African Congress) an illegal organization. The words of its former President, Chief Albert Luthuli, remain as an epitaph on the period: 'Who will deny that thirty years of my life have been spent knocking in vain, patiently, moderately and modestly at a closed and barred door?' He who always 'strove with zeal and patience', now joined his people, he said, 'in the spirit that revolts openly and boldly against injustice'.

The shootings at Sharpeville and the banning of the ANC is the essential turning-point in political strategy. Thus, in its final year, the Treason Trial was the trial of an organization that no longer had legal existence; of policies that no longer had validity. It was a trial of leaders who defended discarded attitudes at the very time they were confronted with new challenges which they must either meet, or renounce all claims to leadership.

The Treason Trial, and with it the Congress adherence to a policy of non-violence, had passed into oblivion. Many had chafed at the reluctance displayed by responsible leaders to move on to more militant action. But the Nationalist Government had finally clamped down on all methods of non-violent protest.

South Africa cut its final ties with the Commonwealth. On the basis of a referendum held among white voters only, Dr Verwoerd declared that South Africa would become a republic on 31 May 1961.

Two months previously a representative conference of African leaders, the 'All-In African Conference', had been held in Pietermaritzburg. It had elected a Continuation Committee to organize a three-day stay-at-home strike as a protest against the decision to declare a republic without any consultation with the majority of the people.

Nelson Mandela, formerly Transvaal president of the African National Congress, had been elected to head the Committee. To avoid arrest, he had left his home and family and had directed the strike campaign from underground.

Years before when Nelson Mandela had first come to our house, one of the children ran into the kitchen shouting excitedly: 'There's a giant in the front room!' After that, in our family, he was known as 'the giant'. But it was not only his splendid physique and attractive personality that made him an outstanding popular leader. He responded to challenge. And when

21

confronted with difficulties his political strength and understanding grew.

From lawyer to strike organizer. To work underground, Mandela had left a flourishing law practice and an office filled with clients from early morning until late at night. He was never again to return to normal life. He was the first African leader to leave his home and live in hiding. This in itself was a sign of the passing of old ideas and old methods of struggle.

The apartheid regime prepared in earnest for the challenge to the Republic Day celebrations. A new General Law Amendment Act had been passed which empowered the police to arrest and detain anyone without charge for a period of twelve days; previously any arrested person had to be charged and brought before a court within forty-eight hours of their arrest. Armed with this new law, the police had been picking people up all over the country to hold them in jail during the crucial period of the planned strike.

Nelson Mandela's home was raided and searched twice in that week. Many homes were searched for hours in their owners' absence.

But the most unusual part of the police operation was not this — raids had by this time become part of the South African way of life — but the large-scale military-like expeditions into African townships, particularly on the Witwatersrand, and especially in Soweto. Heavily-loaded three-ton lorries moved into the South-West Townships before dawn, as torrential rain flooded down, churning the streets to mud and slowing the trucks to a snail's pace: in the trucks were hundreds of policemen, armed with rifles, revolvers, bayonets and torches. The trucks fanned slowly out into the ill-lit streets, headlights reflected back by the solid curtain of rain. Reinforcements stood by at all major police stations and barracks. Radio patrol cars cruised through the locations. Helicopters with enormous searchlights fixed underneath, hovered over the houses turning night into day.

While Radio South Africa blared out the call-up of troops, Mandela broadcast for the first time on an underground transmitter — Freedom Radio. The broadcast was heard by only a few, its range was limited, the technical problems not yet overcome. It was a small beginning of the new policy of struggle that no longer sought to work within the framework of what the Government declared legal.

31 May 1961, Republic Day. The papers declared the strike a failure before the first morning had passed; only a minority of workers stayed at home, they proclaimed. Yet this was not the truth. The extent of the strike was far greater than anyone realized at the time; later, bus companies produced figures to show how they had run empty services to the townships that day. In the industrial towns, and in those industries with Africans in trade unions, many stayed out for the full three days. In some areas, the great majority of workers stayed at home.

But in other respects, success was impossible. Workers in three key industries — mineworkers, railway workers and dock workers — were forced to work under military conditions. Railwaymen were escorted to work from the compounds where they lived by armed police; dock workers were kept on Salisbury Island, just off Durban, and could not return to the mainland; the mineworkers were closely guarded in mine compounds and could not be reached.

The outcome was a clarification of political attitudes and activities. The old methods are finished, the people said. The lesson of the stay-at-home was implanted deep in the minds and hearts of every South African: peaceful protests can no longer take place.

Non-violence! Legality! It is all in the past. In the locations people spoke of other methods. None even thought now of all the arguments for non-violence that had been paraded through four and a half years of Treason Trial evidence in the form of documents, speeches, Congress policy statements, leaflets. Finished, gone, buried. The Government was rule by violence, repression by force of arms and force of law; in themselves, 'unjust laws have the nature of violence'.

This was the radically changed and more menacing situation, that we faced. It was winter like all other winters in Johannesburg, sun-warmed all day, clear and cold at night. Like all others, and unlike any other. We knew that in the past the police kept some sort of watch on us. Only now, for the first time, the minder was posted more or less permanently across the road behind the stone wall, recording day and night all our comings and goings and the car numbers of our visitors.

23

*　　　*　　　*

All those years of raids. All those papers, books, pamphlets, letters they had seized, sorted, listed, receipted, carted away to The Grays (headquarters of the Security Policy in Johannesburg); studied, graded, filed — what happened to them all? What was the importance of them? What did they want with handbooks issued annually by the South African Institute of Race Relations, copies of which were freely available in every library throughout the country? With copy after copy of the Freedom Charter, at a time when it was still legal to have copies? With newspaper cuttings? With drafts of novels that were never finished?

What did they want with all the books they took? And who at The Grays was concerned with *Short Stories* by Anton Chekhov, or *A Dictionary of Quotations*, or *Women of Asia and Africa*?

The raids are merged in my memory into a picture of two heavy men — there were always two, but not always the same two — moving with deliberation among Rusty's architectural plans and my verses and scribbled notes and sketches.

Painfully slow, they would concentrate with furrowed brows on every single item, seeking in it the secret of subversion to the State that it might conceal. In the end, what was the value to them of it all? And why were they so reluctant to return anything, even after months and years?

'Have you actually *read* all these books?' one asked. 'What's this — a library?' asked another. They discussed the problem of our books with each other. They seemed to feel that their very number was suspicious; if you had one book, what did you want another for?

Lips moving, brows contracting, one man had taken a book from the bookcase, examined its cover and the spine, read the title page, turned a few pages, hesitated, turned to his companion: 'Are we looking for books about Russia?'

'Yes.'

The book went on to the pile on the floor. It was *Russian Fables*. The next book. The long, difficult examination, the turning of a few pages. 'Do we want books about philosophy?'

'Yes.'

One took down an Everyman edition of Marx's *Capital*. Read

24

the title. Opened it and studied the title page. Leafed through it. Closed it and put it back on the shelf and took down the next one …

Three books later something clicked in his mind. His eyes shifted back again. 'Are we looking for books by Marx?'

'Yes.'

Back he went to *Capital*, and added it to the pile.

Out of a cupboard came a list of educational films available free from the United Kingdom Information Office.

'Are we looking for stuff about films?'

'Yes.'

A book by Nehru, a book on the re-building of English cities after the war, a book by Tolstoy …

The raids in earlier years had been exploratory. If you raid enough people enough times sooner or later something will be found. Many people were terrified and tried to keep the fact that their homes had been raided from becoming known.

There was a new crime by 1961 — being in possession of literature that had been legal at the time it was issued, but had subsequently become illegal. All material issued by the African National Congress for the last forty-eight years fell into this category. We cleared house, yes, we had periodic clear-outs, particularly when a rumour of coming raids was whispered around. But even after years of clearouts, we would come on a page torn from a banned newspaper, caught within some old files or papers.

On one occasion, a constable kept turning up copies of radical journals and asking his superior officer: 'Have we got a copy of this?' as though The Grays was some sort of reference library and the raid was to ensure that the collection was complete. He was told irritably to put it back — his superior at least was one man who knew what he wanted.

'What are they looking for?' a woman who was working for me once asked.

'Oh, I don't know — papers, documents …'

'Will they find it?' — a breathless whisper.

'No.'

She was an African and hated the police, so she gave a great sigh of relief, 'Oh, that's all right, then.'

Did they find it? Who knows! Books and magazines and

articles would appear as exhibits at trials, typewriters would lie for months at The Grays, books were kept for years, some to be returned, some gone for ever. Morning raids, afternoon raids, evening raids and night raids. Raids at half past two in the morning. Coffee on the kitchen table, and cigarettes, and more coffee. Lights burning in our house when all the neighbourhood was quiet.

The old excuses. Some of the police, particularly in the earlier years, were apologetic. 'No need to get rude.' (Rusty was always aggressive and it put them on the defensive.) 'We're only doing our job.' Or, 'We have to do it — it's our job.'

It was as though they were practising their plea for a day yet to come: 'I was only carrying out orders. Just doing my job.'

2
'Black Man in a White Man's Court'

The sound of an explosion in the night. Was it thunder? Often summer storms sound like an explosion.

Rusty gets out of bed and looks out at the silent garden behind the curtain. 'Can you see anything?'

'No, nothing.'

What could he see in any case? The kopje across the road obliterates any view.

'It wasn't thunder,' he says. 'It's quite clear — no clouds.' It was a reverberating boom; it sounded quite close.

'It seemed to come from somewhere near Marist Brothers School.' 'Yes, somewhere in that direction.'

We lie awake and listen. Will there be cars, sirens, hooters? There is no more sound, only the silent tension of the night, the feel of a million people sleeping.

Any night now there may be an explosion somewhere in the city or the surrounding areas. There have been acts of sabotage up and down the country from the end of the year. The first explosions went off in the early hours of 16 December 1961; leaflets were pasted up on walls and torn down by the police, but here and there they stayed up long enough to be read:

> The people's patience is not endless. The time comes in the life of
> any nation when there remain only two choices: submit or fight.
> The time has now come to South Africa.

The posters, in English and Zulu, announced the formation of a new organization, Umkhonto we Sizwe (the Spear of the Nation). Umkhonto claimed to have members of all races in its ranks and called itself 'the fighting arm of the people against the Government and the policy of race oppression. Violence will no longer be met with non-violent resistance only', it said.

27

From the time of the Republic Day strike, there had been a ferment of discussion in the Congress movement. The lessons of the strike, conducted with such emphasis on 'non-violence', had become clear; that it is now impossible to stage any peaceful protest, whatever its form, without calling out the full military might of the State, with all the repressive and terrorist powers of mass raids and arrests.

Sabotage started tentatively, experimentally. The saboteurs chose for their targets Government offices or installations which they could damage without causing loss of life. Terrorism was no part of their policy. Pass offices, post offices, electrical substations, pylons, these were the targets of bombs; and power supply lines and telephone wires were slashed.

There was an increasing number of arrests. The casual violence that has always been part of South African police stations and prisons began to assume the nature of carefully organized physical assault and selective torture: brutality and sadism as the rule, not the exception; the similarity of methods throughout the country suggested co-ordination from highly-placed authority.

We, Rusty and I, did not join Umkhonto; we did not participate in its sabotage acts. If we were innocent, why was I afraid? Because we were not innocent of involvement, we knew of the decision to form Umkhonto, we were associated with the whole movement, and when reprisals were taken we were sure to be among the victims.

*   *   *

We did not have long to wait. In May 1962, Rusty was served with an order confining him to Johannesburg and prohibiting him from entering black areas and factories.

In May the then Minister of Justice, Johannes Balthazar Vorster, introduced the General Law Amendment Bill (which became known as the Sabotage Bill) designed, he stated, to 'render subversive elements and communists harmless and to punish saboteurs'.

This Act is the foundation stone of the repression, imprisonment without trial, torture and murder that was to follow.

It laid down a minimum sentence of five years, a maximum of

death for 'acts of sabotage', which included damaging property, possessing firearms, weapons or explosives, endangering law and order, or hindering essential services; conspiring with others or encouraging them to commit such offences; putting up a poster, going on strike, causing hostility between sections of the population, being on the premises of certain buildings unlawfully, painting a slogan on a wall even slipping a leaflet under a door. All this could be sabotage, punishable with the death sentence.

The new Act provided for secret trials, and for re-trial on the same facts after acquittal, and for repeated trial and conviction on the same charge, under different Acts.

It altered the definition of a 'gathering', making it virtually illegal for a banned person to go to a cinema or have a cup of tea with a friend and many people would be sentenced to jail for such offences.

These were general powers. But the General Law Amendment Act also gave the Minister special powers to deal with persons banned or 'listed' in terms of an earlier act, the Suppression of Communism Act.

The Suppression Act had spread the definition of communism to create 'statutory' communists; so anyone became a 'statutory' communist who had broken one of the many clauses of the Act such as, for example, taking part in the Defiance of Unjust Laws Campaign. Statutory communists, whether they were political communists, non-communists, anti-communist or anything else, were 'listed' together with former members of the Communist Party.

All of them were liable to be issued with ministerial orders banning, proscribing and curtailing their activities. So too were thousands of others, also 'listed' as former members of other organizations since illegalized by the Government, such as the ANC.

Rusty and I were both listed, as were nearly all our friends and colleagues. We had both been banned for many years from gatherings, from various organizations, and from what amounted to all public activity.

Nothing written or spoken by any banned person could now be published or reproduced in South Africa.

The most sinister provision of all gave the Minister powers to place people under arrest without hearing or trial. He could confine a person for any period he wished to any place he defined, he could prohibit such a person from performing any specified act, or from receiving any visitors, or from communicating with anyone at all, other than a doctor.

*   *   *

By July, the new Sabotage Bill was law. The Commissioner of Police, Lieutenant-General J. M. Keevy, speaking at a police function, publicly thanked the Minister of Justice 'for the able way in which he had piloted the General Law Amendment Bill through Parliament. This legislation will provide the police with the necessary equipment to rid the Republic of its enemies'. The Republic of South Africa had become equated with the Nationalist Party and its government; the law had become equated with sten-guns, handcuffs, batons and other equipment of the police.

The courts were filled with case after case arising out of the events of the past few weeks. On one day the Johannesburg magistrate's court resembled a conference of the liberation movement, when about twenty members of the Congress organizations appeared on various charges; nine members of the Congress of Democrats charged with 'acts calculated to further the objects of an unlawful organization' (they had put up posters supporting the ANC); several Africans, members of the Women's Federation and others, charged with 'creating a disturbance' on the City Hall steps during the protests; photographers and journalists from African newspapers arrested during the scuffles, when they tried to photograph the attackers; and Walter Sisulu, arrested and charged under the Suppression of Communism Act.

I sat in court next to Mary Turok when her husband Benny was sentenced to three years' imprisonment for attempted sabotage. The sentence was comparatively light because he had been arrested under less stringent legislation and charged before the new Sabotage Act became law. Three years seemed, then, such a long time. Afterwards Benny would consider himself one of the lucky ones, others being sentenced for life. As we waited in

30

the lobby of the court to wave goodbye to Benny when the trial was over, members of the Special Branch threatened that we would be next.

*　*　*

Vorster had said he would use his new powers speedily. As he often boasted, he was not a man to threaten idly, and I think we all expected that we would be slapped under house arrest the moment the Bill became law.

I simply could not visualize the operation of a law that, under its new definition of a 'gathering', might stop me from speaking to people with whom we associated so closely, with whom I had shared so many things and whose friendship brought warmth and pleasure into a now constricted life.

We will find ways, I thought; we had always found ways in the past to circumvent the restrictions; but knew that it would not be so easy. The new law held more potential danger than those of the past.

'I want to have a few friends around,' said Amina Cachalia, an Indian friend of ours, 'because who knows it may be our last chance to spend an evening together.'

So we had dinner with Amina and her husband Yusuf, and enjoyed the Indian delicacies she had prepared for us; and joked about 'last suppers'. But it wasn't funny; a coldness lay over the evening that could not be dispelled by the hot food. We could not know it was the last time we would be in their house, but, as in everything we did then, we were under the constraint of waiting for something inevitable without knowing exactly what it was.

We felt the sands running out, and an urge to see people, to move around, get out of town while it was still possible. Not many places within reach of Johannesburg are worth visiting; and in winter everything is brown and dead. The winter is beautiful, the air brilliant, sparkling like polished glass; the sky cloudless for weeks on end, light blue and pure by day, spectacular by night with great drifts of stars down the milky way, the whole night illuminated from horizon to horizon. But it is dry in winter, electric dry; I recoiled from the shock of touching the door of the car after driving; clothes sparked and crackled when I undressed; hands became rough and hair flew to meet brush or comb.

One sunny warm day, with dead countryside everywhere, we went for a picnic. The grass was brittle and yellow, pricking us even through blankets laid on the ground; the sun burnt through the thin, clear air; we felt we would splinter and snap like the dead bushes along the roadside under their layer of red dust.

Early in August we felt the first blows of the Sabotage Act; the Government issued a list of 102 people under what was termed the 'Gagging Clause' of the Act; no speeches or writing of these people could now be published. Politicians, novelists, journalists, poets — by decision of Vorster they were silenced.

Among those gagged: Dennis Brutus, teacher and poet, awarded a literary prize for a poem which cannot now be read or published in his own land; Alex la Guma, journalist and writer, whose story *A Walk in the Night* received international notice and praise, but may be read in South Africa only illegally. One hundred others, deprived of the right to communicate publicly, were being isolated and removed from 'the vast empire of human society'.

Probably there were no Pasternaks among us, or perhaps it was for other reasons; there *were* a few protests, but no wave of indignation came from writers abroad who speak so constantly of the need to uphold the artist's right to freedom of expression.

Rusty and I were on the list of people whose writings could not now be published. Rusty had served on the editorial board of the monthly magazine *Fighting Talk* almost from the time that it was started at the end of the war; he had written countless articles for it, some under his own name and some under pseudonyms. I also contributed regularly to *Fighting Talk*, and from time to time wrote for the weekly newspaper, *New Age*.

Vorster had threatened to ban both these papers, but meanwhile they continued to appear. But now the editors of both publications and all their regular contributors had been silenced.

All we were concerned about was to continue writing as long as possible. This was not through bravado or mere habit of defiance of such laws; it was simply that we believed we had something which should be said out loud, and the fewer people who

32

were prepared to say it, the more important that we carry on and circumvent the silencing ban.

*   *   *

Nelson Mandela had been arrested in August 1962, having lived in hiding for nearly seventeen months. In that time, since he had gone underground to direct the Republic Day strike, he had attended meetings all over Johannesburg; he would get up when a meeting was over and walk off alone in the night, tall and straight-backed. If he sometimes felt nervous or afraid, if he found his life lonely and depressing, he never revealed it. He moved around the country, then one day slipped across the border into Bechuanaland (now Botswana), and made his way up the long hot route through Africa, visiting heads of African States, and going as far as London. When he slipped back into South Africa he was fulfilling the promise he had made not to leave permanently, to return.

But, conscientious in everything he did, he insisted on going to Natal to report personally to ANC members on his trip. He met too many people; someone could not resist boasting that he, too, had met and talked with Nelson Mandela; there were police spies and informers waiting to pick up every whisper of a rumour; so the police knew he was in Natal, and put out road blocks. They waited for three days; then, on his way back to Johannesburg by car Mandela was stopped and arrested.

Now he was appearing in court on two charges, one of incitement to strike, the other of leaving the country without a passport.

I walked into the spectators' gallery and found it crowded out with leading members of the Special Branch: Colonel Spengler, Detective-Sergeant Helberg, Viviers and others.

The proceedings were short; Nelson was remanded until October, refused bail, and we emerged from the small courtroom into the corridor to find it packed from end to end with people who had been unable to get in. We became wedged into this huge crowd and a lot of police both in uniform and plain clothes and all ranks from colonels downwards, were wedged in with us. We could not move, the crowd did not seem to want to move, and the police were working themselves up into some kind of anger so that they could deal with the situation. Some had truncheons, young men in uniform were fingering their revolvers.

Suddenly the people started singing.

Doors from the courts and offices opened, the hearing of cases stopped at the ringing, unusual sound. Singing the African national anthems in Xhosa and Sesotho, 'N'kosi Sikelel' iAfrika' and 'Morena Boloka' ('Lord Bless Africa'), the crowd started moving slowly towards the entrance of the building as the police, annoyed but cautious, began to force us out.

So we moved, in a unit, a solid mass; we were not separate people but a single living whole, singing as only South Africans can sing, singing contempt of the court, its trappings and flunkeys, singing defiance of the police, their arms and power, singing belief in the future, in freedom, in the possibility of happiness. Each of us felt enlarged and released, as though the sound of the singing alone could liberate us from the sorrows and terrors of our lives and lift us above the possibility of defeat and despair.

I was wedged in together with Amina Cachalia and an African friend, Ruth Mompati; at the door we three found ourselves cut off from the main body of the people by rows of armed police. In front of us the police joined shoulders and stood in a phalanx, then pushed against the crowd dispersing down the steps, so that women fell and were trampled and everything became confused. Ruth and Amina and I stood behind the police, watching this, until we found the opportunity to get safely past them and down the steps.

Out in the street the people picked themselves up and re-formed into a procession, still singing. But I would be arrested if I walked with them. This was clearly a gathering, so I left them and went my own way.

*   *   *

The trial of Nelson Mandela attracted a great deal of attention, for during his period of hiding he had become something of a legendary figure, sought by the police but always evading them.

34

His daring in leaving the country, travelling openly in other countries and then returning again, had captured the people's imagination.

In the week before his trial, the Minister of Justice issued a notice banning for a period of six months all meetings that were held as a protest against the arrest, custody, trial or conviction of any person, for any offence, anywhere in South Africa or South-West Africa.

The trial was transferred to Pretoria which meant that not many of his supporters could attend and also minimized the possibility of any demonstrations taking place in defiance of the ban.

Police blocks were out on the road between Johannesburg and Pretoria, stopping all cars with Africans in them, searching people for documents, arresting some, delaying others, sending others back to Johannesburg. Still, there were about 350 spectators at the beginning of the trial.

When Mandela entered the court, all the spectators rose together as though he were the judge himself, and giving the ANC salute of a raised fist shouted '*Amandla!* (Power!) Nelson saluted in acknowledgement and turned to smile at Winnie, again regally beautiful in traditional dress.

'I challenge the right of this court to hear my case!'

The words were more than mere bravado. They showed the extent to which this leader of the African National Congress had finally broken with the legalism of that organization's past. It was the first time that such a leader had risen in any court and challenged its jurisdiction — said in effect, I do not recognize your court and your justice, and *your laws no longer have any meaning for me.*

It had taken a long time to reach this position of defiance, to shake off the deference to legal procedure and respect for the law, even wrong law, which had become ingrained in organizations steeped in many years of legal struggle. 'What sort of justice is this,' he said, 'that enables the aggrieved to sit in judgement over those against whom they have laid a charge?

What is this rigid colour-bar in the administration of justice? Why is it that in this courtroom I face a white magistrate, confronted by a white prosecutor, and escorted into the dock by a white orderly? Why is it that no African in the history of this country has ever had the honour of being tried by his own kith and kin?

... I hate discrimination most intensely and in all its manifestations. I have fought it all during my life; I fight it now, and will do so until the end of my days. I detest most violently the set-up that surrounds me here. It makes me feel I am a black man in a white man's court.'

He challenged the right of the court to hear his case, on two grounds the first that the court was not an impartial tribunal but an instrument of punishment for those who sought to end white supremacy, and thus he would not be given a fair and proper trial.

The second ground: 'I consider myself neither morally nor legally obliged to obey laws made by a Parliament in which I am not represented.'

The application for the magistrate to stand down was refused. Mandela then conducted his own defence, calling witnesses and cross-examining them. At the end of four days the Prosecution closed its case, and the magistrate asked Mandela if he had anything to say.

He said, 'Your Worship, I submit that I am guilty of no crimes.' There was a considerable pause, and the magistrate asked rather taken aback: 'Is that all you have to say?'

'Your Worship, with respect, if I had something more to say, I would have said it.'

The magistrate reserved judgement until 7 November; when Mandela was found guilty, he addressed the court in mitigation of sentence. He described with vivid sincerity the background to his life, his youth, his struggle to become a lawyer, his involvement in the struggle for rights for his people.

He outlined the history of events leading up to the decision to call a protest strike on Republic Day, and declared: 'If I had my time over I would do the same again, so would any man who dares call himself a man.'

He showed how the Government had used the power of the law to handicap him in his personal life, in his career, and in his political work; described how he had been banned, trailed around constantly by police wherever he went, not allowed to pick his own company, to participate in political and social activities or join organizations and all this not because of anything he had done, but because of what he stood for, what he thought, because of his conscience.

Every attempt of the African people to obtain some redress for their grievances had been met with force, and he warned of violence to come. Finally he spoke of his own decision to leave home and family and become an outlaw. 'No man in his right senses would voluntarily choose such a life in preference to the one of normal family, social life which exists in every civilized community.'

Whatever sentence would be imposed, 'rest assured that when my sentence has been completed, I will still be moved, as men are always moved, by their consciences; I will still be moved by my dislike of the race discrimination against my people when I come out from serving my sentence, to take up again, as best I can, the struggle for the removal of those injustices until they are finally abolished once and for all ... I have done my duty to my people and to South Africa. I have no doubt that posterity will pronounce that I was innocent and that the criminals that should have been brought before this court are the members of the Verwoerd Government.'

The magistrate sentenced him to a total of five years' imprisonment, emphasizing that Mandela showed no remorse for activities which were not only unlawful but undemocratic; that he seemed proud of his achievements; that he had stated he would continue his activities whatever sentence was passed on him, and that the court was not concerned with politics but with the maintenance of law and order.

Mandela's speeches in court could not be legally published. But not long afterwards an illegal pamphlet of his words was circulated in the townships. When the case had ended, the spectators left the court singing 'Nkosi Sikelel' iAfrika'. In spite of the Government's ban on demonstrations they marched down the street chanting a new freedom song, *Tshotsholoza Mandela* — Carry on, Mandela!

3

House Arrest

October 1962, summer. Our front door was open at night because it was so warm. We were eating supper and from where I sat I looked straight up at the ribbed glass of the door, partially closed. The shadowy forms of two men appear behind the glass.

I said, 'Who is that?' and Patrick, who had finished supper and was fiddling with the radio, glanced up and said casually, 'The Special Branch.'

And it was Sergeant Kleingeld with a young man, who wore an open-necked, coloured shirt. They did not raid, but simply handed Rusty two notices.

The first notice prohibited him from having anything whatsoever to do with the preparing, compiling, printing, publishing or dissemination in any manner whatsoever of any publication. The second gave the conditions of house arrest similar to those which had recently been imposed on Helen Joseph, then National Secretary of the Federation of South African Women, Walter Sisulu, former ANC Secretary General and Ahmed Kathrada, a prominent member of the Indian National Congress. Home confinement between 6.30 p.m. and 6.30 a.m., all weekends and public holidays; to report to Marshall Square every day between 12 and 2 p.m.; no visitors whatsoever in the house; prohibited from entering any factory, and any black township or location; confined to Johannesburg; and prohibited from communicating with any other banned or listed person, with the exception of his wife, Hilda.

The weekend exploded in a blaze of publicity for us and the four others served with notices that same night — all whites, this time. The Press came and took pictures of the family; the children willingly obliged and posed, except Patrick who was silent and alien.

The Special Branch came, too, twice in two days, just to 'check up', as they said. The second time was Monday night.

Toni had invited two friends for dinner, one a young doctor, Johnny, and the other a student, Lorna, from Toni's college. Lorna had never been to our house before and never came again. They had been invited before the house-arrest notice. Because Rusty could not now receive visitors we had divided ourselves into two groups; he ate his dinner in the kitchen with the children to keep him company, while I ate with Toni and her two friends in the front room.

We had just finished dinner when the Special Branch were with us. They were aggressive and rude; they behaved in an intimidating manner towards our two guests and demanded their identity cards, escorting Johnny back to the hospital where he was houseman to check his identity. They searched the house and questioned Rusty about his movements. Then they said to Toni: 'You are aware that visitors are not allowed to come here?'

She was defiant. 'I'm not under house arrest — you haven't served me with any notices prohibiting me from having visitors.'

'Your father is under house arrest. He is not permitted to have visitors.'

'That's right. These are my visitors, not his.'

'They are not allowed here.'

There was a fierce argument. They left threatening 'further action'. It was not a very happy evening.

Toni launched her own campaign for the right of the children of persons under house arrest to have their friends visit them. She used the methods she thought would be best — Press publicity. Over the past few years she had become friendly with some of the reporters who regarded our family as a perennial source of news. She phoned them and gave them her version of the story.

She told the Press she would continue to ask friends to visit her. She could not see why she and the children should be precluded from having friends. 'It would be hard to make the little ones understand why they couldn't ask friends to come home with them. But however it affects our lives, we are proud of our father and will put up with all the hardships and sacrifices.'

The reporters telephoned her daily for further developments. She made a point of asking friends to come around ('at a time like this you get to know your friends'). There were statements from the authorities and counter-statements from Toni; and at the end of the week she had won from Vorster a public acknowledgement that the children of parents who had been put under house arrest were not debarred from having friends visit them.

There were intricate points of law that had not been settled. If Toni had a friend and Rusty walked into the same room to fetch a book, and the Special Branch arrived and saw him there, could it be said that his action constituted 'receiving visitors'? If he sat in the same room as visitors, but did not converse with them, was this 'receiving' them? The lawyers suggested that these were matters which could only be decided by a court, following on a prosecution. We were not anxious to be guinea-pigs in any test cases. Therefore we re-ordered our life to conform to the new restrictions, and after the glaring publicity tried to settle ourselves into new routines of behaviour.

Because our home was also Rusty's office, salesmen called with new products, samples and price lists; I had to tell them he would contact *them*. For discussions with builders, structural engineers, and firms supplying materials for his jobs, he had to go out to their offices — they could not come to him. So the difficulties of keeping his practice going seemed to increase constantly and reporting to Marshall Square every day took a big slice out of his working time.

The phone began ringing at night. People in Johannesburg do not keep late hours; there is little night life in the city and it is unusual for people to phone after eight-thirty. The sudden penetrating ring of the phone late in the evening in that quiet house, or shattering sleep in the middle of the night, was always frightening. Abusive harsh voices swore and threatened — it doesn't matter, I would think, replacing the receiver softly and crawling back to bed; but my heart seemed to take a long time to become slow and silent again, and I would lie stripped of sleep waiting for the shrill impersonal summons of the telephone again. There was a regular caller at about six every morning: the sound of someone breathing, but nothing was said.

Anyone could walk down the front path at night unheard, until they stepped on the front porch; there was a loose paving stone on our porch that made a soft, distinct 'clonk'. The sound would bring our eyes up from the books we were reading, there were a few moments of intense listening. It could be one of the two dogs, Pepe and Nyama, who were always dashing out of the kitchen door and running round to scratch on the front to be let in again. The silence of waiting. Perhaps the bell would ring — *they* would be there again to check up if Rusty was observing house arrest and sitting at home alone, communicating only with his wife.

This was the time when we first started to close and lock our front door, because any evening they would be there, standing right in the front room. I bought bamboo blinds to pull across the ribbed glass at night, so they could not see our shadowy shapes within the room.

And now, in summer, on those highveld nights when the air is cool and beautiful, we sat with closed windows behind drawn curtains, we checked where the curtains met and at the sides to make sure there were no cracks through which they could see. It must be done carefully, methodically, continuously. The children might have a friend, or someone might come to see me, and if Rusty walked into the room or stood in the doorway, and if *they* saw, it would mean jail. We dared not slip. That was what they came for, that was what they wanted. They didn't mind how often they came; time was on their side, sooner or later there would be a slip.

Home has changed, it is no longer ours, it is no longer a place of refuge and relaxation.

Our pattern of living had become muted, played in a minor key. Strange Saturday nights, once the occasion for relaxation, Saturday nights, when friends came to our home, or we went to theirs.

Quiet house, quiet garden. Beyond the closed door the sound of the sprinkler turning round and round to water the flowers. In the room, we play records. The music swells out beyond the walls, to drown the sound of police cars coming down the street.

Curiously quiet Sundays, the pool deserted except for the children. A blaze of summer heat, apricots torn off by torrential rain and hail, rotting in their hundreds under the trees where friends once filled their baskets with the fruit. The dazzle and glare of sun on the pool; from time to time the wonderful summer

41

sounds of children diving and playing endless games in the water, water games that go on for hours and hours, diving, fighting together in the pool, scrambling out, diving in again; until with lacquered hair, dripping and shining like seals, they lie exhausted face down on the burning hot paving around the pool until the sun drives them back into the water.

But at the same time, a drying-up of noise and life, as though under a great iron hand.

* * *

House arrest and other bans were designed to put an end to the activities of individuals who had persisted in spite of everything in working against apartheid. The ban on communication prevented discussion, and therefore plans for joint action. All leading people in Congress organizations were now of course banned from 'gatherings' and from belonging to organizations (and had for years been prohibited from meetings of any kind); yet banned people still carried on political activity, and the Special Branch knew it.

Those under complete house arrest, twenty-four hours a day, were like prisoners forced to provide their own board and lodging. Those permitted out for twelve hours had to live a wary life of limited contact and restricted communication.

These disabilities of house arrest were evident; there were others less immediately apparent. Only the eccentric becomes a hermit by choice. Who can live in a vacuum? The need to work and the need to communicate are primary, basic needs on which man's whole development has depended. To deprive a person of these is ultimately to inflict a punishment worse than ordinary imprisonment, one potentially destructive to the individual.

Those under house arrest were not only deprived of their right to communicate, not only cut off from the stream of normal living, but in addition they became their own jailers. They must themselves impose these conditions, must divorce themselves from the community of man; they must maintain their isolation by their own actions and will, and day and night they must be vigilant to hold themselves away from that world of life in which they may no longer have a part.

Ahmed Kathrada lived in a small flat in a building called Kholvad House in Fordsburg, only a couple of miles from the centre of Johannesburg. Kathy had been a king-pin around whom activity developed and revolved. He was permanently in communication with people, with organizations, with ideas. His flat was a centre to which people came. He drew to himself friends of all races, many of them white.

His flat was comfortable enough inside; outside, the building was run down, flaking plaster peeled from cracked walls, the area was sinking into the mess and dirt of a slum. No trees or open spaces to look out on, only the pound of heavy traffic down the main road to outlying suburbs. Rubbish, bus tickets, paper, straw, the debris of a run-down locality of offices, factories, bazaars.

No more people climbing the four flights of stairs to Kathy's flat (there is a lift in Kholvad House, usually out of order); no more friends sitting around and talking, no more informal parties with their uninhibited mixture of races; most of Kathy's friends are listed people. He can read a book by himself, play a record for himself, gaze out of his window at grey walls and washing lines. Every evening, every weekend, every holiday, within the four walls of a small flat in Kholvad House; house arrest for Kathrada.

Walter Sisulu lived in one of the little boxes in Orlando. We had been there many times in the past, before it became impossible for whites to enter Orlando. In his tiny front room we had sung freedom songs with friends, songs of different countries, a rich mingling of voices and music and languages. All now prohibited.

Two weeks after he had been placed under house arrest, Walter's mother, who lived with him, died. In the African tradition of sitting with the bereaved, relatives and friends came to the house. He could not turn them away — he could not even speak to them; his wife, Albertina, tried to explain that he was not permitted to receive them. In the very small house, with the dead woman lying in one room, the mourners became a threat; Walter sent an urgent application to the chief magistrate in Johannesburg for permission to receive mourners in his home. Permission was not granted. In the evening Minister of Justice

Vorster broadcast a radio statement on conditions imposed on individuals under the Sabotage Act, describing house arrest as 'most humane'. And later in the evening, at 11 p.m., when all the visitors had left and the house was in darkness, awaiting the removal of the body for the funeral next day, detectives raided Walter's home and dragged him to the police cells. The charge: disobeying his house-arrest order and assaulting the police. The charges were later withdrawn, but the sour flavour of police persecution could not be wiped away.

For Alfred Nzo, placed under twenty-four-hour house arrest in Orlando, life became entirely solitary. His wife Regina, a nurse, was living at a hospital. A young boy shopped for him and brought food as far as the wire fence surrounding the small garden in front of his house.

A few people spoke out in protest against house arrest. A few protested against the inhumanity of imposing such conditions on people who had not even been formally charged nor given an opportunity to defend themselves in a court of law. 'Injustice is no longer noticed, sensitivity has become blunted, conscience has become expedient, standards and moral values have become blurred,' an ex-member of the United Party wrote. 'We South Africans are losing our humanity.'

It was going to be harder and harder, and house arrest was not the end of the road, but the beginning.

4

Net of Silence

In the early months of 1963 there was no pause between new Bills, orders, edicts. In January, the suburbs were filled with thousands of African women desperately walking the streets seeking out old employers — white Madams who peered at them and did not remember them — to piece together enough letters, documents, papers of some kind to prove they had lived in Johannesburg for fifteen years. If not, by 1 February, the date set down by which every African woman would have to carry a passbook, they would be 'endorsed out' of the city. The great protests against passes for women lay in the past. Women had resisted the pass laws since July 1913, but now, with leaders banned and organizations proscribed the struggle had dwindled away.

In January and February police raided Alexandra Township, nine miles outside Johannesburg, day and night in the first stage of an operation to break up families, remove homes, separate husbands and wives and children, and build single separate hostels for men and women employed in Johannesburg. Small children wandered around Alexandra uncared for while their parents were in jail. Women crouched and listened in the dark, waiting for the sweep of lights over their rooms, listening for the police cars.

Yet summer moved on with all its glory of sun and heat, and our land had never been as flourishing and prosperous as now. At this time of the year we used to go to the coast. A thousand miles from Johannesburg to the Cape. We would start one morning and drive all day, and go on driving through a night of shooting stars with the children asleep in the back of the car.

February brought great summer rains, but in the Northern Transvaal there was another season of drought, with crop failure and hunger which had been accumulating for years. The country was full of surplus food: millions of pounds of butter and cheese, tens of thousands of unsold beef and sheep carcasses cluttering the coldstorage rooms; thousands of tons of top-quality bananas hacked to pulp to keep up prices; huge, hidden dumps of oranges and other citrus fruits, a great sea of yellow and gold, taken away to remote hills and left to rot — while the babies died of kwashiorkor and gastroenteritis and tuberculosis. Food that rots and children that die, all through this beautiful, bountiful summer.

In the same month came the 'Censorship' Bill, which had the effect of shutting down independent newspapers and magazines including *Fighting Talk*, and which ultimately put me out of work. *Fighting Talk* was both a political and a literary magazine, and many new, black writers were first published in its pages. The Minister's signature on an order and *Fighting Talk* no longer existed. A part of us died with it.

The Bill was not simply a measure for political censorship. Culture had become an enemy, as it was once for Germany, and the enemy had to be suppressed and destroyed. The poet is dangerous — his words break through barriers of race and language; the artist is dangerous — his brush and pencil reflect what exists around him and create commentaries on his life and times.

On 22 February a new ban was directed against the progressive weekly newspaper *Spark*, an inheritor of the fighting press tradition which began a quarter of a century before with the weekly newspaper, the *Guardian*.

The *Guardian* was banned in 1952. Within a week, a new paper appeared, *Advance*, banned in turn in October 1954, and succeeded by *New Age*. Except for five months during the State of Emergency of 1960 when it was summarily suppressed, *New Age* appeared regularly for eight years until banned, giving birth to *Spark*.

The three papers had not been content merely to record, but had also campaigned ceaselessly against injustice.

Some revelations, that became national scandals and were finally taken up by the big newspapers, began as exposés in the pages of these small weekly papers. The story of the abuses of African labour on white farms, the near-slave conditions of workers locked up by night and whipped by day, was first told

46

in *New Age* by Ruth First. The uprisings in Pondoland, the hidden famine, the police contraventions of the law, cases that were never reported in other papers, all came to light in the 1950s in the pages of the *Guardian* and *New Age*.

In the last three months, *Spark* carried on the tradition under enormously difficult circumstances. The editor was prohibited from talking to his own business manager, and not permitted to go to the printer so he could not see his own paper through the press. Still, somehow, they had kept the paper going. Now it became impossible.

The last issue of *Spark* had an article headed: 'REMEMBER THE MEN AND WOMEN IN JAIL!' and listed the names of some of the ever-increasing number of people serving sentences for political offences. Without *Spark* and *Fighting Talk*, who was there to remind the country of those in prison? A clause of the Sabotage Act made it illegal to possess any banned paper, under a penalty of three years' imprisonment. *New Age*, *Advance*, the *Guardian* and *Fighting Talk* all suddenly fell into this category. I could not bear to destroy the copies of *Fighting Talk*, so I wrapped them up and sent them overseas for safekeeping.

The *Government Gazette* notice prohibiting listed people from printing and publishing deprived me, too, of my job in the mornings for the magazine, *Amateur Photographer*, which was owned and run by a friend of mine, Mannie Brown.

Now I was not only prevented from having anything published, but was also stopped from entering the premises of any place where publishing took place such as the offices of *Amateur Photographer*. I could not return to my job of copywriter in an advertising agency; advertisements that I wrote could not be reproduced.

The problem of jobs became a serious one for many of us, something like the atmosphere of America's McCarthy era. We were marked. We knew how those blacklisted Americans must have felt, pushed out of their jobs and professions, their children isolated by playmates, forbidden to speak to them. Small things, perhaps, but they hurt; the young couple with whom we had dined so many times in their beautiful house on top of a hill, who now kept from us in a silence harsher than words; Frances's school-friend from the Children's Home, who used to stay with us for weekends, but was not allowed to come any more.

Mannie, who was listed, was asked to resign from his bridge club, which played in rotation at each member's house; it was becoming embarrassing, the others said, when the Special Branch came to inquire what they were doing at his house. The police had even visited his mother one day to ask what Mannie's car was doing outside her house.

But the job situation was more important. After a great deal of hesitation, as any sort of request to those in authority was repugnant — to ask *them* for favours! — I wrote to the chief magistrate of Johannesburg who theoretically had the power to grant exemptions from the ban on entering publishing premises (in fact he only acted on the advice of the police) and asked permission to continue working for *Amateur Photographer*. When no reply had been received by the end of the month I telephoned the magistrate's office and received my reply: 'You must cease working there forthwith, and sever all connections.'

At Rusty's suggestion I registered for an Art class at the university, because listed people without an occupation were liable to be put under twenty-four-hour house arrest. He felt that if they decided to house arrest me, they might at least let me out during the day to attend university.

Although I had never been to university, I had no difficulty in enrolling as an 'occasional student' attending courses but not studying for a degree. It was a reminder that because the majority of South Africans are debarred from the universities, whites who wish to attend any course have little difficulty in finding a place.

From the moment I stepped inside the university gates on Mondays and Tuesdays each week, I walked into a new world, quiet, unhurried, relaxed and pleasant, and all the special circumstances that hounded and hedged South African lives melted away.

The problem of earning a living remained. Rusty had obtained one worthwhile architectural job just before he was put under house arrest. The job he was working on was a new wing for a private clinic, and the fees would keep us for a year. But our financial position was precarious. I began to concentrate more

48

and more on writing articles for magazines and papers in Europe and America.

There was never any doubt in our minds about the morality of defying laws that were essentially immoral; nor was it a conscious decision taken at any particular time. The law had ceased to have validity. Political influences were becoming more evident in the courts as they began to reflect the harshness and non-legality of the Government itself.

Caught in the net of silence cast around us by all the restrictions, we felt like helpless watchers in the playing-out of a tragedy. The country seemed to be building up towards a disastrous situation, a future threatened by destructive and punishing violence.

The stage was being set for something more extreme than even the house arrest and restrictions of the past. The excuse would be a short-lived African organization, Poqo. This was the Nationalist's Frankenstein. To destroy it, Vorster was now preparing his 'further means', which he would then use against us as well.

*   *   *

A small, plump, smiling African woman, Christine, came to our house every Tuesday to do the week's ironing. We had a washing machine; I did the washing during the week, and stacked it to await the arrival of Christine.

She was like a beautiful brown ball; every portion of her was soft and round and jiggled when she moved, and she was always good-natured.

One Tuesday Christine arrived unsmiling and upset.

'My brother — he has been arrested.'

'What for, Christine?'

'Poqo.'

'And was he mixed up with Poqo?'

'Madam, no, I swear it, no. He never take part in politics. He never go to meetings. He had good job, and he mad about football. Football, football, all the time. He never even had time for meetings.'

'Then why do you think they arrested him?'

49

'They arrest dozens of boys. They come in the night and bang on the door and just pull them out. He go round with someone they think is Poqo, or someone just give a name.'

We obtained a lawyer to act on behalf of Christine's brother, and a friend of ours gave a loan of £100 for his bail. The young man was lucky; he was able to return to his job and for the many months before his group was brought up for trial was working and earning. Other young men caught up in the Poqo arrests, almost without exception, sat in jail for months and months awaiting trial, because they could not raise the bail money.

When his case was eventually set down for trial, the charges against him were withdrawn for lack of evidence.

At the outset, few knew the extent of the nation-wide police raids directed against the mysterious Poqo; for some weeks there were swoops on townships all over the country, including the Transkei, and hundreds of men, nearly all young, were filling jails all over the country. The Chief of Police, General Keevy, stated that the police dragnet had become so wide that it was almost impossible to say how many Africans were being arrested daily.

Poqo — the word means 'pure', 'alone'. The name had first appeared in the Press the previous year during a trial of farm labourers who had been accused of collecting pangas and other weapons for the purpose of killing whites.

Poqo was similar to organizations that had arisen in African territories farther north; a return to something more primitive and tribal. The very sound of the name with the Xhosa click, so alien to white tongues, was fearful and strange; for whites it evoked distorted memories of the Mau Mau, secret rites, secret oaths, secret plots by Africans directed against the whites.

Poqo grew out of the Pan-African Congress, itself a breakaway wing of the African National Congress. It was hardly an organization at all. A number of acts of violence that took place at this time were attributed to it. Five white people were murdered by a party of Africans at a place called Bashee Bridge in the Transkei. Then, in the wine-farming town of Paarl in the Cape, there were riots in which both Africans and whites were killed.

There had been five riots in Paarl in the space of three years.

50

Africans who worked on the wine farms and in the fruit-canning factories of Paarl lived at Mbekweni, a location, but for men only. The men lived twelve to a room, six concrete bunks on either side, with a space between the walls and roof through which the wind blew in winter.

In the heart of this picturesque and peaceful-looking countryside, life at Mbekweni was unbelievably bleak. The men lined up behind huge communal stoves to cook their food, and queued for the inadequate showers and insufficient lavatories. Tough African policemen — blackjacks, they are nicknamed — patrolled incessantly.

The conditions were aggravated by particularly corrupt officials, from whom Africans could obtain relief, a work permit or other concessions — at a price: white officials trading on the hopeless position of African workers.

A band of about a hundred of these labour units marched out of the location one night and into Paarl. The men marched to the police station, perhaps with the idea of releasing some who were in jail.

Police shot at the marchers and killed some, then retired into their police station to protect it, so they said. The marchers went berserk and murdered three white civilians.

Poqo was overwhelmed and crushed, its members arrested and tortured. They told their plans, named their associates. Their punishment was extreme: twenty-three sentenced to death and executed for the five whites murdered at Bashee River. Four-hundred arrested in Paarl; seventeen sentenced to twenty years' imprisonment each, one to twenty-five years, two to death.

The Government appointed a one-man commission of inquiry into the Paarl riot, a Mr Justice Snyman, who produced an 'urgent interim report' for the Minister of Justice.

He stated: 'Certain whites appear to use the Poqo movement. These include communist agitators and whites who purport to be liberals and even members of the Liberal Party.' There was evidence, he said, that whites played a leading role in the murders and outrages in the Transkei and Eastern Cape.

No evidence was ever produced, either in his report or later to support his assertion. Whites — liberals, radicals, whatever they are — were in fact quite ill-informed about Poqo; they did not

51

know of its existence until it was at the point of disintegration; nor would whites' racial exclusiveness have been acceptable to the men of Poqo.

'Poqo plans to overthrow the Government by revolution this year,' stated Justice Snyman. He called for drastic and immediate action to break the organization. His suggestions included retrospective legislation, the elimination of preparatory examinations in certain political trials and the introduction of special courts. Vorster, stating that this was 'the psychological moment to have this power', presented a new Security Bill, a law which finally ended the rule of law in South Africa. The new Bill gave Vorster powers of arrest and confinement without trial. It provided for sentences ranging from a minimum of five years up to death for anyone receiving training in methods of violence outside South Africa; or for furthering the objects of a banned organization. People who asked for armed United Nations intervention in South Africa could be found guilty of treason and liable to the death sentence.

The clauses of the Bill concerning military training overseas and advocating armed intervention in South Africa were made retrospective for fifteen years.

The Bill gave powers for continued imprisonment without further trial — at the Minister's discretion — of people who had completed jail sentences, a clause that would later be known as the 'Sobukwe clause' (after the PAC leader whom the Government would keep jailed indefinitely). A summary trial could be held without preparatory examination, where this was considered to be in the interests of the State. And among many other clauses it gave any police officer the powers to arrest anyone without charge or warrant and hold them incommunicado for ninety days for the purposes of interrogation; it totally prohibited the courts from interfering with this form of detention, and deprived the prisoner so held of the right to see anyone including a lawyer. And it permitted the repetition of ninety-day arrest of any individual any number of times.

Power from then on resided in the equivalent of the S.A. guards — Swanepoel (against whom there would be repeated allegations of torture in court cases), Rossouw, van der Merwe, Viktor, de Villiers, the men of the Security Police. They would exult in their power — 'the ninety-day law is a mighty weapon in the hands of the police,' one claimed; it puts them beyond the courts.

The Bill was rushed through Parliament in record time, through both the House of Assembly and the Senate, in a total of thirty-two hours of debate. The opposition, the United Party, decided to support the Bill 'because of the Poqo danger'.

*　　*　　*

I am in the kitchen one evening at about six preparing supper when a family deputation descends on us, consisting of Rusty's brother Harold, and Harold's wife Jean; his sister Evelyn, and her husband Felix. They have come to tell Rusty that he must now leave the country and are determined to try and influence him.

Supper needs constant attention and cannot be left for long; so I shuttle back and forth between the kitchen and the front room, trying to listen to the arguments.

'What is the point of staying any longer?' says Harold.

'Because it seems to me important that those who object to such laws should stay and say so.'

'But you can't say anything any more. You haven't been allowed to go to meetings for years, and for the past six months you've been under house arrest. What do you achieve just by staying shut up in your own home.'

'Just by staying, even shut up in my own home, I achieve something; I don't give way before I am forced to, I don't voluntarily throw in the sponge. That's exactly what the Government wants — it wants to be rid of all its critics; and I don't see why I should cooperate with them.'

'But others have gone — look at those who were put under house arrest at the same time as you were. Cecil Williams has gone, Kotane, the Hodgsons have gone, Marks has gone —'

'What others do isn't the criterion for what I do. I do what I think is right from my point of view.'

'Isn't it time you thought about your family as well as yourself? Don't you think you should take a different decision for the children's sake?'

'Yes, I think I should consider the children, and I do. In the long run the most important thing as far as the children are concerned is what sort of country will they have to live in. There must be some white people at least who take a stand against what's being done, so that in the end it's not all decided on a racial basis, it doesn't just become entirely a racial question. That *some* whites stood with the Africans, regardless of the consequences, and refused to run away — that must be important for my children in the end.'

'In the end! But before that end comes, where will you be? How does it help them for you to be in jail? How does it help your own ideals and your cause? What good do you do sitting in jail?'

'I don't know if I will do any good, inside or outside jail. But this is my country, this is my struggle. And I'm not prepared to throw in the sponge when it gets tough and let them have it their own way.'

'You'll be able to do more for your country and your cause from outside than you can under house arrest or in jail.'

'That's debatable. I don't want to join the exiles. There are enough of them in any case. I will not voluntarily go into exile.'

The argument goes on for quite a long time. The children listen silently and intently. They have no desire to leave South Africa but they know this is important. I do not join in, I only pick up what I can of the discussion between short trips from the kitchen. In any case, I support Rusty's stand. I like to hear him argue — perhaps it helps remove my own secret doubts.

*　*　*

Ten days after the Ninety-day Bill became law, the first arrests were made. The police did not reveal names unless it suited their purpose; information filtered through slowly. We had not anticipated where and how they would start, and in that we showed our ignorance.

They wanted most of all to discover the whereabouts of the growing number of Congress leaders who had gone into hiding. Walter Sisulu had disappeared from his Orlando home while under twenty-four-hour house arrest — he had been gone for some days before the police discovered it. Ahmed Kathrada had also broken house arrest and disappeared from his flat. Govan Mbeki, from Port Elizabeth, was in Johannesburg, and ordered to return home when the house-arrest order was served on him; from that time he too had disappeared. The police knew they were still in the country (it is virtually impossible to cross the borders of South Africa without the fact becoming known in a few days). Attempts were being made to seal the borders over which people had once passed freely without documents. Fences were being erected for hundreds of miles, and police posts set up on the roads running into the three Protectorates.

The Special Branch were determined to find these men, and to locate the whole machinery of the underground movement and all associated with it. We tended to assume that as long as the underground leaders remained undetected they had not succeeded.

On 26 June, celebrated for many years by the Congress movement as Freedom Day, the voice of Walter Sisulu was heard in a broadcast made from some unknown place, by an illegal transmitter. 'Join our ranks and fight for national liberation ... In the face of violence, men struggling for freedom have had to meet violence with violence ... Freedom will come!' The police stepped up their search and the methods of interrogation they were now using on detainees began to show results.

Somewhere in a prison cell a detainee broke and confessed to knowledge of Walter Sisulu's hide-out. He did not know the exact location but knew it was a house in extensive grounds somewhere in the outlying suburb of Rivonia. At the beginning of July, the police were searching for the house, driving up and down the lanes and byroads and adjacent areas for days on end.

For more than a week they drew a blank. Then they obtained a second piece of information. The house was circled on their maps — Lilliesleaf Farm in Rivonia.

On a Thursday morning — 11 July — Lieutenant van Wyk of the Special Branch had a task force ready to raid the house where they now believed Walter Sisulu was. At midday they were about to go when there was a last-minute delay. Colonel Venter, head of Security, insisted that van Wyk obtain a search warrant to prevent anyone obstructing the search of the house. Van Wyk had deliberately not taken out a warrant to prevent any possible leak of information. Everything was held up while he went to obtain it.

At midday Rusty left home to report to the police at Marshall Square, to deliver some architectural plans to an engineer, and then go on to Lilliesleaf for a secret meeting.

As he left our house, Lieutenant van Wyk was postponing his raid to wait for a warrant.

Rusty was reluctant to go to Rivonia; too many people now in detention knew where it was and what it was used for. He had been persuaded to go 'just this once more' — the last time, they said.

So strong was his sense of foreboding, so heavily weighted with the knowledge of danger, that at the last minute, even after driving up the road away from the house, he returned once more. He had taken a document that was to be discussed that afternoon. But he took it from his pocket, concealed it in the garage among the nuts and bolts and boxes that held his carpentry equipment, and went out without it.

I wanted to say *Don't go*, but I could not.

Then he drove off again.

PART II
NINETY DAYS

1
Mourning

The back door is open. Claud in the kitchen warns me: 'The police —' and I say, 'I know, Claud,' and go into the house.

Rusty is there, unshaven, with heavy, pouched eyes, standing in Toni's bedroom while two Special Branch men search the room. They allow me to embrace Rusty just for a moment. He says, 'You know what happened? They arrested —' and I interrupt, 'Yes, I know. All of them.'

'We were so anxious.' In front of the SBs I cannot add — *we guessed what had happened.*

'Didn't they inform you that I had been arrested?'

'No. We just waited and waited the whole night.'

'I asked them to phone and tell you. They said they would,' he says with bitter hate.

'It doesn't matter.'

As the search continues, Rusty tells me of a few things he wants me to do in connection with his work. The police take him from room to room and I follow, hovering on the outskirts because they keep telling me to stay out of the way. We talk very briefly, Rusty and I; the Sergeant, in a sour, resentful way, is being permissive; often they will not allow any conversation with an arrested person. We keep it to a minimum, in case he stops us altogether.

The search is thorough, for documents, papers, names and addresses. The Sergeant asks for my handbag, which now has nothing in it except a purse, comb and spectacles.

Keith is still in our bedroom. After they have searched the room, they tell Rusty to pack a bag. He puts in a change of clothes, pajamas, and toilet articles. When he tries to put a book in the case, the Sergeant seizes it and says, 'No books.' He is aggressively short-tempered when Rusty tries to protest and will not argue about it. 'No books allowed.' It is final.

Keith silently observes. After they have gone he asks for a

pencil and paper, and prints awkwardly in his left-handed writing a letter which he asks me to send to Rusty. *Dear Dad, If they won't give you any books to read let me know and I will send you some, love keith*. I take the letter and keep it for sentimental reasons, not telling Keith that Rusty is not allowed to receive any letters.

Two reporters from the *Star* have come to the house and have been driven away by the Sergeant. One is a friend, Tony Hall, the other a photographer. I ask, 'Please, Tony, no pictures.' But Tony has no power to stop the photographer. From beyond the gate he takes pictures with a telephoto lens which appear in the *Star* that evening, one of the Special Branch Volkswagen and the Sergeant's back, captioned: 'Two police officers piling seized books and documents into their car in the driveway of Mr 'Rusty' Bernstein's home after a two-hour search of the premises today.'

The other photo shows two people with frowns on their faces and is captioned: 'A policeman leaving an outbuilding of the Bernsteins' home with confiscated documents. Mrs Hilda Bernstein can be seen in the background.'

They search the garage (Rusty must have stood there turned to stone) and find a box of old papers and pamphlets which they take away. The document he had put there the previous afternoon is not found.

I manage to give him a brief kiss before he is taken away, and repeat once more: 'Don't worry about us. We will be all right.'

Then they are gone.

* * *

The house is in mourning; Claud and the house are quiescent; they have no way of protesting except by silence. Keith, Claud and I are left in the house; Toni has gone on holiday with friends, reluctantly and with many misgivings, but at my insistence. Frances is on a camping trip with friends, and Patrick has not yet returned from his holiday.

Friends come and ask me to stay with them, but I cling to the house. And Keith clings even more than I. He will not even leave the house for half an hour to come to the shops with me.

From the house, through the vista to the bottom of the garden which opens up only when the trees are leafless and the obscuring vine thin and bare, I see Claud moving around the garden with Keith close beside him. He potters around the compost heap, making preparations for spring planting, cuts away the brittle strings of creepers and dead bean plants, moves a wheelbarrow with Keith riding on it, or helping him to push. Their voices reach me sometimes when I am in the kitchen, through the uncluttered winter air. Claud talks softly to Keith all the time he is working; the two dogs follow them, Nyama leaping for a stick or a ball, or dancing on dainty black paws when Claud sweeps up leaves with a broom.

I want to be here. I resist well-meaning attempts to make me stay with friends, or to have someone come to share the house.

Harold, Rusty's brother, says, 'You can't stay here alone with Keith at night. If you don't want to leave, ask someone to come and stay with you.'

'We will be all right,' I tell him. Leave me, I want to be alone at night! We do not want anyone, they will be intruders.

Even Claud does not leave our home on his free days, but sits outside his room in the sun, or inside talking to a friend. Keith and Claud share a pot of porridge in the mornings beneath the quince tree on the grass; the days are still; the evenings pass away with their magenta skies; at night, when Keith is asleep, I play records so loud that the music soars through the room and seems to fill the street and echo from the hill beyond. Music and silence, on and on, late into the night. The later I go to bed, the less hours to lie awake.

For a few days, no one comes near the house except relatives, Harold and his wife, Jean, and Evelyn, Rusty's sister. The women visit in the afternoons and have tea; Harold comes when he leaves his office and collects books and bills, to assist and advise me.

Only these close relatives and a few political friends come for a while; people are afraid of our house, they shun it. Still, a few who were not frequent visitors now phone and call. The front door bell rings one evening, and it is my friend Vera; we embrace and are both near tears when she says: 'My husband forbade me to come, but I could not keep away.' The phone rings one evening, and Gerhard and Gertrude Cohn, who were never close friends, ask if they may come; and they call again.

I write to anxious relatives overseas: 'Remember, for both of us, it was a free choice. Do not nurse illusions — I don't. Rusty will not be out of prison this side of Freedom Day. Only when this whole place bursts open will he be free again.'

I have not said this to the children. The first night after the raid, before she had gone on holiday Frances had asked when she was in bed, 'Is Daddy under ninety days?'

'Yes.'

'And will they keep him for the whole ninety days?'

'I'm afraid so.'

'And after that, will they release him?'

'I don't know, honey — I hope so, but I don't know.'

From that moment she has calculated the date of his release at the end of ninety days and counts each day towards it. But the little ones must first gradually get used to the simple fact of living for the time being without him, and later on they will have to endure what I know is going to be a difficult and cruel trial conducted in an atmosphere of hostility towards them all.

'We are settling down to ordinary living again, and I know I will become accustomed to living without Rusty, as I must do for a very long time ...', I write to the friends and relatives overseas. I know I will never get used to living without him. I tell them everything except the truth — and the other fear that hangs over us, rumoured in the Press and among the legal men at Innes Chambers, hinted at by close political friends who still hesitate to put it into words: *They are going to get the death sentence.*

Every time my mind starts pursuing such thoughts, I try to bring something else forward to occupy it. Physically I am constantly busy, most of all it is necessary to drive away from that agonizing circle of reproach for mistakes made ... they should not have ... I should have told him not to go ... how could they all be together like that ... why wasn't Rivonia abandoned ...?

How to cope with the idea of Rusty and Nelson and Walter and Kathy being sentenced to death. In my heart I think the Nationalists do not have the terrifying conviction of their own rightness or the grim thoroughness of the Germans, they do not really believe in themselves and their cause, and this means hesitations and weaknesses even at the same time as it drives them to greater extremes. To uphold a lost cause, lost in the eyes of the whole world, must inevitably lead to doubts and conflicts. I feel they could not carry out the death sentence even if it were passed, they could not carry it out! And there would be an out-cry from all over the world …

What is the point of worrying at this stage? It is still far ahead; face it when the time comes; there are more immediate things, and step by step I must bring myself and the children to meet them. First we must live through ninety days, then be prepared for the more public ordeal of the trial. Already the police are feeding bits and pieces of information to the Press, to create the atmosphere of fear, hostility and hate in which they will conduct the Rivonia Trial. That's enough, without thinking of the sentence.

There are two things of burning importance that I have to con-sider. The first is my own involvement; they are in jail and we who remain outside can try and pick up some of the broken strands. Or we can leave them. That seems the quickest road to betrayal of what they had attempted to do. If it were not for the children there would be no hesitation. Even so, I cannot hesi-tate. I cannot. I watch Keith through the kitchen door: he comes in, he follows me from room to room, he sleeps in Rusty's bed while the others are still away, to be near me; what right have I to consider a course that will take me from him as well? Yet how can I not do what must be done? 'A call to battle, and the battle done'.

So I decide, and meet with others, and the strands are caught up.

The second burning thing is to make contact with Rusty. I know with every fibre of my being that he will, somehow, some time, find a way of establishing contact with me. I have to be ready when he is, to notice what even the constantly vigilant warders and Security men may miss, and so help to forge that link. I think about it constantly, while busy in the house, while driving the car, while shopping. I project myself into the jail, I picture the cell he is in. In the 1960 emergency I was in jail in Pretoria Prison for a while. The men's sections of the jails are always more formidable and probably more closely guarded than the women's; but there must be some similarities of routine.

I know he has been stripped of everything, all books except the Bible, therefore all paper and writing instruments. But there must be ways. What will he do? How will he make contact with me? I think about it, and do not know, but keep myself ready …

* * *

Because Harold insists that it is not safe for me to stay alone in the house with Keith, and because I am so reluctant to move out, we reach a compromise.

I call in a local electrician to install a button next to my bed, which rings a bell in Claud's room in the yard outside the kitchen. The button is on a bookshelf, level with the bed, and the electrician puts in a tiny globe, so that at night there is a small circle of light around the button which is immediately visible. This satisfies Harold, and I also find it remarkably reassuring. When I turn off the light at night and the house is very dark and quiet, I lie and look at the little circle of light; when I wake in the night, I look for it, it makes me feel safe.

In the past I did not like being left alone in the house. The iron roof contracts in the cold night air with a sound that can be loud, sudden and startling; the floors creak. There are a lot of burglaries in our neighbourhood. It is not difficult to break in, in spite of the burglar-bars on the windows; but we have never had anyone actually try it, only 'fishermen' stealing through the open windows.

The 'fishermen' go round at night with a long stick, hooked at the end. They fish for clothes — men's jackets and trousers lying over the backs of chairs in bedrooms. One morning we found one of their poles discarded in our garden; it became most useful for reaching lemons on top of our trees. But one night we left it out on the lawn and it disappeared again.

Whether it is the effect of my glowing bell-push, or because thieves seem such a minor trouble in present circumstances, I seem to have lost my nervousness about being alone at night, and am no longer bothered by the sounds of the house.

In a few days Denis Goldberg's wife, Esmé, arrives from her home in Cape Town, to see if she can get permission to visit Denis, who was also arrested at Rivonia, and she comes to stay with me for about a week. Esmé is short and plump, and moved to easy laughter or tears. Esmé and I are women who do not like being without men.

I can mend fuses and do other odd necessary jobs around the house, but don't like having to take decisions without ever discussing them first, disciplining the children, deciding on questions concerning schooling, pocket money, how late they can stay out at night. I don't like having to take the car in to be repaired. Something goes wrong with the record-player and I don't know where to take it to be fixed; Rusty used to fix it himself. Everything that was shared is now mine, and most of it seems to be responsibility and decisions.

Rusty has been around so much during those prolonged months of house arrest, available for so many chores, never out after about six in the evening, always able to share the fetching of children from school and other domestic jobs, that it now seems worse than if he had never been under house arrest.

There are nights when I awake to unusual sounds and believe there are prowlers round the house, but I never press the illuminated bellpush to Claud's room.

I sleep badly. I go to bed late at night, taking an apple, orange, newspapers, a book. I spread the fruit and papers over the empty bed next to mine, and use Rusty's pillow to prop myself more comfortably while reading. Being alone has advantages. You can crunch an apple or make the whole bedroom smell of oranges, without disturbing anybody. Rustle the papers and book pages. There is plenty of room for everything. The lights burn. I read till my eyes burn, and the night burns silently down.

Then I switch off the light and thrust out a hand to feel the flat bed next to mine and weep.

I dream a great deal. Dreams and nightmares, often forgotten on waking, sometimes hauntingly real.

I sleep one night, then I am awake, lying in bed in the intense darkness. It is so dark that not even a faint light seeps in from the street lamp beyond the hedge, between the drawn curtains. I turn for the reassurance of my bell-push light — it is not there, all darkness, the small glowing circle has gone. I stretch my hand to switch on the bedside light. I press the switch but no light comes, all darkness.

Then I feel panic, and climb out of bed and press the light-switch next to the door. Darkness, no light. And then through the house, room by room, I turn on every switch and not one light goes on, none of them are working. Dark, solid dark throughout the house, dark in the garden. Dark outside in the street, the street lamp is out. Darkness that can never be penetrated, dark in my home, dark in the world outside, dark in my heart.

It is not fear I feel but awful sadness and somehow I crawl back and I am lying in bed and crying. My eyes are closed, my own tears forcing their way through closed lids seem to wake me. I open them with effort. The light-switch glows dimly and steadily. I try the bedlamp — it works.

I switch off the light again and lie watching that tiny warm circle. Claud would come any time that I pushed the button. But I don't need the bell. I never use it.

2

The Pretoria Road

Three wives of arrested men — Shirley, wife of Bob Hepple; Iris, whose husband Dr H. Festenstein was arrested on the evening after the raid on Rivonia, when he went to visit Arthur Goldreich, and myself — present ourselves at Johannesburg Security Police Headquarters on Saturday morning for an interview with Colonel Klindt, Chief of the City Security Branch.

The Grays, situated where commercial Johannesburg begins to merge with small industries, is an oblong block of concrete, old by Johannesburg standards; probably built in the 1940s. Security Police occupy two floors of the building, and Colonel Klindt's office is on the seventh floor. There are two lifts with clanging metal gates, and there is always some seedy Special Branch man, white or black, lurking in the semi-dark of the hallway.

Our immediate object is to ask permission to visit our husbands, on the grounds of discussing urgent personal matters, disrupted by the arrests. Rusty has always handled everything connected with payments of rent, insurance and household accounts; and I have already had calls requesting copies of plans, and need his instructions on what to do about various jobs on which he was working.

Our underlying purpose is just to see our husbands, to establish the essential thread of contact that we know will be so vital to them, to give them the reassurance that we ourselves are still free, and capable of coping with the situation.

Colonel Klindt says he will see us, but one at a time. Why do we come together? He is not going to receive any deputations. If we have anything to say to him, it must be said privately. The tone is immediately set for all those future interviews with Colonel Klindt.

Irascible and aggressive though he always is, he will never refuse to see me except when he is actually in conference; the door of his office stands open and the approach to him is direct, not through secretaries or subordinates. I had expected to have to overcome obstacles in the form of the lower-ranking Security men, lieutenants or sergeants or captains. Many Security Branch men who are lower down in the scale install themselves behind the barrier of an inner office; but not Colonel Klindt. You must present yourself just outside the door — to his line of vision — and wait for his impatient order to come in.

I already know about the mental preparation necessary for going to The Grays. This is the citadel of the enemy, the seventh floor is the nerve centre of their operations. I am known to every one of them, and there is no protection here. When they come to our homes they are invaders on our grounds, usurping our privacy; when they watch us, follow us and serve bans and notices, it is an intrusion, and they know it; but when I go to their headquarters it is as a supplicant and they know this too.

They eye me standing at the lift gates, waiting in the corridors, or when they walk into Colonel Klindt's office. A few give a polite greeting, most of them do not, but simply look. Their look says, 'What the hell are you doing here?' and, 'So your husband's in real trouble now, isn't he? You'll be next.' The red-faced stormtrooper, Swanepoel, beefy Dirker, van Wyk who is 'slim', clever, and looks at people from the sides of his eyes, and all the lesser-known, even the ones I don't know — they have all studied my photographs and my record — look, look at me as they pass. They are in the ascendancy; they have more importance and power than ever before.

Then Klindt; there would never be an interview with Klindt in which we would not exchange angry words. I would come to a standstill outside his office door to steel myself against that impatient, 'Yes? Yes? Yes?' the opening salvo in a battle for which we are both prepared; I do not stop then to analyse why this man is so much on the defensive, so aggressive and yet so touchy; always claiming to be 'fair' — what does it matter to him whether I think he is fair or not? The lower-ranking Security men have no such qualms — imagine Dirker, Kleingeld or Swanepoel caring a damn if I or any of my political associates think they are 'fair'.

The trouble is that he *is* fair — by standards that have passed, in methods that no longer operate. If he were truly 'fair', as he

68

claims, he could no longer sit at that desk as head of the Security Police in Johannesburg.

Colonel Klindt never takes part in physical assaults or torture. But before what judge could he plead ignorance of the things done by those under him? He knows. Could he stop it? Does he want to?

One by one Iris, Shirley and I enter his office to ask for our visits. We trot out our prepared reasons: I want to obtain my husband's power of attorney; I need to discuss financial questions; repayments of the bond on our house and so on; and I must find out what to do with various clients and their plans.

I had intended to tackle him on the question of books; it becomes desperately important to get something in to Rusty; I already have an inkling of the long ordeal of ninety days, and the need in some way to penetrate its emptiness. But Shirley has wisely advised against it. 'Let's get these visits first,' she says; 'one step at a time.'

So I don't ask for permission to send in books, but I do ask permission for Rusty to finish doing some architectural drawings, and this is curtly refused.

'No. Definitely not! You know your husband is under ninety days? It is not permitted.'

'The regulations don't prohibit him doing work.'

'It is not permitted,' he shouts angrily; then quietens and says, 'You may take him a change of clothes and collect his dirty washing from the jail once a week.'

He looks up from his desk, grey-faced, grey-haired, prominent pale blue eyes the only colour in the drabness of uniform and skin.

'When do you want to see your husband?'

'As soon as possible.'

He speaks with the pronounced accent, the hard vowels and slurred consonants, of the man whose home language is Afrikaans. All the Security men are Afrikaans-speaking, and many speak English only hesitantly and poorly.

He says: 'I am giving you permission for a ten-minute visit on Monday. You will go to Scotts Buildings in Pretoria, take this note to the Captain, he will give you an escort to the jail. You will discuss immediate family and business matters only. If you attempt to discuss anything else, the visit will be terminated immediately. Have you any transport to Pretoria?'

I then ask him for permission to collect our car, which is parked in the yard of the Goldreich house at Rivonia where Rusty left it when the police took him away. He says he will tell the Rivonia police to let me have the car and tells me when to go and fetch it.

The pattern of visits during the ninety-day period is always the same: first obtain the note with permission for the visit; this must be taken to Security headquarters in Pretoria where two Special Branch men are delegated to accompany you to Pretoria jail. They stay throughout the visit, standing close and listening carefully to every word and for any remark on either side that is not related to the purpose of the visit — except greetings and mutual inquiries about health and the children, which they permit.

Over the weekend I collect the car from the Goldreich house. It is a depressing sight, police at the gates, police emerging from the bushes, and Special Branch men at the house, demanding the names and addresses of the people who drove me out to get the car. It is as though the house itself is under arrest — they are still searching the grounds.

The house, set among trees in many acres of ground, is beautiful, with large cool rooms decorated with African masks, sculpture, handicrafts; and containing long shelves of Arthur's expensive art books. Arthur and his brown-eyed wife Hazel, who is a nursery-school teacher, were not at home when the raid took place. They came home in the early evening and were both arrested and held under the ninety-day law. Their two sons, little boys, were left alone in the house with an African maid. The thought of Hazel and the two little boys is painful beyond words.

On Monday I drive to Pretoria for my visit, with a list of things to ask about, most important of which is, 'Which of your clients owe you money that I can collect?'

Ten minutes behind thick mesh and glass. I see his face dimly: he is haggard and red-eyed. He appears to have difficulty in concentrating on what I am saying, as though he is so infinitely tired that just to stand and talk is too much effort. The Security men stand close to me, watch my face with concentration; as

70

though they may learn something important by my expression.

Ten minutes that seem like two. All the things unsaid. Did you understand also what I could not say, Rusty? That we are crushed, but not destroyed? That I am strong and will not fail? That there is no room for self-pity, only to concentrate on how to adapt?

And I am back again on the Pretoria road, heading towards Johannesburg. From now on for nearly a year I will travel to Pretoria and back at least once a week, usually more, sometimes every day, and come to know every inch of it; outwards from Johannesburg with intense anticipation; back again with flat resignation. It will seem sometimes that a great portion of my life is consumed with the petrol along those forty miles of the road to Pretoria.

From our house it is not far to Louis Botha Avenue, the main road to the north that passes through Pretoria. I drive through streets lined with jacaranda trees and gardens with high hedges, swimming pools, tennis courts. Once into Louis Botha Avenue it takes time to shake loose from the thick traffic, the many stops at traffic lights, the snarl-up of cars and vans, and to emerge among the cluster of minor industries — venetian blind firms, flooring-tile manufacturers and makers of old-world cement garden ornaments — that fringe the outskirts of the suburbs.

Then come the road-houses: Pickin Chicken and Dairy Den; the last few garages; and there is Alexandra Township on the right, what remains of it now that the population has been reduced by half, the families destroyed, the back-yards emptied, the smoke so much thinner, as though even the haze that obscures Alexandra morning and evening has also been 'endorsed out'.

After Alexandra, open land with hedges and trees, and then the big screen of the Drive-In Cinema dominating the skyline; it was the first Drive-In built in South Africa, and Rusty designed it; he would probably have done the others that followed as well, but for the Treason Trial, in which he was one of the accused, and imprisonment during the 1960 emergency.

Under a fly-over bridge, and now the road opens up, the car speeds past the country estate townships of Kelvin and Buccleugh, where tired Johannesburg businessmen build their luxury homes in acres of grounds; houses with huge rooms, china cupboards, great thick glass ashtrays and settees with ball-and-claw feet, where the wives eat themselves up with boredom and vacuity, bridge games, tea-parties, the servant problem, the hostility and ingratitude of children and servants alike — particularly *them*, those ignorant, unclean, lazy creatures from Alexandra over the hill; and the husbands have high blood pressure and die of thrombosis while playing golf or while sitting at the huge walnut desks in their carpeted office.

Then farm stalls with honey, eggs and home-made preserves; up the hill to the Snake Park where children are taken on boring Sunday afternoons.

At the Yukskei Bridge slacken speed; provincial traffic policemen watch for cars overtaking over the white line; but in any case it is a steep dip and a narrow bridge approached on a sharp curve. The other side rises steeply and, inevitably, there is an enormous slow chugging truck which cannot be passed until the hill has been cleared.

Shortly after this an untidy clutter of petrol stations and stores. Halfway House reduces speed to forty; then once more into countryside, several miles of roller-coaster hills lined with bluegums, their spiral bark white and twisting in contrast to the black-trunked pines; countryside stretching to distant hazy hills. This is the longest stretch of open road, and the most beautiful. There is one place here, at the summit of a hill, from which the highveld rolls away in orange earth, tawny grass and muted olive-green trees to the far-distant Magaliesburg mountains, a breathtaking glimpse of space and Africa, where nothing intervenes between hills and sky. Almost of its own volition the car slows down each time for a quick greedy gasp at those open spaces.

The last long hill ends in a small bridge where there is always a traffic jam, someone very slow ahead with cars crawling impatiently up the next rise to a built-up area called Valhalla, with Voortrekkerhoogte on the right. Valhalla is just a mess of sprawling shops and red-roofed suburban houses, and Voortrekkerhoogte (it used to be called 'Roberts' Heights'; the change of name signified the ascendance of Afrikaans over English in the Air Force) is the Air Force training headquarters.

The road winds down and down; up on a hill are the sharp angles of the new Air Force memorial, severe and impersonal; and on the crest of the last hill a huge office block stands by itself — Iscor, the iron and steel works administrative block, turns its modern blue facade towards Pretoria — while on the other side of the road is the heavy stone lump which is the shrine of Afrikanerdom, said to be a replica of a Chicago synagogue, where the master race gather each year to give praise to God for their bloody triumph at arms over the black savages — the Voortrekker Memorial.

The road drops so swiftly that your ears become blocked; suddenly and without any preliminary statement of straggling houses and garages, the road emerges from between rows of trees right into Pretoria. The fir.., the very first, building is a red brick wall that runs along on the left and rises to old-fashioned brick towers with crenellated edges — Pretoria jail.

The first part of the jail is the black section; outside African women permanently cluster with shawls and paper bags waiting to visit husbands or sons, or to hand in food or a change of clothing for prisoners awaiting trial. They sit at the kerbside in the glaring sun or stand for hours at the foot of the steps.

There are no relatives waiting outside the white section, right next door, because we are provided with a waiting-room inside the jail. Even so, we sometimes stand in that sweating hot sun for a long time before they find time to open the door and let us in. Just inside, the small waiting-room with three wooden benches. In all the long hours spent sitting on one of those benches, I have studied every inch of this portion of Pretoria Prison, the face of all the warders, and of each individual who sits there and waits.

On the wall is a calendar and some yellowing notices. One notice reads:

Kennisgewing.
Huurders neem kennis.
Drosters moet onmiddelik
gerapporteer word.

Afrikaans is the language of the civil service in South Africa;

English is scarcely spoken in the jails. The notice appears only in Afrikaans and literally translated means, 'Hirers take notice. Runaways must immediately be reported'.

Pretoria Local is a short-term prison. Prisoners serving long sentences are taken to other prisons usually in outlying places, away from the towns. Africans serving short sentences are kept at Pretoria Local and hired out to local farmers by the Prisons Department.

The farmers come to fetch them from the jail in trucks, the backs of which have been converted into locked cages.

African prisoners do not pass in and out of this front door — it is for whites only — so we do not see them being escorted to the trucks outside. But the white farmers, on the other hand, the 'hirers', cannot go through the non-white entrance, so they sit in this waitingroom as the warders prepare their load of convict-workers, and the necessary papers for them to sign.

A 'hirer' waiting for convicts is immediately recognizable. Khaki shirts and shorts and a wide-brimmed hat, his overweight body was once muscular; his face is burnt red from the sun and is thickly lined, small blue eyes sunk into its flesh.

Runaways must immediately be reported. How many runaways are there, and what happens to them when they are caught?

Apart from the 'hirers', the only regular visitors to the waiting-room are an elderly couple, immigrants from Greece, whose son is in trouble; they bring him home-cooked food almost every day (prisoners awaiting trial are permitted one meal from outside each day). The mother, shawl-wrapped, wrinkled, defeated, cannot speak English; the father explains with halting words that his young son fell in with a bad set and they stole a car; later I find the boy was leader of a gang involved in much more serious crimes. Everything about the parents speaks of failure, failure to find the bright new world for which they had emigrated, failure to bring happiness and security to their children, failure to understand what the forces were with which they had to contend.

Nobody sits in the waiting-room as often or as long as I. Arriving to deliver food and clean clothes; sitting and waiting for the warder to find time to unlock the cells and bring out clothes that are to be washed. Trying to read — who could lose themselves in a book in the waiting-room at Pretoria Prison? I sit and wait and watch the time and calculate how late it will be when I get back to Johannesburg and how I can adjust my schedule of things to be done. And wait for Rusty's clothes; he will know I have been here again when they come to collect the clothes, even though the warders do not speak to him.

Cold in that jail. Outside the blue, blue sky and the hot enclosed sun of Pretoria. But always cold inside Pretoria Local prison.

3
Ninety-day Dialogues

Through the prison grapevine, from the African side of the jail, a message comes out that Govan Mbeki and Raymond Mhlaba are suffering from the cold and are in need of clothes. Neither of them have any relatives in Johannesburg. With friends I collect some warm underwear, buy two thick jerseys, and borrow two overcoats, knowing how intense is the cold of sunless stone and cement in the jail.

Esmé has been granted a second visit to Denis before returning to Cape Town, and she takes the clothes with her to deliver to the black side of the jail.

When she returns she brings the clothes back.

'They wouldn't accept them.'

'What do you mean, they wouldn't accept them? You just leave them there — they *must* accept clothes.'

'They would not accept them,' Esmé repeats. 'First I tried handing them in to the warder who let me in. He said he couldn't accept clothes for natives, they had to be given in at the other side. Then after my visit I took them to the non-white door. When the warder opened, he said I wasn't allowed on that side, I had to go to the European side. When I told him I just wanted to leave some clothes for African prisoners, he said he couldn't take clothes for a native from a white.'

'It's ridiculous.'

'Of course it's ridiculous. You go and tell him. I told him — he just repeated a white can't leave clothes for a native.'

Next time we go to Pretoria, Shirley and I take the clothes. We call on a white woman we know to ask her if she can find an African willing to hand the clothes in on the African side of the jail.

Esmé returns to Cape Town deeply depressed. Denis had seemed cheerful on her first visit, but morose and quiet the second time.

76

A week after the Rivonia arrests the police make another catch: Harold Wolpe, arrested on the border of South Africa while attempting to cross into Bechuanaland. On the day after the Rivonia arrests when he saw me at Innes Chambers, he had left his home and stayed in hiding. His association with Arthur Goldreich had been close and he was afraid his own arrest was imminent. He shaved off his thick, black beard, dyed his hair red and drove to a farm owned by a relative, near the Bechuanaland border.

His escape was to be simple and well-planned. There were some overseas visitors at the farm, who were going to a neighbouring farm for a *braaivleis* (a South African barbecue). The second farm was on the border. Some time during the evening when it was dark, he would slip away from the fireside, walk to the border fence, and climb over into Bechuanaland.

What went wrong was unpredictable. The driver of the car taking Harold and the other visitors to the party stopped to ask a farmer the way; they were not quite sure which track led off the road to the farm they were to visit.

The farmer, who had been leaning idly and peacefully on a gate deep in the country, miles from anywhere, turned out to be a policeman keeping a watch on the border. He asked the occupants of the car to establish their identities, which they could all do except Harold. He was taken to the local police station and brought back to Johannesburg under arrest — ninety days.

* * *

Some of the ninety-day people are being kept at Marshall Square. Harold has been taken to Marshall Square and so has Arthur Goldreich. Shirley and I take and fetch clothes twice a week from Pretoria for Denis, Bob and Rusty. In between, I battle with Colonel Klindt for the right to send food and books to my husband. 'It is not permitted!'

I have already found that the important thing with Klindt is not to accept his 'No!' however fiercely and forcefully delivered. He is full of inconsistencies. After he has delivered the first angry refusal I stand my ground, plead, argue. On the question of books he is adamant; we are both aware that this is a fundamental

77

issue; something to do or read would make the weeks of solitary confinement endurable; deprivation is part of the whole process.

'Detainees in Cape Town are getting food.' 'Who says so?' 'We heard from relatives.' 'What happens in Cape Town has got nothing to do with me. I'm in charge in Johannesburg, not Cape Town. They make their own rules.' 'Well, you could make a rule permitting food here, then.' And on another occasion: 'Food is being taken to detainees in Marshall Square — why not in Pretoria?' 'The conditions are different in Marshall Square.' 'Then let my husband come to Marshall Square; it would be a lot easier for me.' 'No, no, no! Your husband is NOT going to be brought to Marshall Square, not under any circumstances!'

But after a month, we are permitted to take food to Pretoria. There are endless difficulties in actually taking it in; the rules are changed almost every week; the conditions laid down by the Security Branch differ from those imposed by the prison authorities at Pretoria Local, but just the same a supply of fresh fruit, biscuits and chocolate to supplement prison meals is sent in.

One day we are informed: tinned food, or food in sealed containers only; nothing that has been opened, and no home-cooked foods. A few days later the Head Warder at Pretoria, Breedt, refuses to accept tins. 'Everything must be opened!' he orders. Then tapping the tinned foods with his baton: 'Guns have been sealed into tins before now!' Shirley and I repress our giggles until we get outside; the thought of sealing guns into tins of meat or beans had never occurred to us.

As far as the African detainees are concerned, some of them have relatives who can make the tedious journey to Pretoria to bring them food and take away their washing, but many of them do not. In Pretoria there is a wonderful Indian woman who lives in a slummy black ghetto called the Asiatic Bazaar, not far from the main part of the town. Mrs Pillay has no more money than any of the other struggling and segregated families of the Asiatic Bazaar, and no more time than any of the other women with large families and numerous relatives. Yet for years during the Treason Trial she prepared meals for the people on trial and brought them to the court so that they had hot food at least for lunch. Now Mrs Pillay is making meals again. She sends her male relatives around the Bazaar to collect donations of bread, vegetables, fruit from the small traders. In her own house she prepares innumerable sandwiches, cooks curries, parcels up meals into containers. Part of her work is ascertaining the number of detainees and their names, information which is not easy to get, so that she can see each one has something sent in.

My life has now become split into separate lives, almost wholly compartmentalized.

There is the routine domestic life of home and children, picking up to its normal furious tempo as they return from the winter holidays and go back to school. I meet Patrick at the station. In the car: 'Patrick, Dad's been arrested.' 'I know.' 'How?' 'One of the boys at camp — his father wrote and told him and he told me.' I had hoped Patrick could finish his holiday without having the misery of the arrest at the back of his mind.

The second part of my life is the battle at The Grays and the trips to Pretoria and back again, eating away at mornings, physically and emotionally exhausting.

'Colonel Klindt, I want to see my husband.'

'Why do you want to see him?'

'I want to trade in our car — its a Chev. and its too big for me — and get a small one. But it's his car, and I must get his permission.'

'Then you can write him a note — sit down here, you can write it here. I'll see he gets it. One of my men will take it to your husband, and I'll see you get a reply.'

'No, Colonel Klindt, that won't do. I must see him to discuss it with him.'

'Well, you can't see him' — rising annoyance — 'write a note. I'll see he gets it.'

'I must discuss it with him. I want his advice on what kind of car to get. Besides, I don't want to sell his car without seeing him about it first. He's very attached to that car. I want to discuss the finances of it with him. I can't do it through writing a note.'

It is hard going, and he tends so strongly to erupt in anger, but after about twenty minutes of this he does give me permission for my second visit. But this visit, and this conversation, will have strange repercussions that I cannot possibly foresee.

* * *

Rusty and I have established our thread of communication and through it I am living his ninety days with him; the isolation, the long empty days and nights, the suspense and torments of errors, of things done wrongly.

Rusty to me

My cell is approximately ten by eight. It has a table and a hard wooden stool, backless. In one corner is a raised platform on which is enthroned the sanitary pot — so-called. That is all. There is a square window about eight to nine feet up, barred with wire mesh over glass that is so heavily crusted in dust that you really see through a glass darkly. Through it I can see the sky and just the tip of a brick gable of the jail hospital. Blankets and the felt mat on which we sleep *must* be kept rolled and folded against the table from 6 a.m. to supper. Clothes, food, toilet articles are either neatly laid out on the table or kept in paper carrier bags. For some reason known only to the obscure civil service mind, no suitcases or bags of any sort are allowed, only paper carrier bags or topless card-board boxes. At supper-time shoes must be placed outside cell doors for some equally obscure reason, and must remain there until breakfast. The light is recessed into the wall, behind wire mesh, so as to throw a beam of light across the cell and leave everything below four feet in shadow.

He has the extra privilege of a white man: a backless stool to sit on during the day. Africans do not have stools in their cells, nor tables. They must sit on the cold cement floors when they are not pacing up and down in the tiny cells. How does he pass the time? Twenty-three hours in the cell out of every twenty-four, with nothing to do except read the Bible, the only book permitted.

Rusty to me

I am finding the nights worse than the days. Lights go out at 8 p.m. I try to find exercises to keep me up till 8.30. But then I wake too early and from dawn to 5.30 is spent turning and tossing and having fearful nightmares. Quite awful and I contemplate getting up and pacing. But no shoes! I recount to myself memories of child-hood, not in full, but try and discover what makes a man face trial for treason twice in the matter of seven years. Strange how the more I work at it the more long-forgotten memories come back.

I have a new time-killing device in which I pace the cell for two hours — this is my inventing session — thinking about all the damn silly tedious time-consuming and primitive jobs I have done at one time or another, or seen done, and then inventing new ways of doing them. They are screaming for a pad and paper and some scientific advice. As soon as I can send out letters I must get those ideas down. Incredible how fertile one's ingenuity becomes when there is all the time in the world to exercise it without outside distractions or stimuli at all.

Stories of what was happening to ninety-day detainees crept out. In Cape Town police held the wife of Archie Sibeko who they wanted but could not find. After she had been detained, Lettie Sibeko found that she was pregnant. She sat for weeks and then months alone on the cold cement floor of the cell. When relatives brought food and clothes, the police sent them away saying: 'Tell Archie to bring it!' For five months she sat alone with the burgeoning child. They released her two weeks before the baby was born; then arrested her again.

A note smuggled out of a large police cell where many were herded together said, *We do not have enough water to drink — never to wash.* Four teenagers were held for eighty-seven days during which time they were only twice given water to wash, and their only food was hard corn-porridge.

Next of kin are not informed, and poor as they are, many spend weeks walking from one police station to another in different suburbs and towns, trying to find their husbands and sons.

For some it is physical torture. 'They kept me standing for three days,' said a man who was released. This was the first time we heard of the 'Statue' torture, under which people are kept standing for days and nights enduring interrogation. And the electric torture: the victims trussed like chickens with a pole going over bent elbows and under bent knees, electrodes attached to fingers, head, tongue, testicles. How did Solwandle Ngudle die? Police say he was found hanging in his cell. Later at an inquest a witness stated: 'Ngudle went in with the police a long time. When he came back he had changed in colour. I

81

asked him if he had been in the electric room. He said, Yes. He spoke in Xhosa and said: *Indiphethe kakubi* — it had me bad.'

Mosie Moolla, who had been chairman of the Transvaal Indian Youth Congress, was held for three months at Marshall Square. Three days before the ninety days were up, he was transferred to the police station at Mondeor, a white suburban township some way out of town. At three o'clock in the morning they came to his cell and told him he was being released: 'Take your things — go!' With his clothes in a paper bag, he found himself out on deserted strange streets, and started to walk in the direction of town. He had no money, and in any case there was no transport. He walked for a while in silence along the sleeping streets; then heard in the distance the sound of a car; its head-lamps illuminated the road beyond. They came up behind him; stopped. Police. 'You are under arrest.' 'What for?' 'Ninety days.' It had begun all over again.

Abdulhai Jassat was pulled from his bed in the early hours of the morning a few months previously when three other young Indian lads had been caught in a sabotage attempt near a rail-way station.

He was taken to a room ringed by about twenty big white men.

A welcoming circle for Jassat; the handcuffs were taken off his wrists, the officer in charge told him to confess to being guilty of sabotage. 'No.' A crashing blow sent him into the arms of one of the men forming the circle; he was passed from one to the other with blows on the head and face; any one of these men could have beaten him up by himself, because Jassat is small and slight. But this is a game for them; he was hurled violently back and forth, round the circle, across the floor; thrown down, forced to do physical exercises until he collapsed from exhaus-tion, then the group closed in on his prostrate body kicking, shouting their racist abuse. He stood with a heavy stone on his head, he was beaten on the soles of bare feet with batons, they attached leads to his toes and shocked him with a dynamo until he lost consciousness. A wet sack was tightened round his head; he was swung around by his ankles. By the ankles they sus-pended him out of an open window forty feet above the ground. 'Speak! Or we let go. We'll say you tried to escape.' He did not speak. They hauled him in again, calling him a 'dirty coolie'.

Abdulhai Jassat, whose treatment brought on a form of epilepsy from which he will suffer for the rest of his life, was then charged with sabotage; but there was no evidence against him, and he was found not guilty. He was immediately re-arrested in court and held under ninety days.

Rusty to me
I have been keeping a record and find that I am averaging eighteen spoken words a day. 'Thank you' three times for meals. 'May I have a match, please?' twice at exercise times. I keep my vocal chords exercised with an evening song session, taking advantage of the captive audience, Bob and H, and the two warders outside, and the quite remarkable bathroom-type acoustics of the cell which enable me to go from basso-profundo to mezzo-soprano! Aided of course by the fact that I've cut down smoking to two a day for the second thirty days and intend to drop it entirely for the third. Just one of the gimmicks I'm trying out to ensure that I stay strictly non-obsessional and as non-neurotic as possible in circumstances specially designed for neurosis.

Two American psychologists who made a study of detention under solitary confinement say that from the first three to ten days the effects are anxiety, hyperactivity, sleeplessness, nightmares, steadily increasing loneliness, boredom, fatigue, drowsiness, pain, loss of weight and gradual compliance. From three to six weeks the prisoner experiences despair, utter dependence, inactivity, filth, mental dulling, loss of discrimination, delusions, the great need to talk.

Rusty to me
We exercise in a dreary enclosed yard, slate floor, cells all round three sides, open shower, w.c.s, tap in centre. We are NOT allowed to talk, we pace up and down not talking, really rather grim.

There is sun on one side so we stick to the narrow sunny strip. When we first got here we could only just get our heads into the sun by hugging the wall. A search seems to have been inspired by the finding of a note from one of us in J's Bible — silly clot — Vigilance is at its height and even muttering in the yard is difficult.

If you could only *see* the searches now, they get more and more serious like the FBI looking for atomic secrets. Partly the reason is that they *know* there is a pen somewhere and they suspect B or me; partly it is that this has become a personal matter in which the warder seems to think his standing is at stake if he does not succeed in tracking it down.

* * *

Someone comes to my home one day and tells me that Arthur Goldreich and others are planning an escape from Marshall Square.

We are asked to provide a car to whisk them away once they are out, and to find a safe place to keep them until it is possible to get them out of the country.

If they had taken my advice, they would have stayed in jail. I am convinced the escape will not be successful and afraid they will be caught and punished, perhaps even shot.

After several secret messages, a car is hired for the night they are supposed to make their getaway. The car stands for hours round the corner from Marshall Square, while the driver tries to keep up a pretence of tinkering with the engine; finally, in the early hours of the morning, he cannot wait any more and leaves.

The next message says another attempt will be made on Saturday. The car must be there at a certain time in the evening. I complain that Saturday night is a crazy time. 'It's the busiest night of the whole week at Marshall Square. There'll be too many people around.'

But another car is sent; more hours pretending to fix a difficult engine, waiting and watching all the time in suspense. Around Marshall Square the mining companies have their offices; it is virtually deserted at night. The car waits for nearly an hour beyond the appointed time, then finally drives away.

'They didn't come. Waited for hours,' is the first report I hear. Then someone comes and says, 'Well, they made it. They're out!' I can hardly believe it and am petrified for them.

'Who?'

'Four of them — Arthur, Harold, Mosie and Jassat.'

Jassat is not married — Arthur's wife, Hazel, is already under ninety days. As soon as the escape of the four men is discovered,

84

the police arrest Harold's wife, Anne-Marie, and Mosie's wife, Fubeida, who is seven months' pregnant. Both are bullied, threatened, abused for hours on end. The Security men are incoherent with fury at the escape. Ultimately they release the two women, who could have told them nothing no matter how long they kept them.

They could not have said that, once outside Marshall Square, the four men looked for the escape car which had driven off ten minutes before. When they could not find it, they split into two, Mosie and Jassat walking west towards the Indian area of Fordsburg, Harold and Arthur turning north towards the white suburb of Hillbrow.

Mosie and Jassat had not walked very far when they were overtaken by a car; it was driven by a friend of theirs, a man who had been on night duty and was just returning home. He recognized them; he thought they must have just been released from ninety days and stopped in surprised pleasure. They for their part thought he was the man who should have been waiting outside Marshall Square, and started to upbraid him for not being on time.

Arthur and Harold decided to make for the flat of a man they felt would not betray them. They knew it would not be long before their absence was discovered, and the police would be out in force scouring the streets to find them. The sound of every car in the distance set their pulses racing. They seemed to have been walking for hours, trying to keep to back streets, when, ahead of them, they saw a car parked with its lights on. They drew back into the dark and waited; a man came out of the bushes and climbed into the driver's seat, started the car and was about to drive off when suddenly Harold began to run towards the car, shouting.

It was one of those coincidences that novelists would hesitate to use; the driver of the car was the man towards whose flat they were walking. He was coming home late from a party and could not wait any longer to urinate. He had turned off the main road into a dark side-street, where Harold saw him.

Luck so far. But on the Monday morning the papers had huge black headlines: 'FOUR NINETY-DAY MEN ESCAPE. Police throw out a dragnet for key Rivonia raid figures ... descriptions

85

of the four men ... road blocks erected ... a massive house-to-house search in certain areas ... a group of bitterly disappointed Security officers, including Lieutenant-Colonel Klindt, head of the Rand Security Branch, gathered at The Grays to devise methods to track down the escapers ...'

I had decided some days previously that the time had come to try and get another visit to Rusty, and had previously fixed that Monday as the day on which to tackle Colonel Klindt. It was obviously not an auspicious occasion, and I knew I had considerable nerve to go in to The Grays at all. But it did not seem to me that the escape of the four men had any bearing on visiting my husband, and I had a horrible feeling that if I did not go when I had decided, I would lose my nerve altogether and keep on postponing it.

So on Monday morning, early, I presented myself at The Grays. The place was in a turmoil, men striding in and out of offices, phones ringing, doors slamming, people going up and down in the lifts. I tried to get in unnoticed, but inevitably attracted the startled looks of SBs.

'Colonel Klindt, I want to see my husband.'

The blue eyes stared in amazement, almost shooting out of their sockets, the grey face is lined and angry.

'Out of the question! I won't even consider it!'

'But, Colonel Klindt, I have to see him soon because my younger daughter is starting high school, and we must discuss whether she is to take French or Latin ...'

We are off, the slanging match gets under way, I stick doggedly to my 'urgent and important reasons' for a visit. Colonel Klindt who is totally unable to keep to any one subject under discussion, ranges over the whole field of iniquity of those held under ninety days, the disgusting, unfair, underhand tactics used by Goldreich to effect the escape, the impossibility of trusting such people as ourselves. I simply stand my ground and insert a word or two when I can, and wait for him to exhaust himself. Finally we get to the stage where I say: 'Well, if it's absolutely out of the question now, when can I come and see you about a visit?'

He mumbles, 'You can phone me later on in the week.'

Later in the week I phone and say, 'You remember you said I could phone you to find out when you will let me see my husband?' It takes nearly two weeks to obtain this third visit.

Rusty to me
Ten days already since I saw you. It is a funny thing, the hours of each day seem to drag by slower and slower as time goes on, and yet the days and weeks seem to go past quicker. The first time I waited three weeks between your visits, it seemed an eternity that would never pass. And already I ask myself whether you will get another permit from God about three weeks from the last, approximately ten days from now ...

The thought of being in prison for a long time is awful, but tolerable for a man like me. The discomforts and privations mean very little to me. The worst of it is the separation from you, and the kids and knowing that all the time I am here they are growing out of childhood, the years in which I love them best, and I can never recapture that ... I am unable to think of the torments the children must be having at school. Other kids can be such monsters over things they do not understand ... It is hell, not just the loneliness and solitude of tedium but the devilish neurotic fears, anxieties and tensions with only one's mind for company and nothing to move it to think except one's own troubles. You can't imagine what this does to you. You become not just the centre, but the whole of your universe, your own fate, your own future. Nothing you can do or say can possibly affect the life of anyone else, or so it seems. What little courage I have gradually erodes in loneliness with no one near to sustain me.

Once more I go to Colonel Klindt to demand that my husband be allowed books. We have a really big row, a stand-up verbal fight, both shouting together. He states over and over again: 'It is not permitted! It is not in the regulations!' I repeat over and over that the regulations do not specifically exclude books and writing material — they don't actually mention it, and I know and he knows that it is in the power of the officer in charge to interpret the regulations governing the conditions of detainees as he pleases.

He talks of Rusty's refusal to 'co-operate' — 'if you would persuade your husband to be more reasonable, then we would be more reasonable as well'.

'My husband will decide for himself what he thinks is right. I am not going to tell him to do anything he thinks wrong.'

Finally he stands up and bangs his fist on the table with anger, shouting, 'I don't make the law! I did not frame this law! I am merely here to see that the law is carried out!'

At that, I leave without further argument. I feel that, in a way he himself would not understand, this man has revealed his very soul to me. I take up the question of books with lawyers. It seems to me terribly important to make a breakthrough, not just for Rusty but for all the detainees. They argue that there is no point in pursuing it; it is costly and time-consuming to press such questions. The legal men who are sympathetic enough to deal with political cases are few — and all desperately over-burdened with many important cases.

Eventually I go to an acquaintance who is a lawyer and ask him to write a letter to Colonel Klindt and the Director of Prisons on my behalf over the question of books and writing materials, and the conditions under which my husband is held. He does so, and we wait for the reply.

Rusty to me
Nothing gives me worse torments than the fear that something might happen to you or that you may be dragged into this night-mare situation. This tortures me almost to distraction. On the days when I expect you to bring clothes and food, I age a year with every hour that passes. I keep telling myself that this is madness, but reason doesn't help against unreasonable fear. Yesterday clothes arrived as usual in the morning, but no food until the after-noon — left in some office, I suppose. I spent the morning worry-ing; where were you? why did someone else have to bring the clothes? And then the food arrived, and somehow it looked more Shirley's style of food than yours and for a while this gave me ulcers. I know this is crazy, but it destroys what courage I have; darling, please, I beg of you, don't get into danger.

Huge headlines in the papers and pictures printed every day of the four missing men: 'South Africa's biggest manhunt police appeal to the public — reward offered —'.

* * *

'We've just got to find another place for Harold and Arthur. What about their bloody families? Can't we get the families to find a place?'

'All right,' I say, 'I'll go and see Jimmy Kantor.'

Jimmy Kantor, Harold's brother-in-law, runs a well-known legal practice in Johannesburg specializing in criminal cases. Harold was in partnership with him at the time of his arrest. I have met Jimmy, but do not know him well; only that he has created a public image of himself as a fun-loving playboy, and that he has no interest in politics whatsoever.

I sit at a desk opposite Jimmy, and after greeting him ask him for a piece of paper; it seems very likely that his office is bugged. I write: 'We have Harold and Arthur, but must move them. They are not safe. Can you or any other members of the families find a place?'

Jimmy takes the pad and writes: 'I don't know any place, but will try to think of something.'

I write: 'How soon?'

He writes: 'Come tomorrow morning.'

While we pass notes, we keep up some sort of conversation on a pretended legal problem.

In the morning I try him again and he suggests a house that we consider totally unsafe.

The next conversation on the subject is held in my bathroom, with Bram Fischer. We go to the bathroom because it seems the least likely room in the house to have a listening device. We take a radio with us and keep it playing loudly as well.

Sitting on the edge of the bath I say: 'When are you moving them?' Bram says, 'Tomorrow night,' and outlines the plan.

It has been decided to take them to a cottage in the garden of a house in Mountain View, a suburb not far from where I live. The cottage was originally rented by Denis Goldberg, and has been used by people in hiding. The owners, who live in the main house only a few hundred yards away, are Maureen and Louis Kreel. They do not know anything except that the man who rented the cottage is away a great deal. They leave the place alone.

The cottage is risky; by all the rules, it should be completely abandoned. But we are forced to move them and are desperate. Every block of flats in Johannesburg is serviced by a caretaker and an army of African cleaners who have keys to all the flats. Every home has at least one servant. They must be kept at a place where there is no possibility of someone recognizing them from the Press photographs and betraying them for the sake of the reward.

At this stage, too, we still know little of the effects of ninety days, and have not yet had betrayals by loyal people with whom we have worked — not yet. Thus naively, we weigh the loyalty of all those in prison who know about the cottage at Mountain View, and decide to take a chance.

One night, Bram and I go to visit Arthur and Harold at the cottage. I try to disguise myself with long skirts, cushions stuffed into my clothes, an old-fashioned hat, and a string bag with parcels. I leave the house by car, drive to another suburb, park the car and leave it locked. I take a bus back along the route I have travelled, get out half-way home, walk around the corner to where Bram is waiting in a car. He claimed to my annoyance that he recognized me the moment I turned the corner.

Arthur and Harold have now been staying in the cottage for some days, and both are in a state of extreme nervous tension. They dare not put on lights, the curtains are drawn day and night. They eat cold food because they do not want the people in the main house to hear or smell cooking. They do not even flush the lavatory during the day, when there is often a gardener working outside, and a maid walking around talking to the gardener, hanging out washing. From the time it becomes dark until morning they can only sit and whisper, unable to read as they cannot show a light.

The four of us sit together, whispering and sipping brandy that Bram has brought with him. We discuss escape routes, examine maps with the aid of a torch, talk about disguises, transport. They urge us to find another place for them to stay; we tell them to be patient just a little longer.

We seem to be stopping our whispered discussions all the time: a hand placed on an arm, a head tilted to listen. The rustle of leaves outside, the disturbance of a stone — it may be a visitor going to the main house, or a dog chasing through the darkened garden; or something else. We wait; the sound dissipates; we laugh breathlessly and silently with relief. The room fills with

90

cigarette smoke. And finally I kiss them as we leave and say sadly: 'It will be years and years before we meet again.' 'Perhaps not so long,' Harold says.

Next day as I drive down Louis Botha Avenue on my way to Pretoria, and glance up at the roof and trees which obscure the cottage on the hill, the poster reads: 'NET CLOSES ROUND HUNTED MEN'.

'They're probably out of the country by now,' says my butcher, later.

'Probably,' I agree. 'Two pounds of shin and two of mince.'

'They'd be crazy to hang around in Johannesburg waiting to be picked up,' he remarks, and adds, 'Bet they've been over the border for a week. Well, good luck to them if they can get away with it.' He then says with grudging admiration: 'They must have had that escape planned and organized down to the last second. They were probably a couple of hundred miles away before the police even found they had gone. Split-second timing.'

'I expect so.'

* * *

On 23 August, twelve days after their escape from Marshall Square, Arthur and Harold arrived in Swaziland by car, disguised as priests. They were at Francistown in Bechuanaland before the news of their escape from South Africa broke in the Press. A plane sent to Francistown to take them on to Dar-es-Salaam, was wrecked by an incendiary bomb which was put in the plane during the night by someone known to the airport guards while it stood on the airstrip. Afraid of being abducted back over the South African border the men sought refuge in the Francistown jail until arrangements could be made for another plane to be sent. Eventually this was made possible through the help of a newspaper, and they were finally flown out via the Congo.

With the escape of Arthur, the most wanted of the four, the pressure eased a little; Mosie Moolla and Jassat slipped through to Bechuanaland some time afterwards with less publicity, and went on from there to Dar-es-Salaam.

A week before Arthur and Harold had left Johannesburg, I had decided to go to Jimmy Kantor again to see if he had found a suitable place for them to stay. I was on my way to his office when I read in the paper that he too had been detained under ninety days. Perhaps the police thought he had organized the escape from Marshall Square.

It was not illogical. As a criminal lawyer he had a reputation for rather flamboyant actions, and a certain Perry Masonish disregard for the absolute letter of the law. But when the two men succeeded in getting right out of the country, while Kantor was in detention, it must have been clear to everyone that he was not the organizer of the escape. Everyone thought that he would be released. But they continued to detain him. It seemed like an act of vindictive spite: taking out their anger on Harold's brother-in-law and partner. Nobody could realize at that time just how far they would take it out on Jimmy Kantor.

* * *

The newspapers have given up trying to keep some sort of account of how many have been detained. Sometimes a paragraph appears saying that 'five Africans' or 'ten Coloureds' have been seized in this place or that. They are not named, they have become statistics; only their immediate families know who has disappeared.

'Ninety days of nothing' says J. Hamilton Russell, former M.P. '… suggestions become truths, hallucinations become reality, the thought of confession becomes attractive, pride begins to grovel … the spirit cringes, the mind bends, the soul contracts before such sadistic cruelty. The victim longs for company, even the presence of a bullying interrogator … What is true? What is false? Does it matter? Say what I say, says the inquisitor, and all this will end.

'Psychiatrists, psychologists and scientists of world-wide reputation will, without exception, tell you that prolonged isolation is the cruellest kind of torment …'

Rusty to me
It may sound odd, but I am longing to be brought to trial, just to bring uncertainty to an end and also to save us from the prospect of another ninety days like these; the prospect fills me with such awful depression that I cannot bear to contemplate it. I am very

fluttery internally, for no special reason, and feel as though I am as old as Father Time, and shaky as a leaf ... I know I am pretty close to the end of my nervous tether. I am at my worst at breakfast and for a few hours thereafter, then pick up during the day. The prospect is really bleak — unless I am charged, which is what I hope for. Just to be able to talk to people! Only now am I realizing what a beating my nervous system has taken over the past four years of ceaseless tension, made worse by the strain of house arrest when everyone who set foot in the house caused me to tighten up; and finally the weeks, so awful that I cannot even now think of them too calmly, when every day I had to steel myself to go into Marshall Square, expecting to be kept there for ninety days.

* * *

'Suffering,' wrote W. H. Auden, 'takes place while someone else is eating or opening a window or just walking dully along.' It takes place while I shop and look after my family.

'What's the news of your husband?' asks my butcher. 'Have you seen him lately?' What's the news, what's the news — the news is that he sits, night and day, in a tiny cell, deprived of all human contacts, deprived of the right to read, to work, to talk, the things that keep human beings alive. Except for the Special Branch coming each week, with carefully distilled news of only those events most likely to upset him, and with suggested offers of money and immunity if he will 'co-operate'. And a weekly visit from a magistrate who conscientiously writes down his complaints and refrains from doing anything other than passing on what he says to the Special Branch.

My butcher is not a Nationalist; he votes for the United Party. The United Party supported the ninety-day law, subject to an additional provision that detainees should be visited once a week by a magistrate to whom they could put any complaints. This was their safeguard against abuses of the law — safeguarding the detainees.

A magistrate visits Rusty weekly, carefully records all his complaints, goes away and comes back the next week to ask, 'Any complaints?'

One week Rusty says, 'Yes — I want to know what happened about the complaints I made to you last week.'

The magistrate starts to write. Rusty has a facility for reading upside down, and now he reads what the magistrate is writing in his book: *I want to know what happened about the complaints I made to you last week*.

When he has finished writing he looks up. 'Anything else?'

'Don't I get an answer to that question?'

The magistrate writes in his book: 'Don't I get an answer to that question?'

The United Party and their safeguards! My face tightens, my ability to make small talk evaporates.

'Oh well, you people knew what you were doing,' remarks the butcher.

'What do you mean — knew what we were doing?'

'I mean, if you go in for politics, that's what you must expect. Take my advice, you stay out of that sort of thing.'

'You talk like the Germans — turn your back on what's happening and ignore it, it's none of your business. That's how the Jews finished up in gas ovens'.

'It's not the same, not the same at all,' he says severely. He is Jewish himself. 'How can you compare it? There aren't any gas ovens here.'

I stop going to shops where I am known, and where I must make conversation.

So August is over, without the gritty cold winds that usually assail the town at the end of winter, and it is September again, a warm, gentle spring. The swimming season opens officially on the first of September. This year our friends and neighbours, the Schermbruckers, have scrubbed the pool clean and painted it for us.

I make no progress with the battle of the books. Long delays for replies to official correspondence. Threats of further action unless ...

One day Shirley Hepple phones me. 'I collected Denis Goldberg's washing,' she says. 'Something peculiar. The clothes are all torn — there are bloodstains on them. I don't know what to think.'

She brings the clothes to my house. There is a lumber jacket in the back of which are torn two large round holes; a pair of trousers, the bottom torn and splashed with what are obviously bloodstains; a handkerchief soaked in blood; a torn shirt.

94

We examine the clothes feeling cold and afraid. Sometime previously Denis had been moved from Pretoria Prison to a prison in a small Transvaal town, Vereeniging. Shirley took food for him up to The Grays, and the SBs promised to take it out to him. But a week later when she went there again, the paper carrier with the food was still standing where it had been left. We are oppressed to the depths of our souls, not just by the torn and bloodstained clothes, but by the feeling of secrecy and silence that cannot be probed, the impossibility of obtaining aid for someone who must be in need, the whole atmosphere of fear and isolation surrounding the men under ninety days.

'It looks like police dogs,' I say, holding the jagged ends of the trousers.

Shirley replies 'That's what I thought. Why would they set police dogs on to him?'

Only Esmé can even ask to see Denis, so we decide that we must send for her, even though this means an expensive and worrying trip from Cape Town.

When Esmé arrives two days later, she goes straight to see Colonel Klindt and asks to see her husband. The answer is, 'No, no, no. You may NOT have a visit! I will not allow it, not under any circumstances.' He seems very angry, very adamant, and will not give way. Esmé then makes a wise decision. She decides to take the clothes and show them to him. 'What must I think?' she asks. 'I want to know how his clothes got into this condition. I want to see if he is all right.'

Colonel Klindt appears disturbed at the sight of the clothes. The Special Branch have been foolish to let them out; a warder probably sent them through as a matter of routine.

Colonel Klindt tells Esmé, 'Mrs Goldberg, I give you my assurance your husband is perfectly all right. He has not been assaulted or harmed.'

'Then what —'

'He attempted to escape. He didn't get far — he was recaptured.' He gives her permission to visit Denis, who has been brought back to Pretoria prison, and also arranges for her to go to Vereeniging to have a personal interview with the Commandant of the jail there to hear from him exactly what happened.

95

Esmé finds Denis cheerful, still able to joke and make her laugh as he always did in the past. He had become desperate in Vereeniging, where he had been taken because the Special Branch felt he was on the verge of making a full statement. He decided to escape, opened his own cell lock, pulled himself over a roof by scaling a fourteen-foot wall, the top of which was protected by jagged glass and barbed wire. He was actually over the wall and outside running for safety when another prisoner who had seen him gave the alarm, and soon after he was recaptured. His trousers were, as we thought, torn by the teeth of police dogs. Just before the visit is over, Denis remarks: 'Oh, Es, don't bother to send in my pajama trousers; just the tops. I can't get the trousers over the chains.' Both of his ankles are joined by a clanging chain night and day for a month.

* * *

'Colonel Klindt, I want to see my husband.'

I needed more than ordinary courage to ask for this visit — Shirley had warned me: 'If I were you, I'd stay away from Colonel Klindt for a while.

'Why?'

'He's furious with you — at least, I assume it was you; he didn't mention your name. He just kept carrying on about people who tell lies, people who get visits to ask to consult their husbands, when all the time they don't want to consult them at all.'

'But why me?'

'He said someone wanted to consult their husband about the car, and all the time the car had been sold and it was all lies.'

'Yes,' I admitted, 'he must have meant me. I asked to see Rusty about selling the Chev., but I'd actually already arranged to trade it in.'

An unlikely set of circumstances enabled Colonel Klindt to discover my duplicity. When Arthur and Harold escaped to Swaziland it was in a car that was later found abandoned. The South African police traced the car back to a second-hand dealer, visited the firm, questioned the principals and took away the books for examination. Going through them, they discovered my name and that I had traded in our Chevrolet for a Volkswagen. By a careful examination of the dates, it must have become clear to Colonel Klindt that I had actually made the transaction two or three days before I asked for a visit to consult Rusty about the sale.

'But I'm going to ask for a visit, all the same,' I told Shirley.

'What will you say? He's absolutely furious with you. He just went on and on about how he has been fair to us and we must be fair with him, and how he can't stand people who deliberately tell lies.'

'I don't know what I'll say. I'm going to ask for a visit.'

The grey face with slight puffiness, but even more deeply lined, was thrust forward and up from his seat at the desk. His pale eyes blazed with fury and he cried: 'No! Not under any circumstances. You will not be allowed to see your husband again!'

Once more we were joined in the battle of words. He must think I am cold and hard. He does not know how I stand with thumping heart outside his office door, and only come because of a consuming need to reach Rusty, a need far greater than my own fear of coming to The Grays and my repugnance at crawling to him for favours.

He accuses me of lying to him. I defend myself, I say I *did* want to discuss the car, it was true I had already arranged the sale, but still I had to let Rusty know about it; if he had objected, it would not have been too late —

'It is not so! Those are not the facts! The sale was completed before you came to me. I try to be reasonable to you women. I've let you have visits; it is a privilege, not a right. If this is how you abuse the privilege, you are not having it again.'

So we carry on. Again, in the middle of the argument he will suddenly alter the subject completely, so that each time we are about to come to grips, I find myself arguing about something else. Again he ranges over the whole field of the sins of the Rivonia men, of what they were plotting to do, of the escape of the four men, and generally of my ingratitude for the kindness he has shown. I have brought along pressing new reasons why I must have a visit, but he keeps reiterating that I can write a note, he will obtain an answer, but I will NOT get a visit.

When he talks of what the Rivonia men had plotted, I ask 'Are you pre-judging them? They haven't even been charged yet ...'

'Oh, they'll be charged all right, they'll be charged.'

'When will they be charged?'

'That I am not prepared to say. When we are ready to charge them. Are you claiming your husband was innocent? What was he doing at Rivonia in the first place?'

And so on, and on.

After about twenty-five minutes of this, I feel myself bullied and beaten beyond endurance. I am crying, not consciously to try and arouse pity, but simply because I can no longer restrain the tears, because emotionally I cannot endure the tirade any longer.

Somehow, I feel, I must get through to this man, I must make him understand.

I face him with tears I have been trying to conceal and raise my voice to force him to stop: 'Listen to me, Colonel Klindt, just listen to what I have to say!'

He is taken aback by my raised voice, but shouts in turn: 'I have been listening to you — I've listened to everything!'

'No, you have not! You just walk around shouting at me the whole time! You won't let me finish a single sentence, and you don't listen to a single word!'

Perhaps the tears and fury surprise him, for he stops pacing, sits down at his desk, and mutters: 'Well?'

'Colonel Klindt, when we women come to you to say we want to see our husbands, because we want to discuss the sale of a motor-car, or something about the children's education, or rent payments or what to do about the insurance — don't you understand, don't you realize that if our husbands were dead, or if they were ill in hospital, we would manage these things quite easily ourselves? Hasn't it ever occurred to you that we are actually perfectly capable of taking our own decisions about our own affairs?

'When I say to you, I want to see my husband, it's because I want to *see* him. I want to see him for myself. I don't want your men taking messages and bringing me a reply. I want to see that he's still standing on his own two legs, that he's still able to walk and talk —'

'Mrs Bernstein, I assure you, nobody has touched your husband, he is perfectly —'

'I don't want your assurance!' I shout at him. 'I don't want to be told by the Special Branch! I want to see for myself. Even if I don't say one word to him, I want to see him! *I want to see my husband!*

Silence. He gets up, walks to the window, returns to his desk, sits down again, fiddles with a pencil. We avoid looking at each other. I sniff and wipe my face. He pulls a small writing pad towards him. He mumbles without looking up, 'All right. When do you want to go?'

* * *

They go, our friends, the people with whom we had, as the police say, common purpose; they have left on exit permits or fled across the border at night. More and more have gone, and more are going. The ones dodging the police to escape arrest usually end up concealed in Johannesburg before they leave the country, because it is the only way out. Some we meet and talk to before they disappear; others we only hear about. Each escape is complicated, tricky; it is becoming more and more dangerous; each escape involves planning with others, and often money must be found. Once over the border they will have to live for weeks before reaching Dar-es-Salaam or London. It is not an easy journey.

Apart from Alfred Nzo and Rusty, who are both in jail under ninety days, there is only one person left in Johannesburg under house arrest: Helen Joseph. Cecil Williams has gone, and Moses Kotane, and J.B. Marks, Jack and Rica Hodgson and Michael Harmel. Harmel and the Hodgsons left together for Bechuanaland when there seemed no point in sitting doing nothing under twenty-four-hour house arrest, and when Rica had tried unsuccessfully for weeks to obtain a job.

I wonder if we will ever know again what it is like to be light-hearted and to be truly happy. Life itself has become toned down, we live it at a different level from ever in the past. The records I play so late into the night remind me of that beautiful and splendid world which at this time is not ours.

* * *

On 9 October, two days before the ninety-day period has expired, Rusty and the others arrested at Rivonia are released from ninety-day detention, immediately re-arrested, and charged with organizing sabotage and an armed uprising against the South African Government.

They are to be brought to court.

PART III
CONFRONTATION

1

'Violence, Bloodshed and Hellish Revolution'

In September, about three weeks before the Rivonia men were released from ninety days and charged, a nineteen-year-old policeman, Johannes Arnoldus Greeff, was brought to court. The charges: bribery and assisting the four prisoners to escape from Marshall Square. The prosecutor, the Deputy Attorney-General for the Transvaal, Dr Percy Yutar, declared that Greeff was the victim of the evil machinations of two traitors; and that 'Goldreich and his confederates had plotted a violent and hellish revolution, planned on a military basis'. Responding to the atmosphere of the times, the magistrate sentenced Greeff to the maximum possible — six years' imprisonment.

REVOLUTION ON MILITARY BASIS — this becomes the black-type headline impressed on the eyes and mind of every South African. Violence and bloodshed. The Rivonia men have, in a sense, already been tried before the whole country in a way unique in South African legal annals.

It is South African law that any case *sub judice* may not be commented upon publicly in a way which might influence the judgement of the courts. But the Rivonia men, for three months, are not charged; they are simply 'ninety-day political detainees'; the *sub judice* rule does not apply. Since July they have been publicly branded as guilty of plotting violence and bloodshed. Statements have been made by the Minister of Justice, by top military rankings of the police, and by officers of the court in the person of the Attorney-General and his deputy. General Keevy, Commissioner of Police, speaks of 'an end to all subversion' as a result of the Rivonia raid; Colonel Hendrik van den Bergh, head of the Security Branch, says the underground is smashed, its leaders apprehended, and nothing left to be done except mop up the remnants. Trial by public statement and public opinion has taken place, the guilt of the Rivonia men is assumed.

While the whites freeze at the word 'Rivonia', Africans have reacted with excitement and joy. Discussion sweeps through the townships, through the carriages of trains crammed with workers; they stand in groups on the pavements, speculating, hoping. They hope the rumours are true. They hope the Rivonia men planned violence and bloodshed. They hope they *were* organizing a military uprising. They hope others will carry it on now that these men are in prison.

In an atmosphere already so charged against those who will be on trial, counsel must be found for their defence when they appear in court. But who wants to be the instructing attorney in such a case? Lawyers will defend any type of criminal activity; they are ready to appear on behalf of murderers, car thieves or businessmen who have tangled with the law; but they shy off political cases. They stick to their own rules; they do not say, 'I am not prepared to appear for *these* men', they only say, 'I am too busy', 'I have too many cases on hand at the moment'.

And if this obstacle can be overcome, where is the money to be found? Legal fees and general expenses will be very high. A committee was formed some years ago in Johannesburg to provide legal defence in political cases, the Defence and Aid Committee. But some of the committee members decided on grounds of 'principle' not to defend cases of people who have been charged with acts of violence. They refused to defend cases involving acts of sabotage and would not extend aid to families and dependents of alleged saboteurs.

After discussing the problem of finding an instructing attorney with friends, I approach a man I have never met before, Joel Joffe, and ask if he will act on my behalf in the case in which I anticipate Rusty will be involved. It is a vague sort of brief to offer a legal man; he is not yet charged, I say, but probably will be charged soon; I don't know what the charges will be, but they are likely to be serious; I don't know where money will be found for fees.

Joel Joffe is a Johannesburg attorney who closed his practice and sold his home with the intention of emigrating with his family to Australia. He is not a member of any political organization, but he has felt the evils and injustice in the country as something affecting his own life and corrupting for the future of his children. He was on the point of leaving when Jimmy Kantor was arrested. As an act of friendship and because he had finished off his own work, he went to Kantor's office to try and keep the practice going until Jimmy's release. Now he agrees once again to postpone his departure to Australia, and to act on my behalf. In a few days he is approached by relatives of some of the other Rivonia men, and begins to assemble a team of barristers.

Through this case, through his decision to act for us, Joel Joffe was forced eventually to abandon all his plans. Australia closed its doors to him when the South African Government seized his passport.

When the Rivonia men are released from ninety-day detention and charged, they become awaiting-trial prisoners, entitled to two half-hour visits a week with two visitors at each; one meal a day may be sent into prison from outside; they may send and receive letters; and they may have books to read.

As soon as possible I take books to the jail, but there will be many battles to get them to the prisoners. They are given two books each from the prison library's strictly limited selection. Prison officials are united in their deep mistrust and dislike of all books.

The trial is to be held in Pretoria for the sake of 'order and security'. In Johannesburg the bringing of leading Congress members to court would cause tremendous crowds to gather at the courtroom. Even with the ban on gatherings, even with police dogs and the display of military might, people will come — this is the experience of previous political trials. The State does not wish to risk such a show of support for the accused, who are officially said to have no support among the people.

Johannesburg, the greatest industrial centre in Africa, is the heart of action and organization; its busy, restless population is immediately sensitive to atmosphere; and influences State policy. Johannesburg would become inseparably involved with the trial.

Pretoria is like its climate; the town will not react to the trial, but will simply smother it.

The Supreme Court, where the trial will be held, is called the Palace of Justice. Nearby is a dark statue of President Kruger, President of the Transvaal Republic before the British caught the

105

smell of gold. In his long-tailed frock-coat and high top-hat, stern and unrelenting, he *is* Pretoria, the dark figure of authority. Yet the words inscribed on the base of the statue are a quotation from one of his own speeches, strangely apt for today:

Met vertrouwen leggen wij onze zaak open voor de geheele wereld. Hetzij wij overwinnen, hetzij wij sterven: de vryheid zal in Afrika rijzen als de zon uit de morewolken. (In confidence we lay our cause before the whole world. Whether we conquer or whether we die, freedom will rise in Africa like the sun from the morning clouds.)

The freedom of which he spoke in 1881 was for his own people, the Afrikaners.

There are a few palm trees against the background of pillars and the jumble of buildings around Church Square, giving the place a seedy, colonial air. Flights of steps lead up to the Palace of Justice with its columns and undistinguished nineteenth-century architecture. The marble facings make the entrance cold. There are more columns inside, with brass bases, and brass railings along the upper floor; there are always men polishing the brass, white men — perhaps one of those jobs reserved by the Government as a protected occupation for otherwise unemployable whites

On 9 October 1963 eleven men appear briefly in court. Seven of them were arrested at Lliesleaf Farm, Rivonia. They are Rusty, Walter Sisulu, Govan Mbeki, Ahmed Kathrada, Bob Hepple, Raymond Mhlaba, arrested together in an outbuilding on the farm, and Denis Goldberg, who was found in the lounge of the house.

Neither Arthur nor Hazel Goldreich are there; Arthur is in London after his escape and Hazel has just been released, after three months of her own silent agony. The police have used every trick they know on this gentle and courageous woman to force her to talk about the people who came to Rivonia; they have done their best with letters, real or forged, to destroy her marriage and undermine the substance of all her years with Arthur. In this they later succeed, but they have not succeeded in breaking her quiet fortitude. She is free now, but has been

106

warned by Dr Yutar that she may be required as a State witness. They have taken her passport away. Vorster has described the escape of Harold and Arthur as a great loss in the campaign against subversion, and the trial of those arrested at Rivonia without Arthur as 'more or less like producing Hamlet without the Prince, but the show will go on just the same'.

Others arrested at Rivonia three months ago include the farm workers and domestic servants who are still in solitary confinement, and will be called as witnesses. Dr Festenstein, who went to Rivonia on the evening of the same day, is being brought to trial separately, on lesser charges.

In addition to the seven from Rivonia, four others are now charged with them: Nelson Mandela, who has been brought from the prison cell where he was serving his five-year sentence; Elias Motsoaledi and Andrew Mlangeni, who had been arrested weeks before the Rivonia raid and held on suspicion of sabotage. And James Kantor, the man who never joined a political organization or engaged in any political activity in his life, but who had taken his brother-in-law Harold Wolpe into partnership in his law practice.

The accused are handcuffed early in the morning in jail, then taken to a special Black Maria with a separate compartment in front for the white men, segregated of course from the others. A convoy of lorries filled with armed police carrying stenguns, several cars of prison officials and police, including the colonel in charge of Pretoria Prison; all have gathered at the jail to be driven along a prearranged route guarded by armed police to the Palace of Justice. The whole convoy drives into the back-yard of the court, the great iron gates which usually stand open are slammed shut, locked and guarded, and the men wait for three hours in the cells below the courtroom.

The display of armed force is chilling beyond words. Uniformed and plain-clothes police mass around the Palace of Justice; leather-strapped khaki uniforms, service revolvers, grim, antagonistic faces, eyes noting every move of the spectators, watching who greets whom, heavy thick men pressed among us listening to each whispered word. A trial conducted in such an atmosphere can have only one outcome. These are the guardians not of peace and order, but of suppression and death.

A moment of shock when the eleven men, surrounded by warders and SBs, file up from the cells below into the specially-built dock: Nelson Mandela comes first, almost unrecognizable. He has lost about 40 lb. in weight. His splendid figure seems to have shrivelled, his skin has a greenish-grey prison pallor; he is dressed in a khaki shirt and shorts, wearing sandals on his bare feet, and this is what eighteen months in jail, sitting in a cell for twenty-three hours out of twenty-four, being kept apart from other prisoners, has done to the man who was a political leader and distinguished lawyer. Have they so easily reduced this proud and sophisticated man to the dress and status of the African tolerable to whites — to a 'boy'? As he files into his place at the right of the dock, Nelson turns to the public gallery where there are relatives and friends, and flashes that magnificent smile as of old, splendidly confident, full of brilliance and power; this is the Nelson we knew.

Most of the men look haggard and drawn; Jimmy Kantor has been unable to stand confinement and has suffered a nervous breakdown. Rusty looks ill and much older and avoids glancing at the spectators as he comes in. Govan Mbeki, whose hair had been going grey, now seems all grey and for the first time looks his age. Of all of them, Kathrada seems the least changed, as though nothing can shake his secure inner self.

On the bench, Mr Justice Quartus de Wet, Judge-President of the Transvaal, who alone in this special court, will try the eleven men and decide their fate.

Dr Percy Yutar, the Prosecutor rises. 'My lord, I call the case of the State against the National High Command and others.

'I hand in the indictment and the annexure. I also hand in the Attorney-General's authorization that the accused be charged with sabotage, and that they be tried summarily.'

For the first time the defence are given a copy of the indictment, although a special issue of the *Rand Daily Mail* is already on the streets with its whole front page splashed with details under the headlines: 'REVOLT, INVASION, CHARGES — 11 arraigned in more than 200 sabotage acts.' *The Mail* has a beautifully posed photograph of Dr Percy Yutar, 'who is leading the State's team of prosecutors', sitting at a desk studying a bound copy of the indictment.

The indictment charges the eleven men with complicity in 222 acts of sabotage, aimed at aiding guerrilla warfare in South Africa and facilitating violent revolution and an armed invasion of the country, their conspiracy being 'actively planned and envisaged on a military basis and with hostile intent'.

Bram Fischer, appearing for most of the accused, asks for a remand. He speaks of the extreme conditions under which the men have been kept, and says they are not in a fit state to appear. 'In the Criminal Code solitary confinement has always been very carefully regulated. No more than two days solitary confinement and spare diet per week is allowed ... These accused have been in confinement for eighty-eight days.' He also says the defence needs time to prepare for the case. The State has been preparing for nearly three months — yet as late as yesterday the defence were told the indictment was not ready. He requests a six-week adjournment.

Justice de Wet, whose attitudes of annoyance, interest or boredom can be read in his small gestures and the angle of his bespectacled face, is impatient to get the case started. Yutar says they must start quickly because certain witnesses must be called before the end of the month: '*I fear for their safety!*'

The Judge mutters quickly and inaudibly that three weeks is quite sufficient and adjourns the case until 29 October.

He rises abruptly and disappears through a door directly behind him.

2
Visits and Warders

They prepared a special visiting-room for the Rivonia prisoners at Pretoria jail which was also intended for legal consultations: a high counter something like a bank counter with projecting boards separating each person. Between us and the prisoners, a thick piece of glass through which we could see head and shoulders; and to one side of the glass a piece of hardboard with small holes punched in it, through which we talked. It reduced the feeling of personal contact to a minimum and made it necessary to speak loudly.

All sorts of difficulties arose through apartheid regulations. The accused sat side by side in court and in consultation with their lawyers; but were not permitted to have visitors of different races at the same time. We suffered endless waiting difficulties, disappointments.

A few weeks after the trial started, Esmé Goldberg left for England with her two children, mainly to satisfy Denis who thought she might be arrested again, and who wanted his children to be away from the atmosphere of the trial. His mother Annie, came to stay with us for the duration. Annie and I travelled back and forth together to attend the trial and to visit Denis and Rusty. Toni often came with me.

Children under sixteen are not allowed in jails. Patrick was fifteen, but big for his age. After some months I persuaded him to come with me for a visit, pretending he was sixteen. It was not a success. He was so close to tears the whole time, fighting for self-control, that he could barely speak to Rusty. I did not suggest that he should come again, and he did not ask to be taken Frances and Keith were not allowed to come.

Once, only once, I had what is known in prison jargon as a 'contact' visit. On the day of Rusty's bail application I was waiting in court for the application to be heard when a prison official said I could go down to the cells below to see Rusty.

Under the courtroom was a bare concrete hall with a table at which police sat, and, leading off it, the barred gates of two or three cells in which prisoners waited until their case was called. Rusty stood outside the cell talking to the lawyers, police all around. They allowed us to go into the cell together, sit on a bench and talk. The door was almost closed. Lawyers and police left us alone.

I held on to Rusty, touched him, kissed him. We sat clasping each other, alone together. There was nothing in the cell except the narrow bench against the wall. At first we could barely talk, then we began softly, intimately. It was sheer, unbelievable happiness. I thought if I could sit for an hour a day close to you like this, Rusty, just holding on to your hands and talking, life would be completely bearable. That's all I want — just an hour a day in close, quiet contact, alone. At that moment it seemed like the fulfillment of all ambition.

They left us alone for nearly an hour. They could see us if they wished through the peephole in the door, but I don't think they bothered to spy on us.

We were never again allowed a 'contact' visit.

There was an overwhelming desire for physical contact, just to touch each other, hold a hand. I would watch the intense listening backs of the accused when they sat in the dock in front of us, out of reach, separated not only by the dock but by a row of Special Branch men sitting behind them — and would feel my heart twist with longing to touch Rusty. Contact visits. I know now what they mean.

Visiting was not permitted in jail after four in the afternoon. When there were visitors for the other men, too, we found our visit curtailed, and once when we were unable to see our men at all, Annie and I left the jail so bitterly disappointed that when I got home I wrote a letter to the Colonel in charge of Pretoria prison. I asked him why we could not use the ordinary visiting-room when ours was already occupied; and mentioned some of the red-tape restrictions that had lost us visits or forced us to make the journey again another day.

The Colonel did not reply to my letter, but after that we were always given the full half-hour, even if it meant being in the jail after the prisoners were locked in for the night — (at four in the afternoon!)

In January 1964, a list was published of all former members of the now banned radical white organization, the Congress of Democrats. As a former member, Toni's name appeared on the list. Rusty was prohibited from communicating with all listed people, with the exception of myself. From the moment the list was published, he could no longer speak to his daughter.

We phoned the chief magistrate and asked for permission for Toni to visit her father, but he quibbled: *she* was not prohibited from speaking to *him*, it was Rusty who was prohibited from speaking to her. Therefore he had to make the application. Some days passed before I had the opportunity of telling Rusty, who then wrote out an application for permission to speak to his daughter and handed it to the prison authorities for censoring and posting.

Toni was planning to get married and very much wanted to visit her father. On the next visiting day, at the beginning of February, I suggested she should come with me despite the bans. This was Rusty's private affair, his decision, not one for the prison.

A warder called us from the waiting-room and told us Head Warder Breedt wished to see us in his office.

'Your daughter must leave this jail immediately. She is not allowed to see her father.'

I said, 'She *may* see him — it is up to him to decide whether he will speak to her before receiving formal permission.'

Breedt became angry, his face suffused with red. 'She may not see him, *she may not!* You know she is not allowed to see him. He has not had permission!'

'But surely it's only a matter of …'

'I make the rules in this jail! *I'm* in charge here! I tell you she must get out of the jail — *at once!*' And again: '*I'm in charge of this jail!*'

We called for the warder to unlock the front door. Toni had to sit outside in the car and wait for me. Breedt's temper upset me. When I was finally called upstairs to the visiting-room, to my undying shame, I began to cry.

In a few minutes I calmed down, but was upset at breaking down in front of Rusty. It was the only time it happened. I hated myself for it, and for allowing Breedt to upset me.

112

There was no response to Rusty's application and he wrote again. Weeks went by; Toni could not see him, and Rusty could not even write to her. Finally I phoned the chief magistrate and had a verbal battle with him. He kept repeating — echoes of Colonel Klindt! — that he was not *responsible* for the law, but had to see it was carried out. I said, 'Surely it was not the intention of the law to prevent a father from speaking to his own daughter.'

He replied: 'I am not concerned with the *intention* of the law; only with what it says. It is my duty to see that it is carried out.'

In desperation I wrote a letter to Mrs Helen Suzman and asked for her assistance. She personally went to the Minister of Justice on our behalf. Rusty's permit arrived, Toni was at last allowed to visit him again. She and her newly-wedded husband, Ivan Strasburg, were even given an extra visit on the day after their marriage.

Warders were always present during our visits. They stood a little distance away and watched us with constant curiosity; we were so unfamiliar to them.

One appeared rather pleasant. Annie and I always found him quiet and polite, even friendly. His candid eyes and childish face gave him a look of innocence. He was quite normal as long as his orders were carried out absolutely but the slightest infringement threw him into a frenzy.

We ignored the presence of the warders when we talked, but were always aware that the visiting-room was 'bugged'. It was the same room used for consultations; it was not likely the Special Branch would overlook the possibilities of listening in to what was said.

Our half-hour visits always sped by like lightning. When the warder in charge said, 'Time's up' we turned in amazement — so soon? Can it really be half an hour? There were so many things to talk about.

We went down to sit in the waiting-room until the dirty washing was brought to us.

Inside, the chill of stone and cement, the dimness of half-lit corridors. Outside, the overpowering heat of unshaded streets, heat beating down in waves over the hill-locked town. The car

113

seats burned our bodies, the metal too hot to touch, the interior stifling even with all the windows open.

The joy of being outside; the sense of relief as I turned the car and headed out of Pretoria. We waited, scarcely able to breathe, for the wind of speed to cool our burning faces and ease us again. The great expansive golden plains, the vistas of endless freedom that opened up between the dark pines and straggling bluegum trees. Grass, hills, clouds, sky, distance! Who could bear to think of a life shut away from it all? And what makes anyone choose, as the warders do, to move, work and live within the confines of Pretoria Local Prison?

3
The Indictment is Quashed

The head of our legal team was a man who had been involved himself in absolute opposition to the principles of apartheid.

Abram Fischer — to all, 'Bram' — came from a family whose ancestors arrived in South Africa in the eighteenth century. His grandfather, a burgher of the Orange River Republic, rose to be President of that Republic. His father, a barrister like Bram, became Judge-President of the Orange Free State. They were bitter opponents of the British, and true Afrikaner nationalists.

Bram could have followed the family pattern, gaining high honours. In addition to his personal attributes he had powerful connections both in his own right and through his wife, a niece of General Smuts. The *Sunday Times* editor later wrote of him:

> In this well-loved, much-admired family, Bram was himself a model of gentleness and respectability. A brilliant scholar, an outstanding sportsman, a man of character and immense personal charm, he could not be faulted. With his background, his family connections and his own brilliance, his future success was looked upon as a formality: would he be Prime Minister or Chief Justice? That was the only question.

But Bram turned away the professional rewards that were his for the taking. For among his many qualities was a complete and undeviating honesty that compelled him to do what he believed to be right, regardless of any personal difficulties. In the thirties he had joined the Communist Party, finding it the only organization that uncompromisingly rejected the colour-bar. Once he had convinced himself intellectually that the colour-bar was wrong, this was his logical choice. He never claimed special consideration for his social status, and spoke from the City Hall steps, gave out leaflets at factory gates and met with illiterate workers in back rooms. In 1946 he stood trial with us after the mineworkers' strike, and although he himself had been away on holiday at the time of the strike, he pleaded guilty with us because he believed in the essential justice of the miners' cause.

His views were never disguised, yet he maintained a most successful practice, including among his clients some of the largest mining houses who were prepared to profit from his keen brain and meticulous methods of work, and turn a blind eye to his politics. He also acted in a large number of political cases, for which he usually refused fees.

I knew no one with a wider circle of friends, which included people of every stratum and race. He and his wife, Molly, held open house at all hours of the day or night, and were brought every possible problem, from a husband and wife fight to expropriation of Indian businesses under the Group Areas Act. He treated every individual with the same gentle courtesy.

With Bram leading the defence team, we had in addition an unpaid full-time assistant in Molly, who became indispensable to us all. Two junior barristers from the Johannesburg Bar were chosen to complete the defence team: George Bizos and Arthur Chaskelson.

In the midst of the Second World War George had escaped from the Nazi occupation of his native Greece at the age of twelve, setting out into the Mediterranean in a small rowing boat with his father. After some days they were picked up by a British destroyer. George spent some years in an orphanage, finally arriving in South Africa where he later qualified as a barrister. This background made him more ready to take political cases when other barristers had proved reluctant. He was sociable, likeable, with a fund of humorous anecdotes and stories. In addition to his fine legal work, he would become a valuable public relations officer for the defence.

Arthur Chaskelson, younger than George, was regarded by many as the most promising young barrister in Johannesburg. Tall, good-looking, articulate, he was set for a brilliant future. He was not involved in any political organization and had shown no particular interest in politics, but from time to time he had undertaken the defence of people who would otherwise have been unrepresented, some of them charged with political crimes in the 1960s. This he did as a personal duty, not in the sense of any protest against the State.

Although the brief was vague, the charge unknown, the defendants unstated, both accepted without hesitation.

There was to be one further member of the defence team whose participation, at this stage, was not revealed.

As soon as counsel read the indictment they knew that there would be some formidable lying by State witnesses. For example, there could be no documentary proof or truthful evidence on the charge that the accused had at any time prepared for, or asked for, or even favoured foreign military intervention as a solution to South Africa's problems. Yet this was charged in the indictment. There would, therefore, be lying witnesses.

When this became clear, Bram contacted Vernon Berrangé, then on holiday abroad, and asked him if he would join the defence team. Vernon was then sixty-five, still handsome, an immaculate dresser. In his younger days he had been a driver of racing cars, a big game hunter, a fighter pilot in the First World War, a man who revelled in danger. He was the best-known criminal lawyer in South Africa with a reputation for devastating cross-examination. We had seen him in action in other trials, and were always glad not to be on the receiving end of his biting tongue and steely-cold manner. His speciality was exposing lying witnesses, particularly policemen. So high was his reputation that just to be confronted by Vernon Berrangé could unnerve a dishonest witness. His logical brain had led him, as well, to reject the idiocies of apartheid.

By taking the Rivonia brief Vernon was surely aware that it would mean the end of his legal career. He had been listed as having once been a member of the Communist Party, and legislation was being prepared to debar all listed people from the legal profession. To appear for the Rivonia accused will be like signing his own death warrant, excommunicating him from the legal profession that had brought him so much success.

But he accepts.

The Rivonia Trial was a confrontation in which the opposing forces in South Africa appeared face to face; those who stood for apartheid, who defended and protected the apartheid State; and those who opposed it. The court was an ultimate court of morality; the issues were not the guilt or innocence of the accused, but the guilt or innocence of those who opposed apartheid.

On one side was the State with its deep Calvinist roots asserting the unchanging nature of humanity and race, of humans created immediately and in his present form, rejecting evolution, adhering to belief in the rigid and unalterable patterns of human behaviour; fixed laws, the virtues of obedience, attainment as related to heredity not environment. On the other side there was the vision of people as endowed with creative and developing gifts, the ability to learn and change; free-developing, self-fulfilling people, black and non-black.

Each person in the case had to stand on one side or the other. In the Treason Trial which finished three years before, the lines had not yet been so clearly drawn; it was still possible for State witnesses to be honest with themselves and with the court; as when police witnesses testified — correctly at that time — that ANC leaders continuously preached non-violence in all their activities. In the Treason Trial the issue was whether the men and women on trial had resorted to violence to overthrow the State; *the right or wrong of the political ideas motivating their activities was not fundamentally challenged*.

In the Rivonia Trial, a number of the defendants admitted openly that they resorted to violence; therefore the issue was what beliefs motivated them, what situation impelled their activities. They had reached the stage where their acts transcended their need for survival. So the reasons, not the acts themselves, became the supreme issue.

There were three weeks in which to study the indictment. The defence found it shoddy, vague and faulty in law, and decided to apply for the indictment to be quashed.

* * *

Road blocks on the Pretoria road; cars drawn across the road, police waving our car to one side to stop for inspection.

We draw up on the gravel shoulder of the road, the police peer into the car, front and back, then let us go on. The magic pass of a white skin. White women in cool summer suits and dresses, and with the added respectability of hats.

They are not concerned with us. It is Africans they want. It is the opening day of the trial; they know few whites will attend.

118

They want to prevent Africans from going to Pretoria in any numbers. When the cars contain Africans, they order them out to inspect their documents; passes have to be produced. They look for anything — an expired tax receipt, some official stamp not quite in order — which will serve as reason to arrest Africans.

Pretoria teems with police, from the moment we enter the town and pass the prison. Armed police in uniform posted at every street corner in every block round Church Square. Groups of armed police in the road outside the Palace of Justice; police vans with Alsatians; police with satchels of tear-gas bombs in addition to their service revolvers.

It is a nightmare of visible State power, like a sequence from a film of Nazi Germany; a statement about the present, a threat for the future. The sullen stares of young angry faces under peaked caps, disturbed by those whites they regard as alien to their authority; hands groping towards leather-cased weapons, looping taut leashes on straining dogs; high-ranking officers with stars and insignia on caps, shoulders and sleeves, fingering thin batons as they obstruct people on the steps of the Supreme Court; the bulk and thick necks, hunched shoulders and searching eyes of Special Branch men.

The steps of the Supreme Court are cluttered with newsmen and photographers. There are overseas TV teams (there is no television in South Africa). Across the road, in Church Square, groups of Africans are beginning to assemble, unable to obtain entry to the court, but prepared to wait patiently outside if they are permitted.

Among them are African women wearing the green and black blouses and skirts that have always been worn by members of the multi-racial Federation of South African Women; some African women in tribal dress; Indian women in flowing light saris moving with grace and colour; even a medicine man in full regalia of nodding monkeys' tails, leather cloak, feathers, beads.

The prisoners are brought in an extraordinary convoy from the jail to the court — a distance of about a mile. At the head, three cars packed with prison dignitaries and high-ranking policemen; then a lorry with a score of white policemen. Behind that, the Black Maria with the accused, segregated into two separate compartments, a small one for the white prisoners in front, a larger compartment for the blacks at the rear. And this, in turn, is followed by a bevy of cars, policemen and warders and more policemen.

The convoy sweeps through Pretoria's peak hour traffic, drives into the court buildings through the massive iron grille gates at the back of the building, and policemen with stenguns jump out and surround the prison yard while the prisoners, handcuffed, are taken into cells below the court.

There are armed men in every corridor, at every door. We are stopped two or three times before reaching the doors of the courtroom. But there are senior police officers present who know us and give instructions that we be allowed to enter the court.

An hour before the opening of the case the backless wooden benches for spectators — on one side for whites, on the other side for blacks — are already crammed full. There is not even room for us to sit down, and nobody except close relatives of the accused is now allowed to enter. Most of the white benches are clearly filled with members of the Special Branch or their friends. We ask them several times to move up and make room for us, which they eventually do with reluctance, so that we are each perched on the end of a bench.

The police outnumber the spectators; the SBs watch every individual, no word or movement escapes them. We are pressed against their sides. They even fill the small gallery, normally the jury box, on one side of the Judge's bench, which in this case is reserved for distinguished visitors.

When President Kruger laid the cornerstone of this building in 1897 there was little understanding of acoustics. The Judge's bench is an elaborate pulpit of wood, carved and posted like an old-fashioned bed, at one end of the 60-foot court. He is enthroned there, dwarfed in his scarlet robes. On either side of this structure are beige curtains, draped and pleated from floor to ceiling, into which the voices of prosecutor, defending counsel and Judge alike disappear and are lost. A huge-bladed fan, suspended on a long rod from the ceiling directly above the prosecutor's head, wobbles slowly through the summer days, imperceptibly stirring the thick air. Inevitably in the stifling Pretoria summer we dream that this useless object will shake itself loose at some moment when Dr Yutar is standing with finger upraised in dramatic gesture … it does not happen. The fan moves, the air scarcely responds, neither atmosphere nor tedium is relieved.

Judge and counsel can hear each other fairly well as they sit at close quarters facing each other. But counsel have their backs to the galleries and can seldom be heard by the public, and the voice of the Judge rarely carries beyond the well of the court. Even the reporters who are right in front near the bench, to one side, often have difficulty in following the proceedings. For us, the strain of trying to hear becomes intolerable. By catching a word here or there, by concentrating on pitch of voice, expression, gesture, we may guess what is taking place. Apart from the three doors leading into the court, which are closed when the session begins, there is no ventilation. The combination of heat, lack of air, tension, and the strain of trying to follow the proceedings, induces headaches in both Toni and myself. These become part of the price we pay for attending the trial.

The court is not yet in session. On the black benches I see both Nelson's wife, Winnie, and Walter's wife, Albertina. Winnie is banned and prohibited from talking to me; we pass, we look at each other, but dare not risk even a whispered greeting.

Albertina has recently been released from jail after being held as a hostage for her husband; she is not banned and there are no prohibitions preventing us from talking to each other, so I go over to speak to her. We have just greeted each other when a policeman is at my side.

'You're not allowed here.'

'I'll more over to the other side when court begins,' I tell him. 'I've just come here for a few moments.'

'You're not allowed this side, it's for natives.'

I have to go back to the white benches; there is really no place in Pretoria where Albertina and I can sit and talk together. We have known each other for years, worked together in the Women's Federation, and her husband sits next to mine, on trial for their lives, but I may not sit next to her.

Counsel and prosecutors and the various officials take their places. An expectant hush descends on the packed room.

The prisoners enter the dock from the underground cells,

121

Nelson Mandela first, followed by Walter Sisulu. They both wear drab prison uniform; Walter has started serving his six-year sentence for incitement. As Nelson's head and shoulders rise from the stairway which leads directly into the special dock, he turns his head towards the packed benches and raises a clenched fist in the ANC salute. Instantly the people respond with a deep, resounding '*Amandla*!' (Power!) which is repeated as each of the prisoners comes into view. The greeting is not shouted; it is almost as though it is drawn from the people's throats of its own volition, in spite of the massed, armed police and the Security men standing shoulder to shoulder round the prisoners. '*Amandla*!' Only James Kantor and Bob Hepple do not give the salute.

The assertion is made when court adjourns for tea, and again when it reassembles and the prisoners re-enter the dock; this time the full statement: '*Amandla ngwethu*' (Power, strength, it is ours)! Major Fred van Niekerk stands in front of the black benches and states angrily that if there is a repetition of this shouting or any other form of demonstration, the court will be instantly cleared. From then a new procedure. The prisoners are not brought into dock until Justice de Wet has taken his seat; so that the court is already in session, and silence must be enforced.

* * *

Defence counsel have spent three weeks considering the indictment and the nature of the case against the accused; and deciding on the line of defence.

The indictment is a strange document. Seven of the accused — Mandela, Sisulu, Mbeki, Kathrada, Goldberg, Mhlaba and Bernstein — are charged with being members of an association known as The National High Command, The National Liberation Movement, The National Executive Committee of the National Liberation Movement, Umkhonto we Sizwe (The Spear of the Nation). They are also, as are the others, charged in their individual capacities. Kantor is in addition charged in his capacity as a partner of his firm.

Basically the offence charged is the planning of a conspiracy which 'envisaged a military basis with hostile intent', violent

122

revolution and an armed invasion of the country; and in preparation, the commission of more than 235 acts of sabotage. It alleges that 'acting in concert and conspiring and making common purpose' with a list of some seventy named people and several organizations including the Communist Party of South Africa and the African National Congress, they have 'incited, instigated, commanded, aided, advised, encouraged or procured other persons to commit the wrongful and wilful acts of sabotage, preparatory to and in facilitation of guerrilla warfare in the Republic of South Africa, coupled with an armed invasion of and violent revolution'; that they have solicited and received money from inside and outside the country in support of a campaign for the repeal or modification of certain laws, which would further the objects of communism 'as defined in Section 1 of Act No. 44 of 1950'. This is the Suppression of Communism Act in which communism is defined so widely that it covers almost any social, economic or political change.

Counsel consider the indictment to be a shoddy and impossible document, vague and general in its allegations so that it is impossible to discern precisely what the offence was, by whom committed, and in what way the accused either individually or jointly are connected with it.

They had approached the prosecution for further particulars, asking them among other things which of the accused were alleged to have carried out what acts of sabotage; how, when and where the conspiracy was entered into, when each were alleged to have joined the High Command (as they could not be responsible for actions taken before they joined); and had asked for details of how the alleged conspiracy between the Communist Party and the ANC were entered into; and many more similar questions.

Counsel have decided to move in court for the dismissal of the indictment on the grounds that it does not conform with the law and inform the accused adequately and with reasonable clarity of the precise charge or allegation they have to meet.

The decision to attack the indictment does not alter the political stand of the accused, none of whom (with the exception of Kantor and Hepple who have their own lawyers) are prepared to deny association with the bodies they have belonged to.

The attack on the indictment, therefore, is simply to show counsel's resolve that they will not abandon any of their normal legal rights. They will insist that regardless of the whipped-up hysteria and witch-hunt atmosphere, the accused will be assured that the trial will be held according to the normal course of justice. It is this combination of attitudes — on the one hand a tenacious upholding of legal rights and on the other a steady refusal to deny their political associations even with unlawful organizations — that the State counsel, Dr Yutar, proves unable to understand, and therefore unable to cope with.

* * *

In his soft, often hesitant way, sometimes pausing for long periods after making one point before framing the next, Bram begins his careful and devastating attack on the indictment.

He is deeply aware of the responsibility that he carries. The men in the dock are not just his clients, they are colleagues with whom he has worked for many years, close personal friends. On his words may depend their lives.

He is the very antithesis of the public concept of a lawyer, lacking any aggressive demeanour, easy oratory, dramatic gestures. His arguments, delivered in that quiet manner, may appear unimpressive to the public, but they are impressive to legal people.

He traces the defects: lack of particularity; dates and places mentioned in the preamble do not coincide with dates and places in the actual charges; the indictment does not inform the accused of the precise charge they must answer, nor does it comply with the provisions of the code. The accused cannot just be told that they conspired, they must be given information about the time, place and manner in which each became a party to the conspiracy.

The replies given when the defence asked the State for further particulars were curt and repetitive — even ludicrous or simply blank refusals. The almost invariable answer was: 'These facts are unknown', or 'These facts are peculiarly within the knowledge of the accused'. Occasionally facts were more emphatically '*blatantly and peculiarly* within the knowledge of the accused'.

124

The prosecution was following a simple precept: 'You are guilty. Therefore you know what you did. Therefore we don't have to tell you'.

Mr Justice de Wet begins to show signs of irritation and impatience. He is notoriously short-tempered, but whether his impatience is with Bram's argument or with the indictment itself, we cannot tell.

Outside, rain. Heavy summer rain that later trails off to a soft grey drizzle. Some of the people in the square leave, but many stay, the women sheltering under big black umbrellas, standing patiently while argument continues, until court adjourns and the men sweep past in a Black Maria.

The plea to quash the indictment lasts two days. After the restrained and quiet-voiced Bram, it is taken up by Dr G. Lowen who is appearing for James Kantor. He is a German-trained lawyer who participated in dramatic trials of opponents of the Nazi regime before leaving his country as a refugee from Hitler. He is the opposite of Bram — dramatic, emotional and full of rhetoric. He also feels keenly for Kantor, whom he knows personally, and who recalls innocent men he defended against political frame-ups in Nazi Germany.

In Kantor's case, he argues, it is even more necessary than usual that the prosecution state the basis of its case fully and clearly.

Kantor is not being tried for what he himself has done, but is being held vicariously responsible for what has been done by his partner Wolpe. Kantor cannot be presumed to know *anything* that Wolpe has done. He must be told.

His request for such information had been met with replies 'presumptuous — ludicrous!' When he asked if a particular act was alleged to have been committed by Kantor or Wolpe, the State's reply was: 'Yes.' Other replies, 'These facts are not known', and 'These facts are peculiarly within the knowledge of your client'. And finally, speaking with a voice so raised with passion and scorn that even we, at the back, can clearly hear his words: 'Take for example question five. The answer given by the State is dash, dash, dash, exclamation mark!'

Justice de Wet lifts his head. 'In my copy there are four dashes, Mr Lowen.'

125

We know then that the argument is successful and the indictment will be thrown out. Dr Lowen cuts his speech short.

Bob Hepple is the only defendant not legally represented. The Judge asks if he has anything he wishes to say on this matter. Before Hepple can reply, Dr Yutar springs to his feet. Holding his robe with one hand and sweeping the air with his other, he announces loudly: 'All charges against Bob Alexander Hepple are being withdrawn. He will be the first witness for the State against the accused.'

There is a murmur among the spectators. Bob Hepple turns pale and gets to his feet. Lieutenant Swanepoel leads him out of the dock and down the stairs to the police cells. Without a backward glance, he is gone.

* * *

Percy Yutar pleads with the Judge not to throw out the indictment. In some way this trial, climaxing weeks of publicity, is beginning to lose its force.

The day before, Dialo Telli, chairman of the United Nations Special Committee on Apartheid, had interrupted the debate in his committee to announce that the Rivonia Trial had been resumed in Pretoria. 'This is a brazen challenge to the moral authority of the United Nations. We cannot ignore it.' He reminded the committee that on 11 October the U.N. General Assembly voted 106 to 1 to call on South Africa to stop the Rivonia Trial, to release all prisoners unconditionally, and to take steps to end apartheid.

It is clear that the South African authorities will entirely disregard the resolution but even so, it puts them on the defensive.

Yutar now reveals something of his own character and the manner in which he will conduct the whole trial. He ignores all the legal arguments, deals with none of the legal authorities cited, makes no attempt to rebut Bram's arguments. At no time does he — will he — try to argue law with the defence team. He makes his defence of the indictment an attack on the accused who, he says, are not genuine in seeking further particulars; they are merely trying to harass and embarrass the State. He promises to work late every night for a week to provide the defence with everything they ask for. Finally, like a conjuror producing a rabbit, he says that if the defence counsel want precise details he is prepared to hand in a copy of his opening address which would serve in lieu of further particulars.

Defence counsel are astounded. As the man stated to be the most highly qualified prosecution lawyer in South Africa, a Doctor of Laws, he must surely know that an opening address is not a charge. It is a speech in which the prosecution may summarize evidence it intends to lead, to inform the court of the manner in which the State will seek to prove their allegations. It gives free reign to the State to say almost anything; although it is expected to reflect the truth, the prosecutor can make statements as wide as he cares on what he *thinks* he is going to prove.

Joel Joffe commented later: 'Such a speech is so far removed from an indictment that we could not believe the offer was seriously made'.

Bram rises to his feet to protest, but Mr Justice de Wet forestalls him. 'I can see no reason why I should allow you to hand that in, Mr Yutar. Have you any authority that I can do it? Your opening address is not a document that you are entitled to hand in.'

It is now becoming apparent that this showpiece trial is not going as Yutar or the Government expected. If the indictment is thrown out the case will be postponed; and media hysteria will abate.

Yutar's voice is now falsetto: 'I would earnestly beg your lordship, nay, crave your lordship, not to squash the indictment'. (He always says 'squash'.)

De Wet is losing patience. 'The whole basis of your argument, as I understand it Mr Yutar, is that you are satisfied that the accused are guilty. And you are arguing the case on the assumption that they are guilty and that they know all these documents. You cannot beg the question and say that you have got the proof and ask the Court to decide the matter on the basis that the accused are guilty. All preliminary matters like this must be approached on the assumption that the accused are not guilty ... That is the correct approach, and once you adopt the correct approach you are in difficulty with your argument.'

Increasingly rattled, after 'begging' and 'imploring', seemingly close to tears, Yutar offers to change one aspect of the indictment that had been attacked by the defence. Too late he realizes that under law there is only one way to do this — by filing a new indictment.

De Wet begins a lengthy, barely audible discourse on the indictment and the manner in which the State has answered defence questions. The State has in effect conceded it has not supplied sufficient details of the allegations. The reply, 'This is a matter peculiarly within your knowledge,' is one that he has never heard given in a criminal case. It is most improper to give a reply that assumes the guilt of the accused. 'Whether the defence genuinely wants the facts it has asked for is irrelevant,' he tells Yutar. 'It is entitled to ask for them.'

In the circumstances the proper order is to quash the indictment, which he does. He rises and leaves the court. Confusion, in which we rush forward towards the dock. In law, they are free. 'In a country where the rule of law functioned the accused would be released' (*The Times*, London, 30 October 1963).

We hang over the barrier that separates us from the men. The Special Branch gather, their faces grim. Denis is half out of the dock, trying to kiss Esmé, and Warrant Officer Dirker grapples with him, struggling to haul him down to the cells. In a flare of temper Denis shouts, 'Let go! Let go!' and Joel Joffe rushes to intervene. Dirker puts his great hulk between them shouting, 'Joffe, if you ever interfere with me again while I'm performing my duties, I'll arrest you!' Joel replies equally heatedly that his clients are not under arrest, they have been discharged, and Dirker had better keep his hands off them. Swanepoel then rushes into the dock and striking each of the accused on the shoulder, declares, 'I am arresting you on a charge of sabotage!'

In a few minutes it is all over. The prisoners are completely surrounded by SBs and with the aid of warders are being pushed downstairs to the cells again. The spectators stand silently and bitterly.

And suddenly Toni is brought to breaking point by a young policeman who has been harassing her about her headscarf which keeps slipping off the top of her head (women must keep their heads covered in South African courts); as he goes to her a third time, she lets out a wail: 'Oh Mummy, tell him to leave me alone!' and bursts into loud sobs. The whole court turns our way

128

like puppets pulled with strings; the police, the counsel, the Press, the important visitors in the special gallery; their faces startled.

The court is quiet except for the sound of her crying.

4
Jimmy Kantor

Two women attracted the attention of the press photographers, in fact, of all the men: Winnie Mandela, and Barbara, James Kantor's wife. Both strikingly beautiful, it was not merely their features that made heads turn, but a certain quality of bearing: pride, dignity, self-assurance and unfailing elegance in dress. One of Winnie's various bans confined her to Johannesburg and she had to obtain special permission to attend the trial in Pretoria. Whenever she attended court, the police watched her with lustful eyes.

Winnie's work as a social welfare officer made it difficult for her to attend regularly, but Barbara Kantor, together with her mother-in-law, was the most regular attender at the trial. Pregnant with her third child, she managed to look cool and fashionable on the most oppressive days, sitting upright and attentive for long hours on the uncomfortable benches.

Jimmy Kantor was irrelevant as far as the trial was concerned. His firm had handled the opening transaction on the purchase of Lilliesleaf Farm and his brother-in-law and legal partner was clearly involved with the other accused. He thought he was simply a hostage for Wolpe and when the police told him that Harold had escaped to Bechuanaland he exclaimed: 'Thank heaven! Now I will be released.' But he was not released. Now he was joined with others, mostly unknown to him, on capital charges.

In fact his predicament was not only the outcome of police spite, but also of his own integrity. The police had offered him a way out which he had been unable to take.

Although he knew nothing about Harold's escape, he knew someone who did — myself. By exposing me to the police, he might have endangered Harold's safety. Still, he could have bought his release at my expense. He did not.

After he had been charged with the others, an approach was

made to him: if he would report to the police any conversations taking place during their exercise periods between the other whites, Rusty, Bob and Denis, there would be a *quid pro quo*. Jimmy knew Bob and Rusty very slightly, Denis not at all; none of them meant anything to him. He was opposed to their political views and activities. Yet again he refused to take the path of escape offered to him.

The temptation must have been enormous. He had found solitary confinement claustrophobic and could not stand it. He was tortured by the disintegration of his practice of which he had been very proud. It was all slipping away from him: years of hard work that had brought the personal and financial rewards he wanted, expansive living, a comfortable home that Barbara was now compelled to sell, a country cottage and yacht at Hartebeestpoort Dam, the publicity and popularity he enjoyed. All going. The police had swept away from his office mountains of files, all the books and records.

To save what was left he was asked to do quite a simple thing; to turn his back on these men who, after all, meant nothing at all to him. Yet he did not.

Immediately after the formal charge and remand of the men, an application for bail was made on his behalf. Jimmy Kantor's lawyers were convinced of his innocence and certain he would be granted bail.

After hearing his counsel plead, Justice de Wet asked Dr Yutar one question: Are there any indications that Kantor has been involved in the acts of sabotage alleged against the accused?

There was no doubt whatsoever that Kantor was involved, Yutar declared immediately jumping to his feet. Bail was refused. Kantor's counsel, incensed by Yutar's assertion, hurried across to the prosecutor when court adjourned and challenged him to produce evidence of Kantor's complicity in sabotage. Hurriedly gathering his papers together, Yutar mumbled as he rushed out that he had an affidavit made by a responsible policeman stating that Kantor had attempted to recruit Africans for military training as guerrillas.

Throughout the trial the defence waited for this affidavit to be produced but it never appeared.

When the indictment was quashed, a new bail application was

made for Kantor. It was clear this time that de Wet favoured the application, even asking counsel what he considered to be a reasonable sum for bail. The application was nearly completed; Jimmy was relaxed and smiling at his wife, happy in the conviction that he would go home with her that afternoon. Suddenly Major van Niekerk walked into court and handed a piece of paper to Yutar. There was a hurried whispered consultation between the prosecution and the Security Police. Then Yutar was on his feet again:

'My lord, I want to take the court into my confidence. I had arranged with Major van Niekerk to try and meet the request of Kantor and his counsel to release him on bail. Almost immediately after that I was handed this confidential secret document.' He waved the scrap of paper in the air. 'I cannot, I *dare* not read the whole of it. It is to this effect, my lord: there is a movement afoot to get Kantor and whatever other accused who gets bail, out to Lobatsi. And if bail is not granted, to make arrangements and take certain steps to get the accused out of custody, or out of this country ... I must oppose bail.'

Yutar was not under oath or subject to cross-examination, and when counsel asked to be allowed to cross-examine the police officer who had produced the document, de Wet said sharply that no responsible police officer would produce such evidence without justification.

Bail was refused.

Two months later another bail application was made and this time Dr Yutar did not oppose it. Bail of £5,000, with stringent conditions, was given, and Kantor was able to join his family for Christmas.

In the middle of February 1964, as the State case against the accused was drawing to a close, Kantor was arrested again and his bail cancelled, 'because police fear he is planning to leave the country by air', stated Yutar. Just a fortnight before, Barbara had given birth to a daughter and the cancellation of bail was a very hard blow to the Kantors. It was granted again just before the case against him closed. The reasons were hard to see. No shred of evidence had linked Kantor with the charges. It was almost as though the police were trying to provoke him into jumping bail and leaving.

The evidence brought against Kantor hung on Wolpe's activities. One witness was a Mr Cox, senior member of a firm of Johannesburg accountants, who gave evidence on what he had found in the books and financial records at Kantor's office. The questions the State asked him related to 'the norm' in Kantor's books, and departures from 'the norm'. The court was asked to infer that certain transactions in Kantor's office such as the disposition of monies sent to Kantor for the bail and defence of Walter Sisulu (for whom Kantor had appeared in an earlier case) were not according to 'the norm'.

Neither Yutar nor Mr Cox described how they had arrived at 'the norm', and only under cross-examination did Mr Cox reveal that his study of 'the norm' was based on files and accounts selected by the police and forming only a tiny sample of Kantor's records. When his 'norm' was exposed, Mr Cox, like some other State witnesses, found himself agreeing with every proposition put to him by the defence counsel.

As soon as Cox had finished, Mr Coaker applied for Kantor's discharge on the grounds that there was no case for him to answer. The Judge said, 'I have come to the conclusion that the accused is entitled to a discharge. There is no case for him to meet.'

It was March, seven months after Kantor's arrest. The other accused were delighted at his release. The Security Police came forward to congratulate him, and called, 'Goodbye, Jimmy.'

Goodbye, Jimmy — no hard feelings. We stuck you in solitary and gave you a nervous breakdown, we put you up on a capital charge, we ruined your business, lost your home for you; we played cat-and mouse games over your bail; we didn't have any evidence against you, but no hard feelings, goodbye, Jimmy.

It was an extraordinary experience for a man with little interest in politics. And after what had happened, and what he had witnessed while in prison, Jimmy Kantor felt he could never again return to the practice of the law.

*   *   *

The day the indictment is quashed, a bail application is made for Rusty, immediately after Kantor's. Kantor's application was based on his patent innocence. Rusty neither denies nor admits the charges. His application is based on his past record.

Despite all opportunities, it states, and all advice to leave the country since 1949, he has consistently refused to do so. In 1949 when he was offered an appointment as an architect in Kenya, he was refused a passport, and turned down the appointment rather than leave the country without one, thus endangering his right to return.

The application cites his political activities, his listing, bans, arrests, trials; the 1960 emergency when he believed that he and his wife would be detained, but stayed at home, and was in fact arrested and imprisoned; and finally house arrest in the previous October, and the fact that of twenty people in the Transvaal placed under house arrest that year, only he and one other had not fled the country or disappeared underground.

Earlier in the year the Minister of Justice had mentioned Rusty by name in Parliament as 'the sort of person with whom the Government had to contend', as justification for the ninety-day law. This had been a clear indication that he would be indefinitely detained when the law was passed, but he had still refused to leave, although friends and relations advised him to do so. 'I continued to report to the police daily until I was arrested.' He describes how, during solitary confinement, the inducement of an exit permit was held out by the police if he would supply information. He refused. If granted bail, he says, he will stay to face the charges as he has stayed to face equally severe charges in the past.

Rusty is refused bail. I decide to go to Yutar and speak to him myself. My lawyers have no objection although they probably think it pointless. I am not sure of my own motives. Perhaps I want to come face to face with the man who is leading the State case. A personal confrontation.

Short, bald, dapper, holding himself very erect, Yutar's hatred of all criminals is said to stem from the fact that his sister was murdered by a blockman (white) who had refused her advances and attacked her with a cleaver. Whether this motivates him psychologically or not I cannot know, but he is a man who takes an acquittal as a personal failure.

He has a large office at the Supreme Court, filled with members of the Special Branch. I try to ignore them and speak directly to Yutar, asking him why he will not give my husband bail.

'Well — but you know it is not in my power to grant bail; only the Judge can do that.'

'But you know very well that if you do not oppose it, he will get bail.' We have quite a long argument, but he does not say to me: *Under no circumstances will your husband get bail*. Instead, he tells me to come and see him again in about two weeks. In all, I see him three times: a waste of time, but once he has not given an outright refusal, I still go. What I should realize is that his inability to give me a firm 'No' is based on the strange fact that he wishes to be loved and respected by all around him.

On the third occasion there is no one in the office except himself and a colonel of the Security Police, a huge man, tall and broad, with a bullet head. Hands in pockets, he takes a stand near a window with his back to the room. Percy Yutar says, 'Colonel, Mrs Bernstein wants us to let her husband have bail.' He turns his head slowly, looks at me coldly, says, 'No,' and turns back to the window. That is the only word he says during the whole interview.

'You see how it is,' Percy Yutar says. 'I would very much like to help you, I would indeed, but as long as the Security Police — it's not in my power, really. I am sorry, it can't be done.'

As I reach the outer office I turn back and say, 'I hope you will not regret this.'

What I really mean to say is; 'I hope you *will* regret this,' but I haven't the nerve. Certainly I do not intend it as a threat, and am startled at his reaction.

He comes scampering across his office in great agitation, crying, 'What do you mean? What do you mean?'

With all the contempt I can muster, I reply: 'I only meant I hope your conscience will not trouble you too much in the future.'

'My conscience is clear!' he cries. 'My conscience is clear! I am a deeply religious man, haven't you heard that I am a very religious man ...'

'I don't know anything about you.'

'Yes, yes, everyone knows, everyone knows I am very religious!

135

Why should my conscience trouble me? I would not do anything that went contrary to my religious beliefs ...'

The beliefs and personality of Percy Yutar are inextricably bound up with the conduct of the whole trial. Yes, I learn, he is a devoutly religious man, proud of being Jewish, longing to be the first Jewish Attorney-General ever to be appointed in South Africa. Through his conduct of the Rivonia Trial he hopes to prove that Jews are good citizens and patriots, not all communists. He is devious, vain, with passion for publicity, and will contrive to conduct the trial in such a way that he can always get press headlines. At first defence counsel find this irritating; then it becomes ludicrous and a topic for jokes. As the trial progresses, counsel begin to understand that, come what may, dramatic evidence of some sort will always be introduced in court late every Friday afternoon — late enough to be newsworthy for the Sunday papers, that have the largest circulation in the country, and not early enough for the defence to have any time to rebut or to cross-examine on it before the week-end.

The court is to become familiar with Yutar's voice, the rising pitch when things are not going well for him, the squeak of agitation. He gloats when he is winning. This dislike of Yutar, which seems to extend to all his characteristics, is not just my personal prejudice. As the trial progresses almost all members of the defence team refuse to talk to him, and this animosity continues throughout the trial.

* * *

Additional problems in consulting the accused, arising from the idiocy and complexities of apartheid rules, face those who have undertaken the defence.

When the men were first charged and the defence team went to Pretoria to meet their clients, they found the white accused and the black accused were kept in rigidly segregated parts of Pretoria jail. Counsel were told they were permitted to see their clients, but not together. They could first see the white ones in the white part of the jail, then the black ones in the black part. These prisoners, of course, are being charged jointly and sit together in court. It is inconceivable that they may not consult together.

136

The Chief Warder refused to concede. The Colonel in charge of the jail was called. He too, would not agree to joint consultations. Finally the Commissioner of South African prisons — probably influenced by the adverse publicity that could arise from the rule — conceded apartheid restrictions could be relaxed but it should not be regarded as a precedent.

Now, with two weeks before the new indictment, problems of consultation again arise. This time, through counsel's insistence on the right to interview all the accused together, a special office has been set aside for them. But aware that the office would be bugged, and confronted also with the antagonism of prison officials, a complex system has to be devised for communication. Counsel and clients learn to speak a coded language. Names are never used, key concepts are never spoken, only written and passed from hand to hand. With this method consultations become slow, often obscure; so much must be written and passed around.

Prison warders, watching constantly through the door of the office, report the method of communication to the Security Police — slips of paper that are carefully burnt in ash trays before the sessions are over. After a few days Swanepoel is pacing up and down the corridor, his red bull's neck swelling as he casts sidelong glances into the room.

One day when Swanepoel is particularly attentive, Govan Mbeki writes on a piece of paper: 'It's so nice to have Lt Swanepoel with us again'. He waits for Swanepoel to pass the door, then hands the paper ostentatiously to Joel. Joel studies the paper for some time, then whispers conspiratorially to Govan and the others. Then he prepares slowly to light the paper, dropping it into an empty tin that serves as an ashtray, while he fumbles for matches.

Swanepoel dashes into the room, face turkey-red, breathing heavily: 'I think I left my ashtray here. I always have the same ashtray with me in this place'. He grabs the tin, the paper still unburnt, and dashes out.

He did not appear outside the door of the consultation room for a long time after that.

But the problems do not go away. The accused are preparing information and memoranda for counsel about possible witnesses, about events they have been involved in. Knowing that their cells can be raided at any time and any notes will pass swiftly from prison to police to prosecution — perhaps even be used in evidence against themselves — the prisoners are censoring their notes, again devising codes for names and organizations. Gradually the preparations for the Rivonia defence begin to take on the atmosphere of an underground conspiracy within the confines of Pretoria Jail.

At the end of November the new indictment is ready. Yutar has made considerable changes, and defence counsel are dismayed at the length of the document. To the original nine pages are now attached nineteen pages of further particulars and another twenty-one pages of annexures. The three original charges have become four — the additional charge being that the accused prepared for further acts of violence to take place after their arrest. The number of actual acts of sabotage have been reduced from 222 to 193.

'It is a slovenly document,' our counsel say, and draw up a new notice of complaint, listing about forty major errors in the indictment. The decision to request its quashing once again is not based on any desire to harass the court, but on the firm belief that the second indictment is just as faulty in law as the first and should be rejected on precisely the same grounds.

So the scene is enacted once again, but the atmosphere has changed. The display of police force has lessened; the court, both in its approaches and interior, appears less ominous; the fever-pitch of interest has decreased.

This time Mr Justice Quartus de Wet is patently not interested in argument on the faults in the indictment. He wants the case to proceed.

Only a few minutes after Bram starts to speak, de Wet puts down his pencil, fixes his gaze on the skylight and very deliberately ignores the proceedings. Dr Yutar who at first is hunched up over his papers, gradually straightens, sits up importantly; looks around, jokes with the assistant prosecutor.

All Bram's careful arguments are ignored. At lunch we discuss the Judge's changed attitude. Was he 'got at' during the adjournment? Probably not; de Wet has a reputation for being self-willed and obstinate and for a certain impatience with legal quibbles. It is more likely he has decided that, whether the indictment is faulty or not, there is enough material to warrant a trial, and he wants to get on with it.

Harold Hanson, one of the most senior counsel of the Johannesburg Bar, takes up the argument against the indictment on behalf of James Kantor (this, of course, was before he was discharged). In contrast to Bram, Hanson is a powerful speaker who uses his oratorical powers with devastating effect.

He tells the Judge that one of the allegations against Kantor is 'one of the most sinister ever to appear in an indictment'. It is that Kantor had acted as an attorney on behalf of some of the accused in previous cases. 'Am I to refuse to appear on behalf of some of these people because some of them may have committed sabotage; and in appearing for them I may involve myself and thus create evidence against myself?'

He submits the indictment does not disclose any offence by Kantor. Justice de Wet intervenes to point out that although the individual facts may not be particularly weighty, the cumulative effect might well be significant. Hanson's argument is based on the guilt or innocence of Kantor and this aspect of the indictment is not before the court.

'I do not know what you are talking about,' he tells Hanson who is becoming ruffled. 'You are dealing with circumstantial evidence and the cumulative effect is —'

Hanson interrupts loudly and angrily: 'My lord, the cumulative effect of seven noughts is nought. Your lordship started by saying your lordship is not concerned with this indictment, and I say your lordship is!'

The Judge dismisses the application and orders the case to begin.

Yutar opposes defence counsel's request for a postponement, which is not a bona-fide application, he says, and produces another of his pieces of paper. It is a schedule which shows exactly how many hours each day each counsel spent in Pretoria jail in consultation with the accused. 'I don't think I had ever heard of another prosecutor stooping to spying on defence counsel', Joel Joffe writes later, 'and enlisting the prison staff to record and tot up the hours spent by them closeted with their clients ... It seemed to me so outrageous that the prison authorities should lend themselves to such a procedure; and outrageous that the Judge should sit there in silence, listen and accept the piece of paper.' Yutar now argues that as counsel have not been in consultation every hour of their time — which of course they cannot be, as a great deal of other work must be done — the application for postponement cannot be genuine!

The trial must start immediately, he declares, because 'the State cannot guarantee the security of witnesses'. All the witnesses with the exception of police officers and one or two very minor characters have been in police custody for months. Only Bob Hepple has been released. And now Yutar produces the headlines he needs for the afternoon papers: 'Advocate Bob Alexander Hepple has been threatened by the accused or their supporters,' he tells the court, 'and has fled the country.'

The postponement is refused, and de Wet rules that the case proceed the following day.

Later, from Dar-es-Salaam, Bob Hepple told a different story. 'The Government was looking for dramatic effect and wanted to make a scapegoat out of me as a collaborator,' he said. 'I left because I did not want to be a political tool. I believed I was not safe even if I gave evidence for the State, and I might have been re-arrested and placed under ninety-day detention. I left because of broken promises made to me by the police.'

The police had promised to release him from detention if he made a statement, he said. He had made a statement while in solitary confinement as a result of police promises and threats. He stated categorically that he had not been threatened by the Rivonia prisoners or anyone else.

*   *   *

3 December 1963

The formal start of the trial.

The Assistant Registrar puts the charges to each of the accused in turn.

Mandela: 'My lord, the Government, not I, should be in the dock. I plead not guilty to all charges.'

Sisulu: 'The Government is responsible for what has happened in this country. I plead not guilty.'

Justice de Wet: 'I do not want any political speeches. You are asked to plead guilty or not guilty.'

Goldberg: 'I plead not guilty and I associate myself with the remarks of Mandela and Sisulu.'

Each of the accused ignores de Wet's warning and blames the Government for what has happened, with the exception of Kantor who says simply: 'I am not guilty, my lord.'

Yutar rises to his feet with printed copies of his opening address, all beautifully bound and tied up with green tape. As though to emphasize the importance of the documents and evidence he has collected, everything Yutar presents will appear beautifully bound in printed covers.

He hands copies of his address to the Judge and to the defence counsel — the first they have seen of it, although it has been in the hands of the press for some time; and opening his copy, he starts to read.

At this crucial moment Bram stands up. Overnight a small black microphone has grown up on Yutar's desk; defence noticed technicians from the South African Broadcasting Corporation testing it earlier.

The SABC is state-controlled, not an independent or an impartial body. And whatever the traditions in other countries, broadcasting any part of a court case is unknown in South Africa. Defence know that they will not get facilities equal to those provided to Dr Yutar, not now or at any other time.

Bram asks if it is in order for the opening address to be broadcast in this way. Mr Justice de Wet, looking somewhat uncomfortable, says he had given permission to record the opening address 'in order to inform the public', as he had not seen any objection to it at that stage. But now, he states, the position has changed — though how or why he does not mention — and for this reason the previous permission had lapsed. He was not at present prepared to allow the broadcast. Has Yutar any comments? Yutar declares he has no share in the matter at all.

There is a recess. The SABC technicians dismantle and remove the microphone.

Yutar's opening address:

A plot to commit sabotage, violence and destruction as a prelude to

141

guerrilla warfare, armed invasion and the violent overthrow of the Government in a war of liberation, was planned for this year. The plot was the work of the ANC. Their headquarters was Lilliesleaf, the farm at Rivonia, the home of Arthur Goldreich. Here, too, lived Nelson Mandela, Walter Sisulu, Ahmed Kathrada, Govan Mbeki and Raymond Mhlaba, all under false names. Denis Goldberg and Lionel Bernstein were frequent visitors.

The farm, chosen because of its seclusion, was the focal point of the ANC, the Communist Party and the National High Command. The National High Command issued directions and instructions to cells and committees all over the country in conditions of great secrecy. There was even a radio transmitting set, from which Sisulu broadcast to his followers.

It was from Rivonia that the new policy of sabotage, violence and destruction was planned, engineered and directed.

In six months the High Command planned to obtain 200,000 hand grenades and thousands of mines, time devices for bombs and other materials. The police found 106 maps marked with proposed sabotage targets. Young Africans were recruited and sent out of South Africa for military training.

Sabotage was the preliminary step, aimed to produce chaos, disorder and turmoil, to pave the way for the second stage, which was the waging of guerrilla warfare. The accused studied tactics of such warfare as waged in Algeria, Cuba, China and elsewhere.

For the wholesale manufacture of explosives, another property, Travallyn, was bought and workshops were to be erected there. The final stage of the second phase would come when the Government had been brought to its knees and a revolutionary Government would be set up.

Financial support was promised and received from supporters in African states and other countries. In conclusion there remains only to be said that the documents and witnesses will reveal to the court that the accused had so planned their campaign that the present year — 1963 — was to be the year of liberation from the so-called yoke of the white man's domination.

The opening address is Yutar's most effective piece of work in the whole trial, setting out what the State intended to prove; the first indication to the defence team of the lines the trial would take.

The accused have insisted to counsel that although they had considered the question of guerrilla warfare, no agreement to

142

embark on it at any specified date had ever been reached; that at no time had consideration been given to inviting military units of foreign countries to participate in South Africa's troubles and that they all viewed the liberation of South Africa as a long struggle and had never imagined the end would be seen in 1963.

The defence case is clarified. For most of the accused the verdict will be 'guilty'. Their case, therefore, is to expose evidence they maintain is manufactured, lying, incorrect; and to prevent the death sentence being carried out.

5
Victims and Accomplices

We had to learn the psychology of betrayal. There was little understanding and no experience of the past to guide us.

In numbers, in proportion to those appearing in the many trials, there will not be many traitors. The harm each one of them can do outweighs the significance of their numbers. We need to understand them.

We are still quite naive about their behaviour. We think that those who have proved weak in the face of adversity, are still fundamentally the same men who worked together with those in the dock. This being so, once they confront them in court, we think they may change their minds and refuse to testify. Or if they do become State witnesses, they will be ashamed and will falter under cross-examination. We are wrong.

We did not understand that once having changed sides it was virtually impossible for them to change back again, not only for real fear of the consequences, but for deeper, psychological reasons. They have abandoned the safety, the comradeship, the protective understanding of their group, and now they are part of another group to whose rules they must adhere. They have no way out. Attacks from defence counsel designed to shame or shake them simply drive them further into the safety of their new protectors. They dare not be cast out from them. Therefore they must please them in every possible way, carry out their suggestions, adhere tenaciously to manufactured evidence.

The fear of not satisfying their new authority is as great as the simple fear of reprisals — more detention, trials, imprisonment, even assaults and torture. It is the subconscious fear of being totally isolated, plunged into doubt, forced into new decisions, and they would be wholly lost, pariahs to all. The more counsel seeks to prize them away, the more tenaciously they cling to their new security. They have relinquished their right to think freely, to assess independently. They are wholly dependent on powers outside themselves. All that matters is the approval of these powers.

There is no straightforward pattern of behaviour among the traitors. Each finds his own justification, and some go no further than the fact that they have become so terrified that they will now do anything to save themselves.

To defend the indefensible apartheid State witnesses recite evidence they have been taught by the police, manufacture evidence as required. Even when the truth is damaging enough from the State's point of view, they do not leave it at that, but alter and embroider to suit the requirements of the Security Branch. The astonishing fact is that most of this mendacity is completely unnecessary, as all but three of the accused admit to the main charges. They are admitting what is true. To secure their conviction, it is not necessary to manufacture evidence.

They are drowning men who clutch the hair of their best friends, pressing them down into suffocating seas of jail and death to save themselves.

One of them (Adrian Leftwich in a Cape Town case) sobbed loudly in court when he admitted under cross-examination that he was giving evidence to save himself: 'It is not easy to give evidence against people you love, your friends, but, sir ...' he broke down and cried, 'if I stood to get only five or ten years, I would never give evidence.'

Another, months afterwards, when asked why he had added so many damaging pieces of information to his evidence, confessed: 'I was only conscious of my own fear.' A third stated: 'I wanted to be the best State witness the police ever had. I wanted to please them.'

We do not yet understand that in many cases the traitor has to justify his betrayal, not so much to the world as to himself. He must find justification that will shift the guilt and responsibility to those he is betraying. Not: I am doing this because I must save myself at any cost, at the expense of all those I cared for and all the things I believed in, still I must save my skin. But: I am justified in doing this, because I was betrayed — *they* betrayed *me*.

So the main State witness in the Rivonia Trial, 'Mr X.' — Bruno Mtolo — can declare in the witness-box that he had not harmed the people against whom he was testifying, 'as a matter of fact, I

145

have done them a favour'. He had decided to make a statement to the police not only in the interests of the ANC, but all the people in South Africa. 'Every person on this earth ought to think of other people,' he declared. 'Don't you think that that is just a bit of sheer hypocrisy?' defence counsel asked. 'No, I am saying that for it is true, from the bottom of my heart, my lord.'

But not all State witnesses are accomplices. Many of them are victims. Twenty-three of the State witnesses are men and women who are being held under the ninety-day law. These are minor characters in the drama, many of them domestic workers and farm labourers who had been employed on the Rivonia property, Lilliesleaf Farm.

They appear at the start of the case, and their evidence is simple; they explain how they came to be employed at Rivonia, and the work that they did. They describe the building known as 'the cottage' — the self-contained flat in the grounds, some way from the house — and which of the accused they have seen there at various times, either staying there or visiting.

The first of these is Edith Ngopani, a middle-aged woman who had been employed by the Goldreichs to help look after their children. Her evidence is quite straightforward, and defence counsel decide to cross-examine her only to find out what has happened to her from the time of her arrest.

She has been in jail for five months, three of which were in solitary confinement. She says: 'I was arrested on the 11th of July, the date of the Rivonia raid. I am still locked up. I have not been told why I have been kept locked up. I have requested them to let me go so that I can see my children, but was refused … They said that if they were satisfied with the answers that I gave them they would release me. I told them what I know. What I didn't know I couldn't tell them.'

Defence are aware of what happens to those in detention. But they want to underline the fact that witnesses were being held in jail for five months, being told that they would only be released after they had given evidence *to the satisfaction of the State*. Can evidence given under duress be taken seriously by a responsible court?

Counsel challenges the legality of keeping her a prisoner for

146

so long. But Yutar jumps up to explain that she was not in detention, she was in *protective custody*.

As he knows well, there is no procedure in South African law for protective arrest; his statement only underlines the illegality of her detention. (Subsequently the Criminal Procedure Act of 1955 was amended by a clause [known as the 180-day law] which permitted detention for up to six months of anyone suspected of having information required by the police.)

Thomas Mashifane, an elderly man, has been foreman of Lilliesleaf Farm. After giving his evidence he turns to the Judge and asks permission to put a question. Told to speak, he describes how after the police had taken his statement, they told him to undress, then assaulted him with kicks and blows as he ran naked round a table.

'I just want to know,' he says in a quiet voice that is audible in the silent court, 'why I should be assaulted like that when I was not committing any offence. I just want to know why they were hitting me.'

'You can tell the police,' says de Wet, 'and your complaint will be investigated.'

'I did complain to the police and at that time pus was still coming from my ear. Nothing was done.'

The Judge to Yutar: 'I take it you will inquire. I am not going to do it.' And to Mashifane, 'Did the treatment influence your statement at all? Have you told the court anything that is not true?'

'What I said here is the truth,' Mashifane answers slowly, 'but certain things I said I did not say as I would have wanted to say on my own. I want to explain it this way that when a person is being "killed" then he can't speak as he would have wanted to speak if he had not been suffering pain. A man speaks better when he has not been hit.'

Later Dr Yutar tells the court that a senior police officer has investigated Mashifane's complaint, but it is not advisable to disclose the officer's report. However, Mashifane has now approached Dr Yutar and 'begged me not to take the matter any further'.

Mashifane's son, Joseph, has also been held long weeks in a lonely cell, although he is only a boy of about seventeen. He is clearly terrified, clinging obstinately to what he has been saying even when proved to be lying, or when he has contradicted himself. His evidence is important on only one point: he identifies Rusty as the fair-haired man he had seen erecting a radio transmitter mast at Rivonia. It was not Rusty; the occasion was a Saturday afternoon when Rusty was at home under house arrest. The case emerging against Rusty is not strong; this evidence may be vital. Joseph is confused and hesitant, unable to frame his answers properly; but he insists doggedly that it was Rusty he saw. Is he afraid to change his statement, even when it is patently wrong? He made a statement to the police when arrested; he does not know why he is in jail; he does not know if he has been charged with any offence or not; he does not know when he is going to be released the police have not told him.

There is a vital flaw in his evidence, but defence decide not to reveal it at this stage.

An old woman of seventy, Florence Ntombela, seriously ill with a heart complaint, is brought 300 miles from Ladysmith in Natal to give evidence. Two or three years ago she attended a meeting of ANC members in her area and heard Walter Sisulu say something about young people engaging in bombing and burning. She shuffles into the courtroom and climbs the few steps to the witness-box with painful difficulty. She has been arrested and detained twice in solitary confinement in different prisons. She had forgotten Sisulu's words until the second detention. During that period she became so ill that two heart specialists, white men, had been sent for; and when it seemed she might die in her cell, the police released her but ordered her not to leave her own home. She has been brought to court to draw on her last reserves of physical energy and recall from a confused and fading memory some part of Walter's speech that might bear out the State's case. And even so, she tells counsel she might well have heard the words from someone else, at some other time. She cannot really remember.

There are many more who come, usually unwillingly, to add their meagre scrap of evidence, a piece of gossip, a vaguely-remembered story, and induced memories of words said and meetings held. As they come, the State strays far and wide beyond the scope of the indictment. Evidence is led to acts of sabotage not even charged in the indictment. Evidence is led of acts of assault which, if true, could be the basis for a charge of murder, yet no such charge has been made.

At one stage, tiring of the mounting volume of evidence which does not relate directly to the indictment, defence counsel object. Mr Justice de Wet, in a remarkable judgement, slaps them down. This, he says, is not a trial by jury; he is quite capable of deciding what is relevant and what is not relevant. Any objections counsel have can stand over until the end of the case, when they can argue that irrelevant evidence should be struck out.

Seizing on this encouragement, the days, the weeks drag by with the production of material prejudicial to the accused and with mountains of evidence irrelevant to the charge and wholly inadmissible, according to counsel's understanding of the code of the law. With his constant desire to inject drama into the tedium of such days, Yutar would produce either a surprise witness or a very revolutionary-sounding document (usually first priming the press, to obtain dramatic headlines).

It seemed unfair to counsel to base a large part of a conspiracy charge on documentary evidence that might be unknown to all except one of the accused, or possibly unknown to all of them, but known to the co-conspirators named in the indictment though not present in court. Yet despite all the promises made to court, the defence were never provided with copies of documents prior to their introduction. Documents were read piecemeal into the evidence between witnesses.

So the record becomes burdened with reams and reams of evidence on matters which are not in dispute, which defence have no intention of disputing, which they have made clear from the beginning they will not dispute.

To sit on backless benches in the hot court room under the constant observation of hostile SBs, and unable to hear most of what is said, becomes the personal penance of those of us who attend court regularly.

A taxi-driver, Mr A., gives evidence that a few years before he had driven Mandela to a meeting in Port Elizabeth. He is asked to describe Nelson, and how he looked, but cannot do so. 'Was there no particularly distinguishing feature about him?' 'No.' 'Do you recognize Mandela in the dock?' 'Oh yes, I do.' 'Had he looked exactly the same four years ago as he does now?' 'Yes, just the same.'

Mandela is clean-shaven now, as he has been for some months. But at the time of which Mr A. speaks he had a heavy black beard. This is known, and the prosecution's own witnesses have testified to it. The court adjourns for the weekend. On Monday, Mr A. is recalled by Dr Yutar, and somehow over the weekend his memory has improved. He has thought the matter over, he says, and suddenly he has remembered that when he saw Mandela in Port Elizabeth, he had had a black beard.

There is an even more extreme case of coaching a little later. A Port Elizabeth witness tells of receiving materials for the making of bombs and is asked to describe this material which had been carried on the floor of his motor-car. He explains that the powder was like mealie-meal (maize meal), which is off-white. Over and over again Dr Yutar asks him questions about the powder, trying to get him to state that it was black (gunpowder should be black). But he insists it was white. He also describes some plastic tubes which must clearly be transparent if the contents are to be seen, but he insists they were opaque; nothing shakes his testimony about the white powder and opaque tubes — not on Friday, when the testimony is taken.

On Monday he is recalled by Dr Yutar and asked the same questions about the powder and tubes, and this time the answers come out right — the powder is black, the tubes are transparent.

Essop Suliman (defence counsel describe him as a clown and a disgrace to the court) is the owner of a fleet of small vans which he hires out. He is not a licensed bus operator; his 'pirate' company flourishes on the shortage of public transport between Johannesburg and Soweto. He hires out vans for longer trips when required.

Suliman's vans are alleged to have been used by Umkhonto many times to transport young men from Johannesburg to Bechuanaland on the first stage of their journey north for military training. He testifies to many such trips. He is telling the truth when he says the vans were hired to transport young men across the border; but he lies when he testifies that on several occasions, Ahmed Kathrada hired them.

150

He is lying, and the defence know he is lying, and the police know it too. How else can one account for the fact that he has already testified in five other cases about men going over the border; some of the convoys have been intercepted by the police and the men arrested and charged with attempting to leave the country illegally, or attempting to go abroad to obtain military training; Suliman has given evidence in all of them, given all the details required in each case; and in each case he has contradicted himself. His answers are always tailored to fit the needs of the prosecution. In a previous case he testified that Sisulu hired him on occasions; now it is Kathrada. Neither Sisulu nor Kathrada have hired Suliman's vans. But there is very little evidence against Kathrada. Suliman's testimony is important.

Suliman is thoroughly discredited by defence counsel who read back to him differing accounts he has given of incidents in other cases. But Suliman is undeterred. He will go on travelling around the country giving evidence at other trials. He is one of the State's 'travelling witnesses'.

Essop Suliman tells Justice de Wet that he had been kept in custody for sixty-five days before the police took a statement from him, and was then kept a further fifty-five days before the final portion of his statement was taken. He admits giving different evidence in other cases, but claims this evidence is the correct, the true version; he had been confused or his memory failed him before.

His chief driver, Pete Coetzee, proves even less credible. Either he is silly, or he is pretending to be silly. Perhaps he is not as stupid as he appears in the box. He says alternately 'no' or 'yes' to anything he is asked, indiscriminately, and apparently unconcerned which is right. He is asked to identify various people from photographs. Every one of the men who have beards — Goldreich, Wolpe, Slovo — he identifies as Jimmy Kantor. Defence counsel are astonished that the prosecution have called this clown as a witness to facts that they must know will not be denied.

An elderly man, English Mashiloane, gives evidence chiefly concerned with the activities of Motsoaledi and Mlangeni.

He describes meetings of the ANC held in his house at Orlando. He asserts that groups of young men who were to go abroad for military training were picked up by Suliman Essop (the taxi-driver) at this house, and that the two accused had supervised these operations.

This most damning evidence is then developed, embroidered, with stories that the defendants deny and that were patently false.

He tells, for example, how Motsoaledi had brought parcels of dynamite to his house, taken them to the garage and repacked them into smaller parcels, then gone off again, leaving some sticks of dynamite behind the garage door, warning him not to smoke near those sticks. He relates how, on another occasion, a letter had come to his post office box. As he is illiterate he showed the letter to Motsoaledi and asked him to read it. Motsoaledi said: 'Oh, this letter is for me.' He opened the letter and inside there was no writing, only a series of numbers. Motsoaledi said: 'Let me read the letter to you.' Looking at the numbers he reads: 'You are please to meet the recruits who are coming on the Cape Town train on such and such a date and at such and such a time.' Motsoaledi continued to decipher this numerical code in rapid reading while they walked down the street.

There are some letters before the court that are typed in a number code, with numbers obviously standing for letters or words. Yet all the combined resources of the South African Security Police have failed to decipher a word of them. Yet Motsoaledi could, according to the witness, recode them as he walked along, without reference work of any kind.

Mashiloane had himself been a supporter and member of the ANC. What had turned him into an accomplice?

He is a herbalist by trade, and despite his illiteracy, he is not a fool; he is a successful and prosperous business man. He had been allowed to practice his trade while in jail, selling herbal remedies to prisoners and others in jail, and enjoying special privileges which not even awaiting prisoners enjoyed. He had also, of course, earned indemnity for his own participation in ANC activities and for despatching young men abroad.

Yet even as he stood in the witness box he was not free, he insists, from police custody. He seems to feel he is struggling for his own life as fully as those in the dock. He repeatedly asks:

'Am I not also here in court the same as they are?' And at the end it appears that Dr Yutar wants to deny him indemnity from prosecution.

The Judge should have explained the legal position to him clearly before he testified: that, as an accomplice, he did not have to give evidence if he did not wish to do so; but if he did choose to do so, and gave satisfactory evidence, he would get indemnity from further prosecution. Yutar has not told the court that Mashiloane is an accomplice.

Some way through the testimony, de Wet puts the question directly to Yutar: 'You are using this person as an accomplice. Are you not compelled to warn him, should you not tell him, that he should give his evidence satisfactorily or face prosecution?'

Yutar stutters: 'My lord ... I'm ... I do not ... mm ... consider him an accomplice.'

The Judge does not bother to comment, but immediately warns Mashiloane of his position, and orders the State to proceed.

These are among the twenty-nine who were ninety-day detainees. 'I did not use the ninety days for questioning them; I merely used it to keep them in custody to prevent interference from outside,' states a security man during the trial.

And now the police who have prepared and coached the State witnesses also enter the box themselves and take the oath to tell the truth.

Most of their evidence is of a formal nature, of acts of sabotage they have investigated, what they found on the scene, what explosives were used. There is evidence of trials of people in various parts of the country, who have been named as co-conspirators or agents of the accused; evidence of the raid at Lilliesleaf Farm itself in Rivonia, of documents found there. Explosive experts testify about explosives, their effects and consequences, of fuses and methods of sabotage which have been described by various witnesses. In general, these witnesses are not seriously challenged.

But enter Sergeant Card, a man who appears to have a photographic memory. He rattles through a list of some fifty or sixty people from the Port Elizabeth district. He knows all their first names; and each one he gives a title. He says: 'This man I know

153

... he was a member of the ANC ... He was a group officer! ... A commander! ... A Sergeant! ... An intelligence agent!' — whatever title he chooses to give — 'in such and such a branch of the Umkhonto.' He knows, also, all their nicknames, their police records and their present whereabouts.

How does he know all this? When asked he replied: 'Sometimes they told me.'

Under what circumstances would anyone tell a policeman in which branch of a sabotage organisation he had held what office?

On other occasions he answers, 'Through police records' — that is to say, by hearsay, or by word of informers recorded in dossiers, evidence that was not admissable in a South African court.

But Sergeant Card makes one admission worth recording. He is asked how he obtains information from persons who were detained for interrogation. The answer is straightforward: 'We tell them what we want to know, and wait until he confirms it!'

And enter Detective-Sergeant Dirker, who has probably been in the Special Branch longer than any other security man involved in the case. The accused have known him for years, as he knows them. Over those years he has remained a Sergeant while other men, many years his junior, have been promoted to Lieutenant, Captain, even Colonel.

He is six foot tall, heavily built, a paunch swelling over his trousers and almost splitting his white shirt. He wears a few long black strands greased across his balding, egg-shaped head, allowing a couple of strands to fall forward over one eye, to complement his little Hitler-like moustache.

He testifies that the document 'Operation Mayibuye' was found lying open on the table in the centre of the room where Sisulu and the others were arrested. It had in fact been found in an unused portion of a small heating stove in the room. Open on the table, though, it would appear to be the centre piece of the discussion that was taking place, and it was chiefly on this basis that all those in the room that day were alleged to be members of the High Command of Umkhonto. This was important for those of the accused who did not admit membership of the High Command.

Dirker is lying, defence know he is lying. But his evidence is corroborated by another SB man, Kennedy.

But if defence challenge them both on this point, they may well call further police witnesses to show that the document *was* on the table. Would the Judge necessarily believe the accused if they contest this? To avoid a direct dispute, even thought it was of importance, defence decide to leave the document on the table where the police put it.

Dirker recounts an incident in December 1962. He walked into Sisulu's office, he says, and found Kathrada there with his arm round the shoulder of an African barrister, Duma Nokwe, a leading member of the ANC who was later sent abroad. This must be untrue. Kathrada and Sisulu were at that time both under bans prohibiting them from communicating with each other. Both would have been arrested immediately if found in the same office. Dirker lacks the care or the cunning for success as a liar.

After the Rivonia raid, he saw Rusty's car standing in the yard, opened the bonnet and put his hand on the engine block. It was cold. This evidence was to prove that Rusty must have been at the house for some hours; and since the Mayibuye document was open on the table, he must have been at a long meeting discussing it. Ergo, he is a member of the National High Command!

It happened that our car was a model very popular with car thieves and for this reason we had fitted it with a concealed switch that disconnected the self-starter. If the bonnet was opened to see what was wrong, the hooter was automatically set off, and blew continuously until the bonnet was closed. Dirker is unaware of this; when asked if anything happened when he opened the bonnet he replies: 'No.' He is also unaware of the fact that on the day of his arrest, Rusty had reported at Marshall Square just before two p.m. (The time of reporting is registered in the book.) The raid took place at 3 p.m. In between, he had delivered some architectural plans and driven to Rivonia, a journey that takes more than half an hour. He had, in fact, arrived only a few minutes before the raid.

* * *

If so many of these witnesses who are brought to add their piece

155

of evidence are victims, this cannot be said of the State's most important witness, Mr X.

When Yutar announces the calling of Mr X, he asks that his evidence be held in camera, mainly for the sake of the witness. 'He is definitely in mortal danger,' he cries, with a break in his voice. 'I assure this court the State fears for the safety of this witness!'

De Wet asks defence counsel their attitude.

Defence wants all the witnesses to be heard in public, but feel that to insist on this might only lead to a substantiation of the fears expressed by Yutar; so they state that while preferring all evidence to be held in public, they will not object.

While on his feet Vernon Berrangé, who had dealt with the question, takes the opportunity to object to a new procedure which has been introduced at this stage.

The witness box, normally sited in front of defence counsel, has been moved to the opposite side of the court where the prosecution team are seated. The witness thus would stand surrounded on all sides by the prosecution team and the SBs, who are part of that team. Witnesses would face directly towards what in normal cases was the jury box. In the unused jury box is the large and formidable figure of a member of the Security Police, Detective-Sergeant van Rensburg. He has the face of a Gestapo man and the reputation of a thug. Sitting alone in the jury box, glaring menacingly directly at the witness on the witness stand, can only be intimidatory. We object, counsel states, to the presence of van Rensburg.

The Judge upholds the objection. The court is cleared of the public and the jury box is cleared of van Rensburg. The first really substantial witness, Mr X, takes the stand.

Although the court has ordered the press to refer to him as Mr X, everyone knows who he is. Information from the prison grapevine has long established that Bruno Mtolo was talking. He sits and chats with the SBs in the corridor where witnesses wait to be called — a public place where anyone can pass — and where the SBs ply him with cigarettes and treat him as a celebrity, almost as though he is not black. He is a very valuable witness for the State, and proves himself extremely formidable to the defence.

He is a tall, well-built man, relaxed and self-confident, completely at ease. He plays his new role as effectively as he had played another role in the past.

Dr Yutar's opening question: 'Bruno, are you a saboteur?'

'Yes, I was.'

'Did you blow up pylons and other government property in Durban?'

'Yes, I did.'

He describes how he came into the trade union movement and later became an organiser and full-time official. He joined the ANC in 1957 and the Communist Party in 1961. He tells of the meeting in Natal after Nelson Mandela had returned from his secret trip through Africa, and of how Mandela had informed them of the decision to launch acts of sabotage. He, Bruno Mtolo, joined the Natal Regional Command of Umkhonto we Sizwe.

He speaks of the first bombs, planted on the night of 16 December 1961, carried through the crowded streets of Durban wrapped in Christmas paper; describes how he stole dynamite and, in the silence of the near-empty courtroom, demonstrates the making of a land-mine.

Towards the end of three days' evidence he is asked by Yutar why he volunteered to give evidence for the State and revealed all Umkhonto's secrets to the police. The National High Command, he says, let him down.

In June 1953 he went on an assignment for Umkhonto, but failed to carry it out because his heart was not with Umkhonto any more.

Why not? Because he had been in hiding since April, and had been promised a monthly payment. But from June until his own arrest in August the only money he had received was £10. In a loud and bitter voice he claims that the High Command did not care for its recruits — it ran away from Africa.

'Who did not care about them?'

'The High Command ... when they ran away from South Africa, they were not arrested.'

But the only members of the High Command known to Mtolo are those he has met at Rivonia. They are all in the dock in front of him. Not one of them has run away.

The voice is that of Mtolo but the ideas are those of Yutar. Now Yutar asks another key question: 'How did the so-called leadership of the High Command live?'

He, who spent three years as perhaps the most active saboteur in the country, one of the most energetic members of Umkhonto, incriminates everyone who has ever worked with him, everyone he has ever known in the ANC and Umkhonto, including his own brother who he identifies in court as one of the young men recruited by Umkhonto to be sent abroad for military training. He now accuses the men on trial for their lives of having lived in luxury.

He went to visit Walter Sisulu's house at Pafeni. The house and its furniture inside, everything was like that of Europeans. In Joe Modise's house there was a telephone and furniture that he, Mtolo, did not possess. Walter Sisulu paid bail of £3,000, and over and above that, when he came out on bail he had a motor car.

Bruno Mtolo's evidence about acts of sabotage and the people involved — conspirators not in the indictment — contains a fair amount of truth. He is the State's main witness on these points and his naming of many members of Umkhonto is extensive and very damaging. Also he has a remarkable memory. He can recall meetings held months or years before, naming the date, the place, who was present and what was discussed. Much of this is true, and for this reason it becomes very difficult for the defence to sort out the truth from the lies. They are bound together and delivered with the same self-assurance.

The smears on the leadership — they lived better than we did, they have all run away — are untrue. Sisulu's house, inside and out, is identical to a hundred thousand other municipally built and owned homes in Orlando; his furniture and personal possessions are perhaps even below the standard of many African homes; he has never owned a car and cannot drive. Mlangeni's car is not his own; it belonged to Umkhonto and has been used for official business only. Other lies seem to have been suggested to him by the police to make the case more damaging, or to fit what they wish to prove.

Joel Joffe goes off to Pietermaritzburg to interview members of the Natal Regional Command of Umkhonto to find out more about Mtolo and his testimony. It is a difficult mission. All those still available are themselves in jail awaiting trial. They are hesitant to speak to him in prison, doubtful about how much they should say without first consulting their own counsel. But he learns a little more about Mtolo. They confirm his claim to have been a saboteur for three years, perhaps the most active saboteur in Natal. He not only carried out decisions of the Regional Command, but always egged them to greater daring and greater activity. He did not seem to feel himself bound by the Umkhonto insistence never to risk taking human life. He had shown an almost demented passion for violence, and also a singular disregard for his own safety.

Joel also learns — what the leadership in Umkhonto did not know — that he is also a convicted criminal with a record that can be checked.

Gradually Mtolo's character begins to take a coherent shape. Joel feels he is typical of many old lags he has known, swaggering, self-confident, arrogant in the witness box; the ones who 'know the ropes' and even what sentence they will receive, a type he has encountered in the courts and in prisons.

With his phenomenal memory and quick mind he will be a formidable opponent in cross-examination.

As far as his evidence against the Natal Regional Command is concerned, there is little that can be said. Counsel can neither admit the people named as members of the Regional Command were members; they are all themselves accused and awaiting trial on that charge in Natal. Nor can they deny they were members. The charge may be true, but they do not know what these people will say in their own trials. Counsel also do not know the facts about Mtolo's testimony on acts of sabotage, and cannot question the details.

They are left, then, with only two aspects of his evidence that they wish to challenge: a meeting of the Natal Regional Command which he said Mandela had himself attended and addressed on behalf of the National High Command; and the smears on the leadership, the organisation, and the men in the dock.

Mandela, always decisive, makes his attitude quite plain. He will freely admit that he attended a meeting in Natal of the

Regional Command which Mtolo said he had attended, that he reported on his trip abroad and on the arrangements for the military training of personnel. But he will not under any circumstances testify as to who was present, nor admit that those named by Mtolo were members of the Regional Command. He will deny and challenge Mtolo's version of many things he was alleged to have said at the meeting. He will challenge Mtolo's red-baiting smears, his attempts to equate Umkhonto and the ANC with the Communist Party. Mandela says firmly that these allegations are lies, and must be shown to be lies.

Nelson, as a lawyer, knows he is helping to place a noose around his own neck. But even so, defence counsel feel impelled to warn him of his position and to try and argue him out of it. The cross-examination he is suggesting will be an implicit admission that he belonged to Umkhonto, and had held a senior position in it; that he had canvassed and obtained the aid of foreign countries to train military personnel for the struggle against the South African government. It was tantamount to signing his own death warrant, for there could not thereafter be any possible denials of guilt, nor attempts to evade conviction.

Nelson is unmoved. He says he has understood this ever since he took a position of responsibility in the political movement. As a leader he must accept the responsibilities to go with it. Now, he feels, it is his duty to explain to the country and to the world where he stood and why; to clarify the organisation's aims and policies, to reveal true facts. If in doing this his life will be at stake, so be it.

Walter and Govan, both of whom are accused by Mtolo of having had discussions about Umkhonto with him, take the same attitude. They will admit such discussions, but certainly deny Mtolo's version of many aspects.

The problems of defence counsel are compounded. They must now give credibility to Mtolo by freely admitting that parts of his evidence are true. The most difficult witness is not the outright liar, but one, like Mtolo, who relates much that is true, while slipping in lies in places where vital issues are at stake.

In fact he has told many lies, not only about facts known to the defendants, but even more about events in Natal that they know nothing about. Counsel must challenge his version of events without admitting anything that might incriminate any of the Natal men now awaiting trial.

* * *

Vernon Berrangé begins his cross-examination on the question of Mtolo's volte-face. Mtolo repeats, question and answer, his admission that he had, within twenty-four hours of his arrest in August, decided to tell the police all he knew; that his reasons were because he had not received the money he was promised, that Nelson Mandela and Walter Sisulu were well-off and did not care about the security of the recruits, and that the leaders had left the country.

Vernon's questions refer back to Mtolo's careers in the trade union movement and the ANC.

'Did you become disillusioned because you no longer thought that what the ANC and the liberation movement were struggling for was the right thing?'

'I will say this: that I thought all the time that what the ANC was working for was good and I still say so now, that it was good and is good. But what made me feel disillusioned was the action of the leaders.'

'And because you became disillusioned with the leaders you were prepared, within twenty-four hours of your arrest, to go and make a statement, to expose the whole of this movement which you believe to be for the benefit of the black man?'

Mtolo sidesteps rapidly, expertly.

'If I talk about the African National Congress it must be known that I talk about the ANC and not this thing about the Communists.'

'What about the Spear of the Nation?'

'The Spear is connected with the Communists.'

'Did you agree with what the Spear was doing?'

'I agreed with it when it was doing it for the ANC.'

'So you became disillusioned with the Spear when it was doing it for the Communists?'

'Yes, my Lord, in the way in which they were deceiving the people.'

'How were they deceiving the people?'

161

'Because the majority of members of the ANC were not aware of the fact that the leaders were Communists.'

'Now, do you mind telling this court what difference it made to you whether the leaders were Communists, or whether they were members of any sort of party, so long as they were doing something which you agreed to and thought was good?'

'The deception, the deceiving was the thing.'

Berrangé insists he has still not answered the question. 'Because they were not doing it for the ANC, they were doing it for themselves.'

Now Berrangé asks Mtolo a series of questions dealing with his own membership in the Communist Party, and why he went along with them wholeheartedly.

'But what we were doing at that time was all being done for the ANC.'

'That is my whole point!' Berrangé exclaims.

Answers to questions now become so convoluted that Mtolo is beginning to contradict himself and tie himself into knots. At this stage Justice de Wet intervenes, asking Mtolo to explain the difference between the aims of the Communist Party and those of the ANC.

Whether de Wet's intervention was done with deliberate intent or not, he has broken a long build-up to a climax. Berrangé starts once again.

Question and answer lead to: 'And you were prepared, therefore, to betray these members of the ANC for whom you had such soft feeling, merely because of the fact that members of the Communist Party had infiltrated the ranks of the ANC?'

Mtolo: 'As I am standing here I am satisfied in my own mind that I have not harmed the members of the ANC. As a matter of fact I have done them a favour.'

'Are you serious?'

'Yes.'

These are new reasons for Mtolo's 'disillusionment' that he had not mentioned when he gave his evidence in chief.

The cross-examination shifts round. Here the speed of Mtolo's mind is revealed.

'Is this the first time you have ever been in a court?'

'No.'

'In this court?'

'I was here last year.'

'Is this the only case you have appeared in?'

'Do you mean one that is not concerned with politics?'

'I am just asking you, is this the only case that you have appeared in?'

'I have given evidence in other courts.'

Berrangé draws out from him the fact that he gave State evidence in a case involving attempted murder with a bomb, in which he did not reveal that he himself had made the bomb.

He is questioned about his criminal record. He telescopes the number of charges, shortens the years of the sentences (for stealing), finally, reluctantly, admits to being jailed three times for theft.

He finds justification for everything he is doing now, he shifts the guilt of his betrayal on to those he is betraying. *I am justified in doing this because I was betrayed. They betrayed me.*

'But you were talking about a lot of leaders leaving the country. You see a lot of men in the dock here, don't you?'

'Yes.'

'Tell me, other than going to jail for theft, breaking into railway coaches and that sort of thing, have you ever been put under house arrest?'

'No.'

'Have you ever been prohibited from attending meetings?'

'No.'

'Have you ever been sent to jail for your political beliefs?'

'No.'

'Well, that is what happened to most of these men here.' And so it goes on. On the night of his arrest he insists, he decided to give evidence against the men on trial because the leaders had left, and in the interests of the ANC and all people in South Africa. 'Every person on earth should think of other people.'

Defence was intrigued by Mtolo's statement of what he had observed in Walter's home, as Walter insists that Mtolo, to his knowledge, has never been near his house.

Mtolo now constructs a story about having gone to a party one evening when he happened to be in Johannesburg, and he left the party with a friend to have a look at Walter's house. There were only children there. They walked through the house and sat in the dining room, then left. Yet according to his own statement at that time he, Mtolo, was in hiding from the police.

'Did you think it was a very safe thing for you to go to Sisulu's house under the circumstances, when you were supposed to be in hiding?'

Mtolo shrugs. Yutar smirks. De Wet looks bored. Defence is certain this part of the evidence is a put up job. It is followed later by many other attempts to smear the men on trial, to try and undermine their public standing, however little it matches the facts of their lives.

When his evidence is found to be wrong — proved to be wrong by court records or other unchallengeable evidence — he insists he is right and the record is wrong. Here is one example.

Berrangé: 'Do you remember saying to his Lordship that the Rivonia arrests were hard on Billy Nair. Those were the exact words used. You went on to say that you did not care ...'

Mtolo: 'That is correct.'

'Do you remember saying that?'

'Yes I do.'

'Did you discuss these arrests with Billy Nair?'

'Yes, we did.'

'The Rivonia arrests. I see, well that's rather interesting. Because at the time the Rivonia arrests took place, Billy Nair had already been arrested for some time ...'

The interpreter interrupts to say: 'My Lord, the witness is now in deep thought. He is still thinking very hard while counsel was putting that question.'

Berrangé: 'I am sure.'

Interpreter: 'He was softly whispering "Billy Nair, Billy Nair", he was evidently thinking very hard.'

At this stage Mtolo recovers himself. 'My Lord,' he says, 'I think that I should say that in my evidence I said — I think what I meant to convey was that the arrests at Rivonia were a sore point to people like Billy Nair.'

'Oh no! You said that the Rivonia arrests were hard on people like Billy Nair, but you did not care. And you also said only a few moments ago that you actually discussed the Rivonia arrests with Billy Nair.'

164

Mtolo denies saying that; then says if he did, it was a mistake. Berrangé persists: 'Oh no, it is not, I am sorry. Now what did you mean when you said that the Rivonia arrests were hard on Billy Nair, seeing that he was already arrested?'

'I ... I may have expressed it in these words, but what I meant to convey was that the arrests at Rivonia was something that was a sore point. It hurt people like Billy Nair.'

'Is that what you meant to convey, although he had been arrested before Rivonia?'

'Yes, he was arrested before Rivonia.'

'Although you did say a few moments ago that you discussed it with Billy Nair?'

'No, not discussed.'

There were many similar passages that revealed Mtolo's previous court experience. He appeared to have no nerves. He would wriggle out of any situation with a speedy shift of gears, challenging the ability of the most experienced counsel.

In many ways he is a unique witness. His evidence, a mixture of fact and fiction, moments of truth dropped in with downright lies, differs from that of other accomplices in the fact that he covers a much broader span, a longer period of time, a wider number of incidents. And while his knowledge of the real facts is far more extensive than most, his interlarding of fiction is also more extensive.

Yet for all that, he is in many ways typical of witnesses who have been in solitary confinement and interrogated by the police, who have been bullied, bribed or tortured; who have traded the freedom of those in the dock for their own freedom; who know this depends not only on their giving evidence to the satisfaction of the court, as the law demands, but more — to the satisfaction of the Security Police, who can detain them indefinitely if they wish, even after their testimony has been given; even where an absolution from prosecution has been given in court by a judge. They will lie, they do lie. They say what the SBs wants them to — tell them to say.

* * *

'Mr Y.', the next secret witness, is a short bearded man from

165

Cape Town (Cyril Davids). His testimony only affects Denis Goldberg, the only one of the accused from Cape Town, where he lived until a few weeks prior to his arrest.

Davids gives evidence of a weekend camp for 'Coloured' youths held on a farm near Cape Town in 1962, which Goldberg had organized. The camp had been quite openly held and investigated at the time by the police. But Davids now maintains it was held to train young men for guerrilla warfare. Every lecture and discussion at the camp, no matter how seemingly innocent in content, was, according to Davids, for this purpose.

At this time, guerrilla warfare had not even been discussed by the freedom organizations. Later, men were recruited for training outside South Africa. Even so, no sane person would have organized the camp described by Davids inside the country.

Davids had endured ninety days of solitary confinement and several long spells of interrogation, during which time he steadfastly maintained the camp was for 'health and spiritual purposes only'. He was told he would be held for ever until he changed his story. After four visits from the Security Police, a Lieutenant Sauerman came again to interrogate him. 'I told him it was a camp where young guerrillas would be trained, which Lieutenant Sauerman knew.'

'Did he tell you that?'

'Yes. No.'

'Now, please, why did you say yes?'

'It slipped, actually.'

Yet Davids insists under cross-examination that prolonged solitary confinement had nothing to do with it. He likes being in jail, he says, he does not miss his wife, he does not mind being alone. Then he also admits he would rather go to jail for a long time than endure another ninety days again.

Apart from David's own admission that considerable pressure was put on him to change his statement; that he adhered to his original statement through several spells of interrogation; that he was acting under duress, with the constant threat of re-imprisonment; his evidence is, on the face of it, inherently improbable.

What underground conspirator would have broadcast intentions of starting guerrilla warfare to a gathering of people like Davids, who on his own admission is non-political and did not

166

belong to any organisation? Or to employ such people as instructors of young guerrilla trainees? Yet Justice de Wet will find Davids completely credible and accept his testimony in all respects.

How should a judge weigh such evidence? First, it was on record from the witness himself that considerable pressure had been put on him to make him change his statement. Second, even in giving evidence on the basis of that changed statement, he was acting under duress, with the constant threat of re-imprisonment if his evidence did not suit the police. Third, even under duress, in solitary confinement for a long time, he had five or six times repeated that the camp was 'for health and spiritual' purposes, with no guerrilla aspects whatsoever. He only changed his evidence after his first ninety-day period came to an end and he was re-arrested for a further ninety days.

A third 'secret' witness, Mr Z. (Patrick Mtembu) is a member of the Johannesburg Regional Command of Umkhonto we Sizwe, who has been kept in solitary confinement for some months and lost 30 lb. in weight. He admits he was alone in a cell for twenty-three hours out of twenty-four with nothing at all to read or do, but, he boasts, 'I did not go off my head.'

Of all the 173 State witnesses, Mtembu is the only one who has actually worked with the accused, the only senior member of the ANC in the Transvaal who testifies in this case. He has been an accomplice and personally involved in Umkhonto activities. He has been arrested, released, arrested again, each time to be held in solitary confinement. He has been offered an indemnity by the court before giving evidence. He knows he will go free. Yet he chooses, even now, to protect himself at the expense of others. For this the accused cannot forgive him, though they could understand and even forgive those who broke in solitary confinement.

Mtembu still seeks to protect himself by placing responsibility for much of his own part in Umkhonto on the shoulders of Elias Motsoaledi, a man with whom he has had minor political clashes over the years. The case against Elias is not strong; Mtembu has made it strong and exculpated himself. Clutching the hair …

The accused are bitter about this, where the weakness of others only disgusted them. Mtembu lies steadily, although the

167

prosecution probably know he is lying. In only a few months he will reverse his testimony to convict — and send to life imprisonment — another former colleague of his, Wilton Mkwayi.

Even so, during the Rivonia Trial, Mtembu still withholds information from the police. Afterwards, he will be arrested again and then again, and will talk more each time. He will appear as a witness in other trials until the police squeeze from him every last drop of information, everything, all the things they have not known, every name, every home where a meeting has been held. No man can give himself only partially to the apartheid State.

Victims or accomplices? Perhaps of them all, Mtolo is the only willing accomplice. The others had turned around unwillingly, after prolonged periods of solitary confinement and interrogation; and despite all they endured, still stuck to their original statements (as Davids did); but finally take the only way out. The dread of returning to the hell they have been through — plus a prison sentence for perjury — if they change their evidence in court, the need to retain the protection of their powerful new guardians, keeps them adhering tenaciously to inherently unbelievable stories.

Two witnesses from Port Elizabeth give evidence of a conference of the ANC which took place in Bechuanaland in December 1962. The ANC was by then illegal in South Africa, and leading ANC representatives had gone there secretly from South Africa to meet others who lived and worked for the ANC abroad. The holding of the conference was widely publicized in the press after it was over. The South African police certainly knew it had been held; and the British police in Bechuanaland had permitted the conference only on condition that their own representatives were present throughout. No one had been prosecuted for participation in this illegal conference, presumably because there was no direct evidence of the participants except for those in exile who returned to other countries.

Now, twelve months later, two witnesses are produced.

The conference had been conducted entirely in English. Yet these two men, one of whom can only speak and understand Xhosa, show a remarkable identity of memory. Over the two-day period of the conference, they both recall exactly the same two things and both their recollections are untrue. Both only remember that Oliver Tambo who had come from abroad opened the conference, and that Mbeki spoke; and all they can remember was that they spoke about guerrilla warfare and the training of military recruits.

In fact, Mbeki had presided, not Tambo. In fact, the presence of the Bechuanaland Security Police at every session prevented anyone from discussing or even mentioning questions related to violence, military training or guerrilla warfare. But this is all the witnesses can remember. They cannot name a single other person present, nor a single other question discussed. Their evidence is untrue, but not important. Other witnesses tell identical stories that are untrue, but important.

One is the owner of a car for hire — a 'pirate' or unlicensed taxi. He tells a story of a long involved journey on Christmas Day, 1961, after he had been hired by Govan Mbeki. It started in the morning, meandered backwards and forwards from the African township of New Brighton on the outskirts of Port Elizabeth, where Mbeki lived, into the centre of town, back again, and so on from early morning until late in the afternoon. The gist of the story was that Mbeki had first gone to his office in town to fetch an empty carrier bag. They had then travelled around picking up several other people (named as co-conspirators in the case). During the course of the drive, the driver heard conversations relating to electric pylons. This elaborate tale links Mbeki with some dynamite attacks on electric pylons in the district on the day after Christmas.

Mbeki vehemently denies the story. He knows the taxi driver, says that from time to time his taxi was hired by members of the ANC. If the story were true, Mbeki would have no purpose in denying it, as he has already stated that he will admit membership of Umkhonto.

Under cross-examination the witness does not deviate in the slightest from his account of the journey. Defence have added together all the mileage taken that day, allowing the car to move at ten miles an hour, and cannot find more than one and a half hours travelling time. Yet witness says he spent seven or eight hours over it.

Again, the basic facts are improbable. Mbeki lived in an area surrounded by small shops. Would he have hired a car to take him several miles away to his office to pick up an empty brown paper bag — calling at his office, well-known to the SBs, and shown in police evidence to be overlooked by Security Police headquarters in Port Elizabeth? And from a whole day's conversation, could only one single item have been discussed, that item about electric pylons?

Defence are certain the story is false, yet they think it has been built up on a foundation of a journey that the witness had taken at some time; that he had taken someone on this complicated drive; but it was not Govan Mbeki.

The second man also runs a pirate taxi. His story is of a journey on the night of 16 December 1961, when the first explosions took place. He tells how he picked up three or four men and drove them to various places to collect parcels; he then took them to a lonely spot near an electric transformer station. The men alighted and walked off while he waited. They returned, and as he drove them away there was a flash and a dull explosion.

A transformer station *had* been blown up in that area on that night. Yet his story is a lie. He testifies that one of his passengers was Raymond Mhlaba. All the accused know — and the police know, too — that Mhlaba was out of the country for some months from October 1961. He left illegally; there is no way of proving it without admitting where he went and why; and this the police also know, and rely on.

Later it transpires that the prosecution also knew, so they know that the evidence they are leading from their witness is a lie. It is on the strength of this evidence, more than any other, that Mhlaba is directly implicated in the activities of Umkhonto. There is practically no other evidence against him. And it is wholly false.

Cross-examination fails to reveal the lie. For again, the evidence of the journey is probably true, save that the witness placed Mhlaba in the car at a time when he had been overseas. Such lying is not the instinctive, self-protecting lying of someone in trouble. It is purposeful, calculated to fill in obvious weaknesses in the State case. It is evidence designed by the State and proposed by the police to the witness in custody.

A young man, Peter Mbomvo, serving a fifteen-year sentence for sabotage, is brought from Robben Island to testify that as a member of Umkhonto, he threw petrol bombs under orders into occupied houses. His evidence destroys the claim of Umkhonto leaders that they only attacked targets where there was no risk to human life. Even Bruno Mtolo has testified that this was Umkhonto policy. None of the accused know any of the facts of Mbomvo's story.

The record of Mbomvo's evidence at his own trial for sabotage reveals that under oath there he had said quite the opposite and had denied he knew anything about burning houses. The defence exposes this contradiction. But the State have brought him all the way from his cell on Robben Island to lead evidence under oath in court, knowing that it totally contradicts everything said in an earlier case, and knowing that a judge had already rejected that testimony.

How will Yutar rehabilitate this liar?

Next morning, re-examined by Dr Yutar, asked why he had lied about his part in the arson attack during his own trial, he explains that he wanted to tell the truth at his own trial but his attorney, a certain Mr Jankelowitz, had told him to deny everything, including a confession he had previously made to the magistrate. Mr Jankelowitz, he says, told him to say the police had assaulted him. He had followed these instructions, but had been found guilty.

Mr Jankelowitz is one of the few legal men in the Eastern Cape prepared to defend political prisoners on charges of sabotage. Yutar is in fact leading the witness in a damaging smear, which is taken up and headlined in the Press. The defence counsel asks for further cross-examination of Mbomvo to be reserved, so that the facts can be ascertained. It emerges that while under police detention prior to his trial, Mbomvo made *three* separate sworn statements, each of which contradicted the others. At least two of these must have been lies. The first two were made before he had consulted the attorney; the third was made after the attorney had withdrawn from his case. All three differ from the evidence given here.

Vernon Berrangé's cross-examination of this witness, and his exposure of the smear against Jankelowitz, is one of the dramatic highlights of the case. Spectators strain to listen; the attorneys conducting cases in other courts, who often come to listen while waiting for their own cases to be called, crowd the aisles; and important visitors who are allowed to sit in what was normally the jury box are hypnotized by Berrangé's performance.

The jury box stands in a prominent place on an elevated dais on the Judge's right hand, and in front of counsel. As there is no jury in this case, it has been reserved as a public gallery for VIPs; representatives from the Diplomatic Corps of several countries attend from time to time. On the day of Mbomvo's exposure there are in the box two well-known American sociologists, Dr Gwendolyn Carter and Professor Tom Karis, both on a visit from the USA. They have spent the morning with the Special Branch, hearing about the agitators, communists and liberalists, and how the Africans would be placid and happy if only the agitators would leave them alone.

In the afternoon the State P.R. men invite them to come and listen at the trial. Their expressions — fascinated, amused, amazed — are seen by all in court.

Yutar strides out of court and gives orders that in future no one, not even VIPs, shall sit in the jury box. Next day officials from the Dutch and American embassies seeking to take their customary seats there are told they must sit in the ordinary gallery, 'because of what happened yesterday'. Later the Judge overrules this order and visitors are again allowed in the box.

The next day police make arrests among the black spectators. Walter Sisulu's fifteen-year-old son, Max, had come to court to get a glimpse of his father. Children under sixteen are not allowed to visit their parents in jail. Max is asked to produce his pass. Dirker, who gave the order for his arrest, knows very well that as a schoolboy of fifteen he is not required to carry a pass. But the police do not accept this and march him off to the police station. His mother, Albertina, tries to intervene, but the police say they are too busy to worry about her troubles, and he must stay in jail. Only when Joel Joffe threatens an urgent application to court, saying he personally will sue the Commanding Officer of the prison for unlawful arrest and detention, do they grudgingly, without apologies, release Max, after he and Albertina had spent the whole afternoon at the police station.

That day all spectators in the black section of the gallery are asked to give their names and addresses to the police, and two are arrested. One of those arrested is Elias Motsoaledi's wife Caroline. As she is being escorted from the court, Joel approaches the police. 'I am the attorney for Mrs Motsoaledi and I want to know why she is being arrested.' One of the policemen: 'Keep away from us. If you are looking for trouble, you will get it.'

Joel repeats he is an attorney and wants to know the charge against his client. The other policeman: 'If you are looking for trouble, you will get it.'

Joel: 'Are you threatening me?'

'Just keep out of this, or you'll find trouble.'

Joel repeats: 'I want to know what the charge is.'

'Ninety days.' Joel asks the two policemen for their names. One says, 'You know my name', the other warns 'Keep away from me.'

As she is led away, Caroline Motsoaledi cries out: 'What about my babies? They'll be all alone!'

There are seven children. The eldest, who has been left in charge of the younger ones while his mother goes to court, is fourteen the youngest is a breast-fed baby of five months. Caroline lives alone now her husband is in jail. The children will be waiting for her to come home that night, but there is no way of getting word to them. On our attorney's shoulders, already over-burdened with this mammoth case, falls the urgent problem of Caroline Motsoaledi's children.

She will be held for the full ninety days, then re-arrested and held for 156 days in all. She is not charged with any crime.

Before the milk finally dries in her breasts, they will become tight and painful and overflow on the concrete floor where she sits alone. Elias's old grandmother comes from the country to try and cope with the care of the children.

All those weeks and months while she sits in jail, we visit our husbands twice a week. When she is finally released without being charged, the case is long over and Elias far away. The baby does not recognize her, and screams when she tries to take her.

Bram Fischer protests to the Judge. The arrests, he says, are intimidation of the public. De Wet is in an intolerant mood. 'The police presumably had good reason for doing what they did. I cannot see how it affects the proceedings of this court.'

* * *

As the parade of victims and accomplices continues, it becomes clearer and clearer that there is an underground stream running beneath the surface of what may still appear to be a trial conducted according to accepted legal rules and procedures, presided over by a judge in an open court.

We are witnessing the trappings of a trial, and through this trial we are also witnesses to the last stages in the destruction of South Africa's legal tradition, the abandonment of codes of legal behaviour and standards of justice for the sole purpose of hounding and exterminating those considered to be enemies of the State. The State is revealing for the first time the extent to which it will go, that it will stop at nothing, neither in forcing testimony from witnesses under duress, in the suborning of false evidence, nor in the coaching of witnesses. All involved in the court procedures — the Security Police, the State team headed by Dr Yutar (this man so highly qualified in law), the officials, the Judge — yes, and even defence counsel, become participants in this tragedy which will be compounded again and again through hundreds of trials in the future.

Where does Mr Justice Quartus de Wet fit in? Can he sit above the contending sides, in complete impartiality? The overseas Press later praise him for his conduct of the case, and state that the South African judiciary has shown once again its basic integrity. But the truth is that there is no room for impartiality.

De Wet is not to be judged by the standards of a Dirker. He cannot be dismissed simply as an agent of the Nationalist Government. His appointment to the bench was not directly political, as were those of some of the newer judges.

Defence counsel find de Wet temperamental, moody. At the early hearing, when the first indictment had been rejected, he had been cold, impartial and impatient with everyone, especially with Yutar. When the second indictment was contested he had changed, was clearly antagonistic to the defence. He was deliberately rude to Bram during his address, and rude and impatient

174

with Kantor's lawyer, Harold Hanson. He has tolerated outrageous antics from Yutar with indifference, or even a smile, sometimes nodding agreement when no agreement was called for. When the first indictment had been quashed he had stated that a trial with a new indictment could not possibly begin before the 1964 session of the courts, that is to say in February of the coming year. Defence had accepted that, and based their work on it. Then, in November, for no apparent reason, he had changed his mind and ordered an immediate go-ahead.

He is a complex character, obstinate and touchy, handicapped by his father's reputation as a great judge; for he himself is not intelligent enough to live up to the standards his father set in the legal profession. He cannot tolerate anyone trying to tell him how to run his court, even by implication, and therefore hates interventions from counsel. He has little respect for Yutar, whom he calls pointedly '*Mr* Yutar' throughout the trial; yet he sits silent when Yutar indulges in the most outrageous procedures, often seeming to enjoy them.

Whenever State witnesses prove unsatisfactory, or things are not going precisely as planned, Yutar interrupts the calling of witnesses in order to read carefully selected documents, a great number of which had been seized at Rivonia. The usual procedure is that documents must be handed in to the court by the person who found them with evidence as to where they were found. They must be 'proved' before they are read. Yutar does not follow the procedure. The defence do not know what documents he has, nor what he is going to produce. He simply intersperses the calling of witnesses by reading out selected documents, unproved. Always there are others, found at the same place, which he holds back, up his sleeve — perhaps he will trick the defence into a false move. Bram objects to this procedure as unheard of, and asks for all documents to be proved in court in the ordinary manner before they are read. Yutar appears a little diffident.

His purpose, he says, is to spare his lordship the tediousness of having to listen to documents being read one after another for days on end. 'I assure your lordship there is no ulterior motive. I am doing it solely for your lordship's convenience.'

'I can see no objection,' says de Wet. 'Proceed.' From then on

175

Yutar always regains the Press headlines by the revelation of a suitable document at a suitable moment.

The most important State witnesses have appeared, and the trial has been in progress for some weeks. The State begins to produce witnesses whose evidence has no bearing on the charges, but who provide what is in the nature of colourful background material: acts of assault, personal violence; acts committed by other people, material not in the charge sheet; acts not included in the indictment. It is irrelevant, yet inevitably the sensational is headlined in the Press and can harm by the atmosphere of prejudice it creates.

Defence counsel object to evidence not related to the indictment, but de Wet does not want them to tell him how to run his trial. He says testily that this is not a trial before a jury; he is quite capable of deciding what is relevant and what is not; any objections the defence have can stand over until the end of the case, when they can ask for irrelevant evidence to be struck out if they feel like it.

The ruling is a go-ahead to the prosecution: produce what you like, I won't stop any of it. A number of witnesses, whose testimony is most sensational, and many of the documents have no real bearing on the charges. The legal training of de Wet might, as he maintains, enable him to clear his mind completely of this irrelevant material when the time comes to consider the verdict; but this is not much help for the defence. The outcome of the case is not in doubt; some or all of the defendants will be found guilty of the main charges; the fight is to save them from the death sentence, and to present to the people of South Africa the political implications of their deeds as clearly as possible; what they stood for, why they had resorted to illegal acts. The irrelevant material splashed in the Press, helps to cloud the issues and prejudice the public mind.

Some weeks later Justice de Wet gives an entirely different ruling on inadmissible evidence.

The defence wish to call two professors of psychology to testify to possible brain damage suffered by ninety-day detainees, which must render all evidence by such people highly suspect. Both are experts who have made a study of sensory deprivation and studied case histories of many South African detainees. As

176

many of the State's most important witnesses are ninety-day detainees, this will throw new light on the nature of their evidence.

'How can that possibly be relevant?' asks de Wet, when Vernon Berrangé seeks to call the professors, who have been brought from Cape Town and Durban.

'Prisoners who undergo detention may suffer in the mind and brain,' Vernon replies. 'They can incur actual brain damage.' Surely this is relevant information for the court to have in deciding how to value their evidence?

'If you can give me authority on this — I have never heard of it before. I think it is irrelevant.'

De Wet then rules the evidence inadmissible; the court can assess for itself the evidence and decide to what extent it can be relied on. The professors may not testify.

Often his rulings appear contradictory. He was scathing in his rejection of the first indictment, yet the second was clearly just as faulty in law.

Sometimes he intervenes to ask questions of the accused when they take the witness-stand, and the nature of his questions seems to reveal a clear bias against them; yet at other times he will be almost off hand, as when Sisulu refuses to answer a question. The Judge asks him, 'You are not prepared to answer?' 'I am not prepared to answer,' Sisulu repeats, and de Wet then says casually, 'Yes, very well,' as though dismissing the subject with extraordinary tolerance.

The contradictions are implicit in the nature of his position. Yutar, without question, takes his instruction from the Security Police and from the State, from senior officials in the police. He fashions his case to suit the political requirements of the government.

But de Wet cannot be described in the same terms as a stooge of the government. He is obstinate and self-willed and resents interference in his domain. But he is by background, education and association an upholder of the principles of white supremacy. He is not a political pawn — in fact he despises politicians and regards all politics as a dirty business. He probably believes he is 'upholding the principle of independent administration of the law in the face of a hostile executive and intolerance in

177

political quarters close to the Government', as the London *Times* (12 May 1964) comments. But he is full of innate prejudice against Africans, particularly clever African politicians, and is a vivid illustration of the claim made by Mandela in his previous trial — that he could not get a fair trial in an exclusively white court.

He is sensitive to the needs of the white society he has been born into, in which he believes and upholds, and therefore also of the government. He does not need any direction from them, or any form of intervention or informal suggestion. He acts out the role required of him through what he is, through his education, his upbringing, his attitudes, through the moral outlook and values impregnating him in the racialism of our apartheid society.

De Wet states calmly in his summing up that evidence may have been concocted to satisfy police questioning, and that he has to bear in mind that most witnesses appear to fear reprisals. Yet the significance of this state of affairs seems to have escaped him.

Although he does not realize it, he is a tool of the apartheid State, administering laws that can no longer be upheld by honest and impartial men.

6

Interlude at Port Alfred

The moments of courtroom drama are few and far between. Most of the time it is tedious beyond words. We become resigned to sitting for hours on end, day after day, as the weeks move on, not even trying to listen; waiting for the evening paper, when we will read some of the evidence we could not hear.

Over the months, Annie and I go backwards and forwards to Pretoria, sometimes just the two of us, sometimes with others. We are bound together by the Rivonia Trial, by our love for Denis and Rusty, by our mutual belief in their ideals.

Life has not been kind to Annie, whose grey curls and soft brown eyes behind thick glasses give her the trusting look of a child. She is humble, as though forever expecting a rebuff; I want her to stop apologizing for being alive, to assert herself more. Physically she is not strong; but she has laid down a rule: *No tears*, and adheres to it, even in times of great emotional strain. She has moulded into our family life. We will miss her when she flies to join Esmé at the end of the trial.

Molly Fischer often comes to court, particularly when Bram is due to speak. She sits next to me, surreptitiously doing the crossword puzzle in the morning paper. I have a book and pencil and try to sketch without being stopped by the police. Drawing or writing is forbidden. I cut a word game from the evening paper and see if it will last me longer than Molly's crossword.

Molly is constantly busy with the trial, and Bram relies on her tremendously; she is as generous and kind as he is, but sharper and more practical in manner. She shoulders a great burden of work. Only Bram knows how much he depends on her.

Why are political trials so tedious? I watch the scarlet-robed Judge dwarfed in his great wooden canopy, looking bored, amused, impatient. Or watch the faces of the SBs watching me;

179

mostly big men running to fat, often gross. Small eyes; features sunk in fat or distended with muscle; cruel mouths; tempers operating on a hairtrigger.

The children don't like my being at court, and not finding me at home when they return from school each day. I am pleased to have excuses for not attending, but know that the men look round each day when they come up from the cells, searching the galleries for the faces of friends and relatives.

Annie and I are usually silent when we leave Pretoria at the end of a day in court, as though we must both wait to be well away from the city before we can speak.

* * *

December, 1963: and a three-week adjournment for the Christmas recess. I have promised Keith and Frances that we will go to the sea in December, and have invited Ruth First's two younger daughters, Robyn and Jill, to come with us. Now Ruth is released after 117 days in solitary confinement, and she has not been charged; but the two girls decide they would like to come on holiday with me just the same and it seems a good chance for Ruth to have a rest. So I borrow her car, a Citroën, and drive 700 miles to Port Alfred.

The Grand Hotel there is a sprawl of old buildings on a hilltop overlooking the sea. The beach is beautiful with a great curving coastline stretching for miles, the surf running on to white sands.

We had one room with two beds, where Keith and I slept; and an L-shaped veranda with three beds for the three girls. The hotel was full of Kenyans and Rhodesians, refugees from multi-racialism, recovering from the shocks of African advancement, before deciding what part of South Africa to settle in.

The days belong to the children, divided between the beach, the river, the village, and visiting places farther up the coast. The wind blows often along this coastline, particularly in the afternoons, so we take a rowing-boat up the wide river and find places out of the wind.

The nights are a problem, for there is nothing I can do to avoid other people in the hotel. I can stay in the room and read, but it is cramped, without a chair, and lonely in its silence of sleeping children. A lounge overlooking the garden where the hotel guests sit at night: a compulsion to be there, with company; but it is a sterile group compounded of complacency, ignorance, smugness, a cross-section of the ordinary white supremacists.

A professor from Witwatersrand University knows who I am and is pointedly rude. There is an engineer whose youngest child is one of those innocently beautiful children who are the epitome of all childhood. He and his wife and father-in-law ask me to join their party on New Year's Eve. They do not ask questions, but eventually they must know something about me and my odd family of four children, two with olive skins and dark hair, two fair and freckled. We do not discuss politics except on one afternoon before they leave, in a rather indirect way. The father-in-law tells me he has just met a British businessman visiting South Africa for the first time. 'He's amazed at what's happening here — the great achievements in industry and commerce. He says it's fantastic what the white man has done in South Africa and he's going to tell everyone about it when he gets back.' He looks at me and adds: 'But I suppose you wouldn't agree with that?'

'On the contrary,' I reply, 'I do agree, the whites have made a tremendous contribution to the development of the country. But there are two things you cannot ignore: first, for all their technical know-how, the money and the skills they brought, they could not have achieved anything without black labour; all the wealth of the gold mines, the Cape fruit farms, the growth of industry on the Rand — it's all been done with black labour, and it has produced so much wealth precisely because the labour is so cheap.

'The second thing is the belief that everything can stand still — wouldn't it be nice if things could always be this way — tribal natives, migrant workers, nice backward Africans, and on the other hand, wealthy and educated whites. But it can't stand still. The very things the whites brought here — capital and know-how — accelerated the process of change. The world is moving all the time. It is the reluctance to accept the necessity of change that will be the downfall of the whites in this country.'

'I suppose you are right,' he says, sounding doubtful.

181

One afternoon of gentle and steady rain, I am reading in the lounge which is full of adults and children unable to go out, when I hear a voice above the hum of chatter saying loudly, 'Oh, *Rusty* Bernstein!' I look up. A man is talking to Frances. After a few minutes she comes and stands by my chair. 'Come outside, I want to ask you something.'

We go and stand next to the wall in the rain, Keith following us anxiously. 'Don't be cross with me,' she says, and begins to cry. 'First he asked me my name and I said Frances, and he said, what's your other name, and I said Bernstein, and he said, what's your father's name, then I said Rusty, then he ... are you cross with me?'

I assure her I am not cross with her, that she answered correctly and has nothing to be ashamed of; but she is upset, and Keith is upset because of her, and I am upset too. We cannot face the hotel lounge with its curious eyes, so we go for a walk washed by tears and rain and all our unspoken longing.

It is Keith who breaks the tension. Deep among the dripping lush coastal vegetation he suddenly remarks: 'It's like eating peanuts.'

'What is?'

'Thinking about Daddy — once you start, you can't stop.'

Then we laugh, and feel better, and are prepared to face the hotel once again.

* * *

The woman from South-West Africa who lived in a castle outside Windhoek from which she proudly flew the Union Jack during the war, has been on an overseas trip with her husband and daughter. Father is a retired lawyer, elderly and frail, mother is large and forceful, daughter is ebullient. They talk a great deal about their trip and the countries they visited, but all in terms of the virtues or vices of the hotels and the cabins on the ships.

The local paper carries little news, but interspersed among reports on farming conditions and social activities of the district are brief reports of trials of Africans in the area. Two Port Alfred men sentenced to twenty years imprisonment each for cutting telegraph wires; men on trial for sabotage; for being members of the ANC. Who in this enclosed society reads, or understands, or cares? How long can they exist untouched by the living suffering land around them?

More than the defiantly maintained fixed etiquette of their lives is their belief in its static nature. They refuse to recognize that these very things by which they value their standard of civilization — education, money, technology — have in turn acted upon the lives of those around them, a chain reaction of unceasing change that cannot be halted, only delayed. Their traditional ways of life like Victorian flowers preserved under glass enshrine something without basis in the modern world: the Union Jack forever flying from the incongruous German castle at Windhoek, the mud huts with thatched roofs permanently enfolded in the endless landscape, the anonymous 'boy' in white uniform moving perpetually and silently around the tables of their conventions — not machines, workers, schools, mines, the thunder and stamp of machinery under the hills of yellow sand; not compounds, chimneys, townships, crowds jostling on the packed trains, queues at the supermarkets; but the lingering evergreen existence of master over the anonymous 'native'.

By their insistence on a fixed nature of things, by their denial of the processes around them that they themselves have accelerated, they are not only holding down the black man struggling to stand upright and breathe freely, they are also imprisoning themselves in a sterile world.

I cannot wait to go home.

7
The Defence

The State case was formally closed at the beginning of March 1964. James Kantor was discharged and the other nine men remanded until 14 April.

In March, Ruth left South Africa on an exit permit, and in April Toni married Ivan Strasburg. The two events somehow clarified my own feelings and intentions for the future.

Rusty had urged me to consider leaving the country. He worried about my safety and the children. I told him I would not even discuss it until the end of the trial, and so shelved the whole thing.

I was deeply affected by Ruth's departure. She was a close friend; I knew of the prison agony that brought her near death, and believed she should go. At the same time I felt I was being deserted. It was not just a personal matter. She had been an intimate part of the years of struggle, and now she was forced to relinquish it; South Africa would be the poorer. It seemed a personal loss, and something much bigger. So many had left, so many more would have to go.

At the airport I could not talk to her — we were not permitted to communicate — and sat at separate tables in the airport lounge while a Security man watched every move she made. We said a hurried goodbye in the women's toilet — the only place where he could not follow her. And when the plane, so elegant and powerful, rose into the darkening evening sky I felt I had a stone in my heart; and knew I could not go.

I had made a discovery so simple that I could only think most people knew it so well they never thought it worth mentioning. For me it was something new, something I had to arrive at in my own way. It was simply this: that no single course of conduct is necessarily absolutely correct. It was the unresolved problem that had torn me in two. For the children's sake, must I not leave? For the sake of all else, must I not stay?

When I faced the fact that there was no clear solution, and never could be, the agony of trying to make a choice subsided. When Toni and Ivan had fixed the date for their wedding, Toni had come to me and said, 'Ivan and I will live with you as long as Daddy is in jail'; it was an awful pledge for a young couple to have to make to a parent. It could be for life, and Toni knew it. While I privately thought I would never keep them with me for a long time, I needed and wanted them during the trial. Ivan was already one of the family; he put flea-powder on the dogs and went outside to close the car windows when it rained. Keith regarded Toni and Ivan as a spare set of parents.

Patrick decided that he wanted to go to a multi-racial boarding school in Swaziland. He hated school and was full of the dissatisfactions of adolescence that concealed his profound anxieties about the trial. He was learning karate, the whole house trembled to blows of his unclenched hand and showers of plaster fell from the walls. Perhaps his decision was his own form of escape from a situation over which he had no control; but it was a great relief for me; I could no longer exercise the necessary discipline over him, and I worried about his activities over which I felt I had no influence.

So Toni and Ivan converted the basement we had built under our house as a playroom into a bedroom and study for themselvesm, and furnished it with bits of furniture left by friends departing for overseas.

* * *

The defence team had five weeks in which to examine the mountain of evidence and documents presented by the State. They had to decide questions of principle about the overall defence of men regarded as public representatives of organizations and ideas. They had also to consider their individual defences, as all the accused were not equally affected by the evidence against them.

Six of the accused made admissions on some of the charges, which would result in a verdict of guilty. In the case of three, Rusty, Mhlaba and Kathrada, the evidence of any involvement in conspiracy was negligible and they pleaded not guilty.

The evidence was flimsiest of all in Rusty's case. The only real basis for a conviction could be that he was arrested at Rivonia and was in the company of men who were hiding from the police, and were associated with the ANC, Umkhonto, or the Communist Party. What was his association with these men? What was the true purpose of the meeting at Rivonia that day? That had not been established.

The rest of the case against him derived from Joseph Mashifane's statement that a fair-haired man, whom he identified as Rusty, put up the radio mast at Rivonia one Saturday afternoon (the man was Lionel Gay according to Gay's own evidence in a later trial — Gay bore no resemblance to Rusty); Mtolo's hearsay evidence that he had been told by someone that a man named Bunstead or Bernstein came to Durban to instruct on the formation of Umkhonto; and Dirker's lying evidence about the engine block of our car.

Vernon Berrangé was in charge of examining every piece of evidence concerning Rusty, Mhlaba and Kathrada and of helping them with their defence. The evidence against the others was overwhelming. Their concern was not to challenge it, except where they considered it to be lying or distorted. Their wish was to defend what they had done and the principles that moved them.

This they are prepared to do although they know their lives are at stake. The State alleges they had already embarked on the organisation of armed insurrection and guerrilla warfare; and that in pursuit of the plan they had arranged for the intervention of military forces of foreign powers. The State had also led much evidence of cases of murder and of sabotage where murder could be said to have been attempted.

The accused deny absolutely that all their planning was based on guerrilla warfare, though they admit that if all else failed, the time would come when they would turn to guerrilla warfare. They are ready to admit this; but in their view that time had not been reached. They had never contemplated direct intervention by foreign military forces, and felt that to visualize such a prospect was a political error. 'Operation Mayibuye', described as the cornerstone of the State's case, had to be explained and clarified.

The accused, in whatever opportunities they have had to discuss the case among themselves, have laid down very clear basic principles: they will state the facts as fully as possible, but they will not under any circumstances reveal any information whatsoever about their organisations or about people involved in the movement, where such information could in any way endanger the liberty of such people. They would reveal what was necessary to explain and justify their political stand, provided only that it implicated no one but themselves, and that it did not in any way undermine the safety of their illegal organisations.

Once in the witness box, according to law, they would be obliged to answer all questions put to them. This Defence counsel explains, but the accused insist quite simply that they will refuse to answer questions that might implicate colleagues or their organisations. In doing so, says counsel, you may well antagonise the Judge and make your case worse, not better. They remain unmoved. In this case, once and for all, they want to set the record straight and answer untrue allegations and falsifications of the State in public — an opportunity afforded by the case.

Counsel, with the exception of George Bizos, think that they will have to lead witnesses mainly on the evidence of their activities, believing that no prosecutor would tackle the accused on basic political questions. George has more insight into Yutar's character; in his view, Yutar will attempt to debate politics with the accused.

Next they must decide how the case is to be presented. Working on the assumption that the accused will go into the witness box in numerical order, it is assumed that accused number one, Nelson Mandela, would take the first hammering.

In South African courts evidence from the witness-box may only be given in the form of an answer to a question. Defence counsel 'leads' evidence; the witness is then cross-examined on his testimony by the prosecution, and may then be further questioned by his own counsel to clarify points raised in the cross-examination. Counsel may not cross-examine his own witness.

This procedure had obvious disadvantages for those who wished to make a clear statement of their aims. As they worked on the case the accused became more and more unhappy about the prospects of making their views comprehensible in the form of question and answer. What was needed was a single, uninterrupted and cohesive whole.

Nelson Mandela had his own objections to entering the witness-box. In his last case he had refused to enter the box and plead before the court because, he had said, justice could not be done by an all-white court. To enter the box now would be a retreat from his former position.

The alternative was for him to make a statement from the dock. Such a statement could not be interrupted. It could be read, not given from memory. It would not be subject to cross-examination. Such a statement would not have the same legal force in the Judge's eyes. It could be interpreted as an admission that Nelson was not prepared to be questioned about his version of the facts. This would have to be faced, if the other advantages were to be won.

Nothing is simple for the defence. To the immense legal and political problems the case poses — many of which the team have never before encountered, nor expected to encounter in all their legal lives — now are added the practical problems imposed by the minions of the apartheid State. A new consultation room has been set aside for them.

During the adjournment the building staff at the jail have evidently been busy making special arrangements. The room is long and narrow, with a wooden counter partitioned down the centre. The partition is hardboard perforated with holes; a few perspex windows are set into the hardboard, with speaking holes beneath them. If requested the warders can, with great difficulty and sweating and swearing, remove the perspex windows leaving a heavy metal grating in their place. A row of bar stools are fixed on either side of the counter.

Counsel are confined to one side of the counter, the defendants must sit on the other side.

When they are first ushered in to the room, the accused men are already seated on their stools on the other side of the counter, in a long row like customers in a milk bar. Nelson smiles politely, stands up and says: 'What will it be today, gentlemen? Chocolate or ice-cream soda?'

Colonel Aucamp, jail commandant, present for the symbolic opening of this new consultation room, does not like Nelson's remark. He asks counsel how they like the new arrangement.

They tell him bluntly what they think.

The indignity of asking senior counsel to sit perched on high stools holding a consultation across a counter like teenagers in an ice cream parlour is only one objection. More important is the fact that it is now virtually impossible to hold an adequate consultation at all. Five legal men sit on one side, and not one of them can be heard by all the accused simultaneously without shouting; debate is virtually impossible as they are stretched out in single file. Even if they sit shoulder to shoulder, one end of the line is some twenty feet away from the other. Exhibits, notes, must be slid through a tiny space under the bars. Nobody can lean over another's shoulder to read or see what is going on. Special listening devices, of course, have been installed, a supposition confirmed by some events later at the jail.

Counsel protest, but Colonel Aucamp insists that these are his instructions and this is where they must stay. They decide they will take their opposition to these arrangements further, but meanwhile will get on with their consultation.

But now there is a further impediment. Consultation hours are severely restricted. They may enter the jail at 9 a.m. (for which they have to get up each morning at 6.30 to make the long drive from their homes in Johannesburg). Now, they are told, they must leave at mid-day, and may not return until 2 p.m. This, they are told, is to enable the accused to have their lunch; the accused themselves say it is to allow warders to go off duty for their lunch. But it leaves counsel with two hours to kill in Pretoria, with nothing to do and nowhere to go.

Would it not be better, they suggest, to let them work uninterrupted straight through? They could bring sandwiches for the accused so that they would not have to return to their cells.

The Colonel is stunned by the suggestion. It would set a dangerous precedent. Mandela is a convicted prisoner and so, too, is Sisulu, who was convicted on a charge of incitement shortly before his arrest, and has elected to start serving his sentence as he is in jail in any case. Convicted prisoners are not allowed to eat 'outside' food. It was *regulations* — that formidable word repeated so often during these long months. If the other accused, who are entitled to receive 'outside' food sat with them during the lunch hour, there was a definite danger that Mandela and Sisulu might eat 'outside' food, including such luxuries — the Colonel is outraged at the idea — as *bread* (not normally given to African prisoners; they are only allowed mealie-meal).

So counsel must work like this on the preparations for the case: three hours in the morning; a two-hour break idling around restaurants in Pretoria; two hours in the afternoon — the jail closes at four — and then back to Johannesburg to work into the early hours of the morning.

As most of the issues are political, much of the material taken to the jail for the accused to use in preparing their defence is political and all material is subject to censorship by the prison authorities. All books and documents must be handed in at the office and censored before they can be passed on.

As soon as counsel realise that the jail was keeping the prosecution posted on the material they were handing in, they begin to introduce an element of gamesmanship. If they want Dr Yutar to think they are concentrating on a particular branch of evidence, they hand in documents relevant to that aspect. Dr Yutar is duly primed. At one time, partly for real preparation, partly vindictively, they start handing in volumes of the hundred-volume record of the mammoth Treason Trial of 1956 to 1961. Counsel feel the prison authorities will receive some political education while censoring this material: and they like to think of Yutar engaged in the task of reading the hundred-volume record.

When next they call on Dr Yutar, there are volumes of the thick black Treason Trial record piled on his desk.

* * *

Monday, April 23rd. Outside and inside the court building dozens of uniformed police; and plain clothes detectives mingling with the crowds milling about in Church Square. A photographer rests his telescopic lens on the shoulder of a Sergeant and takes snaps of the spectators, to be tagged and filed in the dossiers at security headquarters.

We have, of course, come early to be sure of squeezing ourselves on to the benches; this time the white section is almost completely full; in addition to the usual SBs, many of whose bulk spreads to occupy two places, there is a large contingent of students from Pretoria University — apartheid supporters.

Counsel go down to the cells below the court to have a last half-hour discussion with the accused before the session begins. By this time, even in the Supreme Court, the colour bar is being eroded. When the case first began the three white defendants — Rusty, Dennis and Jimmy Kantor — were regularly locked up in a 'Europeans only' cell; while all the others were in a 'Non-European' cell; and the two groups were only brought together at counsels' special request, for consultation, or just before they were ushered into court to sit together. But this arrangement has broken down; in part it is because the accused themselves refuse to recognise colour demarcations, unless specifically ordered to do so; in part, because colour lines do not operate in this case, either between the accused or between their counsel.

Bram Fischer begins with a statement in which he outlines briefly the case for the defence. He says that certain important parts of the State's evidence will be admitted, but other important parts will be challenged.

Four major contentions which the defence will challenge are:

that Goldberg, Kathrada, Bernstein and Mhlaba were members of the National High Command of Umkhonto, or that they were members of Umkhonto at all;

that Umkhonto was a section of the ANC — the military wing, as the State called it. The defence will show that the leaders of both Umkhonto and the ANC, for sound and valid reasons which will be explained, endeavoured to keep these two organizations entirely distinct;

that the ANC was a tool of the Communist Party, and that the aims and objects of the ANC were the aims and objects of the Communist Party. ["Your lordship will remember that a great point was made of this in the State's opening. The defence will deny this emphatically. It will show that the ANC is a broad national movement embracing all classes of Africans within its ranks and having the aims of achieving equal political rights for all South Africans. It welcomed support not only from the Communist Party, but from any other quarters"];

and fourthly that Umkhonto had adopted the military plan known as Operation Mayibuye and intended to embark on guerrilla warfare.

At this point, Justice de Wet, almost disbelieving: 'That will be denied?' Bram replies: 'That will be denied. The evidence will show why it was hoped throughout that such a step could be avoided. The court will be asked to have regard to the motives, the character, and the political background of the men in charge of Umkhonto we Sizwe and its operations; to have regard to the tradition of non-violence of the ANC; to the reasons which led these men to resort to sabotage in an attempt to achieve their political objectives, and why, in the light of these facts, they are to be believed when they say that Operation Mayibuye had not been adopted.'

At this point Bram pauses; then in the same sober and undramatic voice:

> The defence case, my lord, will commence with a statement from the dock by Nelson Mandela who personally took part in the establishment of Umkhonto we Sizwe and who will be able to inform the court of the beginnings of that organization and of its history up to August 1962, when he was arrested.

Nelson rises, papers in hand, adjusting the spectacles he wears for reading. Yutar has the expression of a man who has been dealt a stunning blow. He jumps to his feet in agitation, resentment in his voice, which rises to the falsetto that the defence recognise as his crisis call. 'My lord, my lord, I think you should warn the accused that what he says from the dock has far less weight than if he submitted himself to cross-examination!'

De Wet, acidly: 'I think, Mr Yutar, that counsel for defence has sufficient experience to be able to advise their clients without your assistance.' And Bram who even when annoyed cannot abandon his gentlemanly manner, manages to conceal his resentment. He appreciates, he says, his learned friend's advice. 'But neither we, nor our clients, are unaware of the provisions of the criminal code.'

The statement starts slowly. Nelson speaks in a quiet but clear voice:

> I am a convicted prisoner, serving a sentence of five years for leaving the country without a permit and for inciting people to go on strike at the end of May 1961.

I admit immediately that I was one of the persons who helped to form Umkhonto, and that I played a prominent role in its affairs until my arrest in August 1962.

I will deal with the relationship between the ANC and Umkhonto, and with the part which I personally played in the affairs of both organizations. I will deal also with the part played by the Communist Party.

I will also indicate what Umkhonto set out to achieve, what methods it used, and why these methods were chosen.

He says the suggestion by the State that the struggle in South Africa was under the influence of foreigners or communists was wholly incorrect:

I have done whatever I did as an individual and as a leader of my people because of my experience in South Africa and my own proudly-felt African background, and not because of what any outsider might have said.

He speaks of his childhood and youth in the Transkei, the influences that were woven into that communal type of society, how listening to the elders of the tribe describing past freedom struggles under African leaders, he was inspired to make his own contribution to that struggle.

Sabotage was not planned in a spirit of recklessness or from a love of violence. 'I planned it as a result of a calm and sober assessment of the political situation that had arisen after many years of tyranny, exploitation and oppression of my people by the whites.'

Umkhonto was formed because he and others believed that violence by the African people had become inevitable as a result of government policy. And unless responsible leadership were given to canalize and control the feelings of the people, there would be outbreaks of terrorism which would produce an intensity of bitterness and hostility between the various races of the country. As all lawful methods of expressing opposition to the policy of white supremacy had been closed, sabotage provided the African people with their only means of defying the Government. The alternative was to accept a permanent state of inferiority. Only when the Government had used violence to crush non-violent opposition had they resorted to violence in reply.

Successive white Governments had remained unmoved by the policy of non-violence followed by the ANC since its formation in 1912. In 1949 it was decided to protest by unlawful but still peaceful means. He had been in charge of this campaign of passive resistance and the volunteers who carried it out. He and nineteen colleagues had been arrested and tried for their role in these incidents. Their sentence had been suspended because the Judge found that discipline and non-violence had been stressed throughout.

Harsh new penalties were imposed in new Acts of Parliament to put an end to peaceful protests, but still they continued.

In 1956 he and 155 of his colleagues had been tried for high treason. When judgement was given five years later, the court found the ANC did not have a policy of violence.

After the shooting at Sharpeville in 1960, the Government had banned the ANC. He and his colleagues decided not to obey this decree, for to do so would be the equivalent of accepting the silencing of Africans for all time.

As a result of the referendum for the declaration of a Republic in South Africa, in which Africans were not consulted, an African conference decided in 1961 to request the calling of a national convention:

I undertook to organize the national "stay-at-home" which was planned to coincide with the declaration of a Republic. As all strikes by Africans were illegal, I was forced into hiding.

Although the strike was peaceful, the Government introduced harsher laws and mobilized its armed forces and sent soldiers and armoured vehicles into the townships in a massive show of force. This decision of the Government to rule by force alone was a milestone on the road to Umkhonto we Sizwe.

We of the ANC shrank from any action which might drive the races further apart than they already were. But the facts were that fifty years of non-violence had brought the African people more repressive legislation and even fewer rights.

For a long time the people had been speaking of violence and the leaders had to admit that a policy of non-violence had achieved nothing, so much so that their followers were beginning to lose confidence in this policy.

In fact, violence had become a feature of the South African political scene.

There had been violence in 1957 when the women of Zeerust were ordered to carry passes. There had been violence in 1958 with the enforcement of cattle culling in Sekukuniland. There had been violence in 1959 when the people of Cato Manor had protested against the pass raids. There had been violence in Pondoland in 1960 when the Government attempted to introduce Bantu Authorities, and there had been riots in Warmbaths in 1961.

Small groups of Africans in the urban areas had been spontaneously making plans for violent forms of political struggle and there was a danger that they would adopt terrorism against Africans as well as whites if not properly directed.

In 1961 the leaders, of which I was one, decided to press for a policy of violence in the national liberation movement, only after serious consideration.

He explains how sabotage had been chosen from the possibilities of sabotage, guerrilla warfare, terrorism or open revolution. Umkhonto was formed as a separate organization to embark on sabotage which, they felt, would not involve loss of life. It was at all times an organization separate from the ANC, although bannings, imprisonment and departures of leaders for overseas had led to some overlapping, some having to serve in dual capacities.

* * *

The court adjourned for lunch.

Outside, opposite the Palace of Justice, in Church Square, a crowd of thirty to forty Africans, mostly women, stood, as they had been standing before the court assembled; and would remain until it adjourned at the end of the afternoon. Some of them wore the green and black blouses that indicated they had been members of the banned ANC.

Uniformed and plain-clothes policemen were also standing around, most of them crowded on the steps leading to the entrance to the court. A burly uniformed sergeant was standing in the centre of the group with a photographer in plain clothes behind him. The photographer had a 35mm camera and a tele-photo lens about eighteen inches long, resting on the sergeant's left shoulder. He was taking individual pictures of each of the spectators. Some of the women turned their backs as the lens turned their way, but by the end of the day, the photographer must have had them all on film. The Raadsaal and the Kruger statue were in the background.

When the court resumed after lunch, Nelson continued speaking, referring from time to time to his sheaf of notes.

He said the ANC was not opposed to capitalism, and explained that the ideological creed of the ANC was not the same as that of the Communist Party. Its creed was one of African nationalism with the concept of freedom and fulfilment for the African people in their own country. The Communist Party sought to emphasize class distinctions while the ANC sought to harmonize them. The co-operation between the CP and the ANC was merely proof of a common goal.

For decades, he says, communists had been the only section of the population which was prepared to treat Africans as equals. It was not surprising when Africans turned to them in their struggle for freedom. Because of this situation, many Africans today equate communism with freedom. They were supported in this belief by a legislature which branded all exponents of democratic government and African freedom as communists. He had never been a communist but his thoughts had been coloured by Marxist literature and he accepted the need for socialism to enable his people to catch up with the advanced countries of the world:

The fight of the African people is against real and not imaginary hardships. Basically we fight against two features which are entrenched by legislation. One is poverty and the other the loss of human dignity. No agitators are needed to teach the African people these things.

Mandela speaks of poverty in the reserves and the squalor and starvation-level living in the towns; of malnutrition and its attendant diseases; Bantu education, job reservation, the industrial colour-bar, the denial of trade-union rights; pass laws and the destruction of family life; living in ghettoes and being confined to one's home after 11 p.m.

He speaks for five hours, with unvarying clarity of voice and of argument. Finally he states:

Africans want to be paid a living wage. Africans want to perform work which they are capable of doing, and not work which the Government declares them to be capable of. Africans want to be allowed to live where they obtain work, and not to be obliged to live in rented houses which they can never call their own. Africans want to be part of the general population, and not confined to living in their own ghettoes. African men want to have their wives and babies to live with them where they work, and not be forced into an unnatural existence in men's hostels. African women want to be with their menfolk and not be left permanently widowed in the reserves. Africans want to be allowed out after eleven o'clock at night and not to be confined to their rooms like little children. Africans want to be allowed to travel in their own country and to seek work where they want to and not where the Labour Bureau tells them to. Africans want a just share in the whole of South Africa; they want security and a stake in society.

Above all, we want equal political rights, because without them our disabilities will be permanent. I know this sounds revolutionary to the whites in this country, because the majority of voters will be Africans. This makes the white man fear democracy.

But this fear cannot be allowed to stand in the way of the only solution which will guarantee racial harmony and freedom for all. It is not true that the enfranchisement of all will result in racial domination. Political division, based on colour, is entirely artificial and, when it disappears, so will the domination of one colour group by another. The ANC has spent half a century fighting against racialism. When it triumphs it will not change that policy.

This, then, is what the ANC is fighting. Its struggle is truly a national one. It is the struggle of the African people, inspired by their own suffering and their own experience.

During my lifetime I have dedicated myself to this struggle of the African people. I have fought against white domination and I have fought against black domination. I have cherished the ideal of a democratic and free society in which all persons live together in harmony and with equal opportunities. It is an ideal which I hope to live for and achieve. But, if needs be, it is an ideal for which I am prepared to die.

The last words are spoken in a lowered voice, so controlled

yet communicating such powerful emotion, that a most profound silence grips the court for some minutes after, until there is a concerted sigh, like the release of breath.

* * *

The ban on publishing anything that Mandela says is eased to permit newspaper reporting of the trial. The papers carry fairly full reports, the *Rand Daily Mail* heading a page: 'MY FIGHT IS FOR ALL. Mandela tells court of ANC objectives.'

It must be remembered that all statements by former members of the ANC, and in fact any information about the ANC whatsoever, has been banned from the Press for years. Except for clandestine leaflets and illegal meetings, there is no way that the policies and ideas of the liberation movement have been put before the people.

Now the bans of silence have been sundered, the trial has become a public forum for these leading spokespeople to make their views, their policies, known.

There is jubilation in African townships when the speech is read. People say joyfully: 'Now we know what our leaders were doing,' and with pride read sections of the speech over and over. They carry the cuttings around in pockets for months afterwards.

At the end of the trial, Justice de Wet was to show an obtuse lack of understanding and a disbelief in the sincerity and truthfulness of Mandela's speech. But to people who matter, the majority of South Africans, the speech is a triumph, a vindication, breathing confidence over the shattered battlefields, restoring hope in the face of defeat. All the blunders and omissions, the failures and betrayals fall into perspective; become no less in themselves, but less in the framework of objectives that can never be relinquished, a struggle that can never be abandoned, just and right beyond any shadow of doubt, therefore as much the goal and destination as ever in the past.

'It is inevitable that any internal war waged in South Africa must result in victory for the oppressed people,' says Walter Sisulu, called by the defence as the next witness. And when asked by counsel: 'Looking back, do you consider that you could or should have acted otherwise than you did?' He replies calmly: 'I can't see how I could have done otherwise, other than what I have done, because even if I myself did not play the role I did, others would have done what I have done instead.'

Sisulu takes the main burden of cross-examination on the political aims of the Congress movement, which Yutar hoped to direct against Nelson. Without notes of any kind, and completely isolated from all contact with lawyers and the other accused, Sisulu is in the witness-box for five days under the most destructive attack Yutar can muster. With Yutar's contempt for blacks, and for all those without a good education, he must have thought Sisulu would soon be tied in knots, contradicting himself, stumbling, getting confused. Walter left school in Standard 6, after eight years of education, and worked in many jobs as an unskilled labourer. Dr Percy Yutar, B.A., L.L.B., L.L.D., is the most highly-qualified public prosecutor in South Africa (from the point of view of degrees). Yutar must have thought it would be an unequal battle.

In South African courts once an accused person starts to give evidence, he is not supposed to discuss the case with his lawyers until his evidence is completed. But it is unknown to isolate a witness completely. This is what happens to Sisulu on Yutar's instructions. He is segregated from the other accused for a week, even travelling to and from court in a separate van. He sees and speaks to no one at all. Defence counsel decide to let the matter rest. Yutar would claim the defence want Sisulu to be coached by the other accused.

Walter Sisulu is fairly small, light-skinned with features that are not markedly African. He wears glasses, smiles a lot in normal circumstances, is deeply attached to Albertina and his children. He is a man who does not act on a hasty impulse. But once he has decided, then he will act with courage and tenacity. He took many years to join the ANC, trying out various organizations of a more limited nature before throwing in his lot with the national liberation movement. Once in, he was rapidly elected to official positions, rising to become Secretary-General. Quietly spoken, he deliberates, tests other peoples' opinions against his own reactions and experience; and his own judgements of people and situations are seldom wrong. He is democratic in methods of work, preferring thorough discussions and many opinions before deciding. His own views carry a lot of weight with all who have worked with him, because they embody wisdom, experience, understanding of what lies ahead, and a generosity of spirit.

Walter befriended Mandela when Nelson first arrived in Johannesburg a bewildered country lad. He discovered Nelson's wish to become a lawyer, he encouraged and assisted him to study. Nelson's appearance and personality made him the more popular figure, but in committee discussions, Walter's views carried more weight.

As the trial proceeded, defence counsel have come to recognise these qualities and, like the accused themselves, they seek Walter's opinion before arriving at a decision.

Bram leads Walter through his own personal story, his childhood and youth, how he came to be interested in politics, the activities of the ANC and the personal hardships and persecutions he suffered as a result: the bans, arrests, confinements, house arrest, detentions and separations from his family.

He also deals with the steps that led the ANC to the acceptance of violent struggle and explains the relation of Umkhonto to the ANC. When Umkhonto was formed, leading officials in the ANC continued to work exclusively in that organisation. Liaison between the two bodies was carried out by Nelson Mandela, who served on both committees. After Nelson's arrest, to maintain contact and to advise them of the political decisions of the ANC, Sisulu had attended meetings of the High Command from time to time, although formally he had not been a member of it.

'Operation Mayibuye' is in many ways the crux of the entire case for the accused. As they have already admitted to the charge of attempting to overthrow the State, defence counsel have focussed strongly on the question of what sentences will be imposed. If the court finds that 'Operation Mayibuye' has, in fact, been adopted, it seems that death sentences will be inevitable. Mandela's statement had not touched on this issue, because the document had been drawn up after he was already in jail.

The paramountcy of Walter's evidence is that, if it is believed, the court must accept that Umkhonto and the ANC are separate organisations with individual identities; and that 'Operation Mayibuye' had not been adopted by Umkhonto, although it had always been envisaged that it might be necessary to prepare for guerrilla warfare some time in the future.

Now Walter must cope with the formidable cross-examination that will be targeted at him, as Nelson has not been in the witness box. The accused all have no doubts about his ability to prove a match for Dr Yutar. Only defence counsel are worried about this.

In the evenings, after leaving Pretoria jail, during the drive back to their homes, the lawyers argue about this. Bizos is backing his hunch that Yutar will shortly diverge from straight matters of fact regarding the guilt or innocence of the accused and will tackle Walter on matters of politics; that his intention will be not so much to prove guilt of the accused as the innocence of the government, its good intentions, its ascendancy over the African majority. The others disagree. They feel that Yutar will keep away from political debate and will examine on the details and meanings of the documents, the places where they were found, their significance in the overall conspiracy and the implications that could be drawn from them.

They take on George's bets. And they lose.

The document was a draft, Walter says, placed before the National High Command by a group of its members. Some favoured it strongly, others were equally strongly opposed. The implications of decisions to launch guerrilla warfare were so far-reaching that the High Command referred the discussion to the ANC. He himself did not feel the document correctly outlined the tasks before the national movement, and no decision on it had yet been taken. He concludes his evidence by stating that he will testify in this case with regard to his own part and some others, but will not answer questions relating to his organization which might lead to the prosecution of others.

On this evidence, counsel believe, Walter will surely face a gruelling cross-examination. But it is not long before the questions begin to drift.

Yutar launches into the attack, determined at all costs to demolish Sisulu, to denigrate him, to smear his motives, to

201

expose his follies and tear his ideals to pieces. He is not concerned with establishing guilt or innocence — it is scarcely necessary in view of Walter's admission to leadership of the illegal ANC and complicity in the forming of Umkhonto. It is to be a political attack.

He is also anxious to extract additional information. Much of his cross-examination sounds more like a Special Branch interrogation than a prosecutor in court, not intended to reveal the validity of the indictment but to ferret out information about people and activities unknown to the police.

The cross-examination begins with an attack on the attitude of the ANC and Umkhonto to the taking of human life. The subject, of course, does not fall within the scope of the indictment at all; there is no suggestion that the accused were concerned in murder or manslaughter, either directly or by default. De Wet shows no inclination to stop this type of question, and even intervenes at one stage to remark to Walter: 'Your argument is that as long as you have not got the intention to kill people it does not matter if you kill people. Is that your argument?'

'No, sir. I am saying that precautions are taken to avoid such a thing. I'm not saying it can't happen, but that precautions are taken that it should not happen.'

Walter explains that in his opinion conditions did not exist at that time for 'Operation Mayibuye'. On the basis of this reply, Yutar reads the document paragraph by paragraph, questioning Sisulu on his opinion. Walter disagrees with some of the formulations, accepts others.

At this point Yutar's cross-examination moves sideways.

Yutar questions Walter on the membership of the ANC — 120,000 at the time it was banned, and Walter explains how an organization that is small in membership may still represent the aspirations of the people. When he remarks that people do want the vote, de Wet leans forward to ask:

'Is that correct, Mr Sisulu? You think they should have the vote, but how do you know that the ordinary Bantu about town wants the vote? You think that he ought to have it, and you are telling him that he ought to have it, but how do you know that he really wants it? You only know that you think he ought to have it, but how do you know what he wants?'

'Well, I have not come across meetings where I have heard people saying, No, we don't want the vote. People always support the idea of the vote.'

When Yutar turns to 'Mayibuye', Walter insists it had not been agreed upon: 'It is a serious matter.'

'Of course it is. It is high treason.'

'I know, but I am not talking about the legal liability!'

Yutar brings his questioning around to a direction which will reappear over and again — what the accused call 'fishing expeditions'. This questioning is not designed to reveal facts about the offences charged, but to extract information from the accused about their colleagues, assistants and co-workers for the benefit of the Security Police. Repeatedly the accused are faced with the fact that they will not answer such questions and that they have no option, despite the warnings of defence, but to refuse.

Yutar (referring to a document issued by the ANC): 'Now where did this discussion take place?'

Walter: 'In Johannesburg.'

Yutar: 'Where in Johannesburg?'

'In the townships.'

'Whereabouts in the townships?'

'Are you trying to get the house?'

Yutar angrily: 'I am not trying to get the house! I am trying to get the truth. Where was this discussion?'

'I am saying in the townships, in the North-Western areas.'

'I want to know the truth. I want to know where in the townships.'

'That means what house it was.'

'Really!'

'I am not prepared to answer that.'

'You are not prepared to answer that?'

'No.'

'Why not?'

'I have explained the position. I am not going to implicate people here. What difference does it make in whose house?'

'Don't ask me questions, please! I want to know in whose house this discussion took place.'

'I am afraid, my Lord, I would implicate people if I answer that question.'

'You are not going to answer that question?'

'No.'

Yutar, holding up one of the exhibits: 'Who was the member of Umkhonto who drafted this leaflet?'

'I can't mention the name.'

'Why not?'

'Because I am not mentioning names.'

Yutar's voice was rising in anger and Walter's low-toned, unmoved responses seemed to feed his fury. He knows that Walter is protecting someone who is still in the country. He says he insists on a name. Again the exchange takes place, and Walter says he will answer only when the people are outside the country. 'Oh,' Yutar cries, 'they're safe!'

'Of course.'

Finally when he reiterates that he is not prepared to answer Yutar's question, de Wet says: 'You are not prepared to answer?' And when Walter again says he is not prepared to answer, de Wet remarks 'Yes, very well.'

This was something new in South African courts. There had been a series of trials of people said to be members of the Pan-Africanist Congress or of Poqo in which many of the accused had tried to exonerate themselves by naming and implicating dozens of others, so spreading the prosecution even wider. The refusal of the Rivonia accused broke new ground. They hoped to set a new standard which would be followed by others in political trials. In fact, the example they set became a precedent and many unwilling witnesses would also refuse to testify and face the prospect of twelve months imprisonment for this refusal.

What is interesting is de Wet's attitude. It was part of his contradictory nature that one minute he appears so biased and sinister, and the next can tolerantly accept Sisulu's refusal to answer the prosecutor. In only a little while he intervenes to ask Walter, with the greatest scepticism, if the ANC really believes the only solution is for black and white to live together.

The main burden of the State's case on 'Operation Mayibuye' becomes forgotten, and the defence case remains unassailed to the end.

'Why should people fear ninety days? The police don't arrest people indiscriminately,' Yutar remarks at one stage.

Here Walter leans forward and raises his voice. 'They arrest many people indiscriminately. For no offence people have been arrested.'

'Would you like to make a political speech?'

'I am not making a political speech. I am answering your question.' As Yutar continues to question him on this point, he recounts how his wife and son have been arrested indiscriminately, how the police arrest without evidence; that he himself was arrested by Warrant Officer Dirker six times in 1962. And for once allows a bitter note in his voice as he says: 'I wish you were an African and could find out what persecution really means. Then you would recognize the situation in this country.'

Yutar is not only fishing, he is also smearing. He is very anxious to bring in the name of Chief Albert Luthuli, President-General of the ANC who in 1961 was awarded the Nobel Peace Prize. He wants to smear Luthuli with the implication of involvement in sabotage, although Luthuli is not named in the indictment as one of the co-conspirators, and therefore nothing he has said or done has any relevance to this case. But as de Wet has already ruled that evidence can stand unchallenged until the end of the trial, Yutar plunges in.

He asks again and again whether Luthuli (with sarcasm: 'the Nobel prize winner for peace') had discussed the new operations. The same exchange takes place until Walter finally insists 'You won't get that from me. You won't get anything from me about Chief Luthuli!'

When Yutar tries to make him disclose the place where he made his underground broadcast, Walter again refuses to answer; and when asked where is the tape used in the broadcast, he says briefly, 'Safe.'

Yutar, discussing another broadcast that was planned from outside South Africa: 'That broadcast would contain propaganda and it would not contain friendly propaganda, would it?'

'The people of South Africa are oppressed, and we have a duty to them.'

The Judge, interrupting: 'And you have the duty to persuade the people they are suppressed.'

'It would be a strange thing if the people in South Africa do not know they are oppressed when freedom is coming to countries in Africa all round us.'

Once, at the end, Yutar again draws an angry retort. He asks Walter if he approves of mass uprisings of the people in a guerrilla war.

'Yes, if the time came for that sort of thing.'

'Like Langa and Sharpeville?'

'How can you mention Sharpeville! At Sharpeville our people were massacred by the Government. The world knows that. The innocent people were shot down by Government forces.' Yutar turns and smirks at his coterie.

But the flare of annoyance is unusual. Walter considers every question carefully, thinking not only of the question, but where it is leading, like a man playing chess. So much so that at one point Yutar remarks with annoyance, not respect, 'You seem to have an uncanny ability to read my mind.'

One of Yutar's accusations, to which he returns frequently, is that leaders like Sisulu kept safely in the background while their followers were sent out on dangerous work.

When the cross-examination is over and Bram has the opportunity of re-examining his witness, he seeks to refute this allegation. He takes Sisulu through the last few years of his political activity.

It is not true that he ever shielded himself at the expense of his followers. He was first arrested and convicted in 1952 in the Defiance of Unjust Laws Campaign; and a second time in that year for organising the campaign and for taking part in it. He was arrested in 1954 and convicted of attending a gathering (he was banned from gatherings). From 1956 to 1961 he was one of the accused in the Treason trial, and during the trial he was detained in 1960 when the first State of Emergency was declared.

In 1962 he was arrested six times; one of these occasions was when his mother died and people came from the neighbourhood to sympathize; he explained the position to the police, but they arrested him, although eventually the charge was withdrawn. After the ANC was banned he continued to play a part in its activities, thus laying himself open to a sentence of ten years imprisonment.

When he was arrested at Rivonia and interrogated under the ninety-day law, he was told he faced grave charges and the death penalty, but he could escape that if he gave the interrogators information confidentially. 'They said it would not be known by anybody. And they said that some of the Europeans had already spoken and given information about me. I, however, said that I would never give information about my colleagues and they could do what they wished.'

Although counsel had not raised the question of Walter's isolation, when the same separation was applied to the next witness after the first day's evidence, Berrangé decides to challenge it.

'On the instructions of Dr Yutar,' he tells the court, 'Mr Kathrada has been isolated and kept away from his fellow prisoners. He is not entitled to have tea or lunch with them, or any form of intercourse. It is an interference with the rights of prisoners.'

Yutar says: 'For reasons which would not be in the interest of the accused himself to disclose in this court, I felt obliged to take that precaution in order, my Lord, to avoid the possibility of consultation between the accused under cross-examination and their fellow accused.'

He then relates that Berrangé had actually spoken to Sisulu during his cross-examination and had concluded the conversation with these words: 'Your colleagues want you to know that they are proud of you, and also the legal team are proud of the way in which you have given your evidence.' And he felt strongly it was irregular for counsel to speak to the accused person under cross-examination and the danger of the co-accused speaking to an accused under cross-examination is a very real one.

Vernon Berrangé, in his capacity as counsel, had asked permission to see Sisulu at the jail during one of the recesses. He had done so specifically to ask him whether he was capable of standing up to his isolation as the long ordeal dragged into a second week. The interview room, obviously, had been bugged, and Vernon's conversation reported to Yutar.

Justice de Wet ignores the implications of this and tells Yutar he has never heard of such a procedure before, and that there was no necessity for it.

*   *   *

Ahmed Kathrada is quite a different type of witness — quick and aggressive where Walter was slow and thoughtful.

His political activities started when he was eleven. He was first arrested at the age of seventeen. He has been charged on seventeen occasions since 1946, not including minor charges like putting up posters or distributing leaflets. Some of his convictions include: participation in the Defiance Campaign; being in the Cape Province without a permit (Indians must have special permits to travel from one province to another); entering an African area; contravening a banning order (when visiting his mother who was ill).

He was placed under house arrest in 1962, and this prohibited him from entering factories, which meant he could no longer work as a printer's representative. Barred from work, from communicating with his friends, from attending gatherings, he decided, when the ninety-day law was introduced, that he would continue to work underground rather than be detained indefinitely.

In the country town where he grew up, Kathy tells the court, he did not experience the colour-bar. He first became aware of it when he had to leave home to go to school. He is a firm believer in the possibility and desirability of a multi-racial society.

Yutar's cross-examination, with its bullying sarcasm, brings out all the sharpness in Kathy's character.

'Do you agree that this proposed broadcast of yours in response to the speech by the Minister of Finance was a very vicious document?'

'I don't agree. I agree that it was in immoderate language, but it was not vicious. I think that what the Minister was saying is vicious.'

'You have called them (members of the Cabinet) amongst other things, criminal?'

'That's what they are.'

Inevitably, Yutar comes round to asking for names of others.

Kathrada refuses to answer questions that might incriminate others. 'Your oath is to tell the truth, the whole truth, and nothing but the truth?'

'I am aware of that.'

'So when it comes to giving evidence which might implicate somebody either in this court or outside you are not prepared to give evidence?'

'I am in honour bound not to.'

'Honour bound to whom?'

'To my conscience, my political colleagues, to my political organization, to all of whom I owe loyalty.'

'What about being honour bound to the Almighty?'

'I am not telling any lies.'

'You are not honour bound to that, are you?'

'Well, I don't know if the police are doing the Almighty's work, but I am not prepared to give the police anything that might implicate other people.'

'Sisulu adopted that attitude in the box, and you are doing the same.'

'Is there anything wrong with that?'

'Don't ask me. I'll tell his Lordship what I think about it in due course. And I'm telling you now that you are adopting the same attitude as Sisulu.'

'That's obvious.'

'And this political organization to which you owe this loyalty, does it include the ANC?'

'Yes.'

'It also includes Umkhonto?'

'If I knew anything about Umkhonto, I would not tell you. If the fact of it was to implicate anybody, I would not tell you.'

'Then how am I to test your story and what you are telling us?'

'I feel very sorry for you, Dr Yutar, but I am unable to help you there.'

Several times, Kathy's quick answers draw laughter from the people in the court, and this Yutar cannot stand. 'You are trying to be funny at my expense!'

At the end, Yutar asks Kathy if he is a member of the Communist Party. He replies that he is.

'Whose aim and object is to secure freedom for what you call the oppressed people of this country?'

'For what *are* the oppressed people in this country.'

'To which doctrine you subscribe?'

'I do, fully and unequivocally.'

'Are you determined to see the fulfilment of the policy, the aims and the objects of the Communist Party?'

'I still am.'

'Which involves the overthrow of the Government of South Africa by violence and force if necessary?'

'When and if necessary.'

* * *

Rusty is in the box. I am not nervous for him, although I can see he is tense and I know it is an ordeal; for I have such absolute confidence in his ability to give rational answers to the irrational Dr Yutar.

The defence feel it necessary to clarify the policies of the various organizations that feature in the case and to explain the functions of certain committees. Names keep cropping up, and general terms: 'the liberation movement', 'the Congress Alliance', 'the Consultative Committee', 'the National Action Council', and so on.

Rusty has a logical mind and can explain policies simply and clearly; therefore his evidence concerns not only his own activities, but is intended to fill in some of the obvious gaps in Justice de Wet's understanding of functions and objectives.

There is less evidence against Rusty than the others in the case. The main — in fact the only absolute evidence — is his presence at Rivonia on the afternoon of the raid. The other evidence consist of the fact that he was the architect for the alterations that included the conversion of an outside storeroom into what became known later as the thatched cottage (where the accused lived, and the meeting was held); that he had visited Lilliesleaf Farm from time to time; that, according to a farm labourer, he had helped erect a radio aerial; that according to Detective-Sergeant Dirker, Rusty's car engine was cold, implying he had been there several hours. And there was also the strange contribution from Bruno Mtolo that a certain Bernsteam or Bunstead had come to Durban to form a branch of Umkhonto. Counsel consider this last piece of evidence is clearly inadmissable from a legal point of view, scarcely worth worrying about; they have only puzzled over why Mtolo, with his clear, photographic memory about everything else, hesitates over Rusty's name, after it has been in the Press for weeks.

Vernon Berrangé leads Rusty through the formal part of his evidence; an account of his political activities starting in 1937 with the Labour League of Youth. He had joined the Communist Party in 1939 at a time when it was legal, and remained a member until its dissolution under the Suppression of Communism Act in 1950. Since then he has mainly worked in the areas of propaganda and publicity; he has written a considerable number of articles, pamphlets and other political material, and contributed regularly to several left-wing periodicals. He had been an executive member of the Springbok Legion, an ex-servicemen's organisation. He helped found, and was on the executive, of the Congress of Democrats, until he was banned from that organization.

He gives his interpretation of the activities and functions of the various organizations and committees, and it is at this stage that the Judge, who began by appearing extremely hostile to the first species of that strange breed, a white communist, begins to show a real interest in what he is saying, intervening with questions to clarify his understanding.

Vernon goes on to lead Rusty in an explanation of what he was doing at Rivonia on 11 July. He visited Rivonia from time to time for meetings. On 11 July he had been invited to take part in a discussion on the conditions of people detained under the ninety-day law, with a view to a campaign of protest for their release, for improvements in prison conditions, and assistance to dependents of political prisoners.

He denies the allegation that he was ever on the roof of the house assisting to erect radio masts.

Defence had expected Yutar to begin his cross-examination on the evidence that had been led about the radio masts, the alleged visit to Durban, the fact of his presence at the meeting on 11 July, and to his visits to Rivonia. But Yutar's first question is about the Communist Party. Were you a member?

'I was, up to the time of its dissolution in 1950.'

'Did you remain a member of the illegal Communist Party?'

Rusty refuses to answer on the grounds that he might incriminate himself in an offence with which he is not charged. He is within his rights, but knows that he will leave little doubt in de

211

Wet's mind that he has, in fact, been a member of the illegal Communist Party.

Yutar persists in the question, then offers him an indemnity for all offences which might arise from his answers, and several times repeats his offer of indemnity. After consultation, defence counsel point out that while the Attorney-General may give an indemnity, the Minister of Justice can reverse it.

Yutar says in any case Bernstein is obliged to answer, and appeals to Justice de Wet to instruct him to reply.

The Judge warns Rusty that he is required to answer the question; if he fails to do so he can be sentenced to eight days' imprisonment for contempt of court; then comments mildly: 'But I don't see that that will make much difference to you in your present circumstances.'

Yutar questions Rusty about a large number of documents, many said to have been produced by the Communist Party during its period of illegality. He is not suggesting that Rusty has written any of them, or even that he had known of their existence. Nevertheless he is asked to interpret them, to comment on their politics, which he does. He agrees with some of the material, and when he disagrees he states so. There is no real relevance to the questions, but counsel make no objection. Yutar is not advancing his case.

Yutar now starts questioning Rusty about the names of leaders of the Communist Party, and Rusty refuses to answer. He asks him several times to name the secretary. He now embarks on the most unsavoury piece of cross-examination in the whole case. He produces a ten-year-old copy of the ex-servicemen's journal *Fighting Talk*, which he must have obtained from police archives as it is not an exhibit and has not been put in as evidence. In it there is an article about Bram Fischer, signed only with the initials LB. It had been written when Bram had been put under bans, and states that whenever the writer despairs for the future of white South Africa, he remembers Bram Fischer and his career, and this restores in him the belief that not all white South Africans are racists. The article describes Bram's political career in various organisations. Yutar puts this article to Rusty and asks him who had written it. Rusty identifies it as his.

Yutar: 'Who was the Secretary-General of the Communist Party?' Rusty declines to answer the question.

Yutar: 'Well, since you are unable to answer that question, perhaps we may conclude that it was the gentleman referred to in the exhibit before you. Will you please hand it to the Judge?'

So the document is handed to de Wet, evidence of nothing at all, not even an exhibit, not found anywhere relevant to this conspiracy or in the possession of anyone. It has one purpose only — to allow Yutar to suggest that Bram held a senior position in the Communist Party, and so denigrate him in the eyes of the Judge.

The next line of questioning, which is quite remarkable, is aimed at discrediting Rusty in the eyes of the Judge. Rusty does not, at first, know to what he is referring.

'Have you ever accused the State of coaching witnesses?'

'I possibly have said that.'

'In this case?'

'Possibly.'

'Have you accused the police in this case of acting improperly?'

'I can't recall if I have, but I think it is possible.'

'You say you might have said that the State coaches witnesses?'

'I might have.'

'That is a reflection on the State Prosecutor?''

'I am afraid so, sir.'

'Have you any evidence to support that *wicked* suggestion?' Rusty begins to answer the question, then turns to the Judge and asks him to rule on its relevancy. 'It is a relevant question, Mr Bernstein, you can answer it.'

Rusty gives the example of the witnesses who changed their evidence between Friday and Monday.

Yutar: 'Did you ever say "Apart from police evidence and documents, all the substantial witnesses other than people who gave purely technical evidence have been detainees who made statements under pressure and while subject to detention in solitary confinement, and subject certainly to the threats of either indefinite detention or prosecution, or both." Did you make that statement?'

'Yes, I did.'

213

'Is it true or false?'

'I think it is probably true, sir.'

Rusty now understands what Yutar is doing. The extracts he reads are from a letter Rusty wrote to his sister in England; which was censored by the prison authorities, then handed over to the Special Branch who passed it on to Dr Yutar; he is using this letter to which he has no right, which is not an exhibit and has nothing to do with the case for the purpose of forcing Rusty to say whether or not he thinks the South African courts administer justice, and whether in fact he himself is getting a fair trial. Could he possibly make such an admission in the presence of the Judge? It would scarcely improve his standing with de Wet, and can only prejudice him. The letter criticizes the coaching by the State of its witnesses, with some bitterness and many examples.

Yutar questions Rusty about individual witnesses, one by one, starting with Cyril Davids. 'He was cross-examined. But it was never suggested to him that he was forced to give the evidence he gave.' In fact, almost the entire cross-examination of Davids had been spent on suggesting just that.

'Now we come to Essop Suliman, he spoke about the conveyance of over 300 recruits across the border. That has been accepted by the defence.'

Rusty: 'I don't think a word of what Essop Suliman said has been accepted by anybody, sir.'

'You remember Harry Bambani, that is a recruit who is serving a two-year sentence. It was never suggested to him that he was either coached by the State Prosecutor or forced by the police to give false evidence.'

Berrangé: 'My Lord, my learned friend is completely wrong. I don't know where he gets this evidence from. In fact it was suggested that he changed his evidence three times.'

Yutar: 'Do you remember the witness Peter Mbomvu who testified to the commission of acts of sabotage? Do you think *he* was forced to say that he committed two acts of sabotage, not one?'

Rusty: 'My Lord, he was either forced, or induced, or persuaded by some fantasy. But it was shown in court that he made three different statements about the same subject, all under oath, at different times.'

214

'So the police must have been awfully inefficient in forcing him to make statements — they got three statements out of him.'

'Yes. And they led all three in evidence here.'

After some more of this, Yutar reads out a passage from Rusty's letter.

'"The whole thing disgusts me, the unprincipled timidity of people and even more the unprincipled willingness, eagerness of the authority to use them." You adhere to that?'

'I adhere to that.'

'But it is the condemnation, of course, not only of the investigating officer but also of the State Prosecutor in this case.'

'A condemnation of the State, sir, which has provided facilities for witnesses' statements to be taken from them under duress.'

Yutar seems to stray further and further from the charges. He gets Rusty to comment, paragraph by paragraph, on a large number of documents found at Rivonia which, it is alleged, have been issued by the Communist Party. Rusty comments freely on the political line and tactics expressed.

A colleague of Joel Joffe's, a counsel from Johannesburg Bar, happened to be in Pretoria that morning. He was sitting in the VIP box listening while Rusty commented on documents dealing with armed uprising, rebellion and sabotage. At the tea adjournment he said to Joel that 'Bernstein had completely cooked his own goose.' Joel explains that the cross-examination is irrelevant. The documents were neither found in Bernstein's possession nor written by him; they were not alleged by the State to have been distributed by him, or even by any organisation of which he was a member. The barrister is completely mystified. So is the defence.

'Is it not a communist tactic to attempt to discredit the police, and has not this tactic been used in this very case?' Yutar asks.

'I think the police succeed in discrediting themselves very effectively without any assistance,' Rusty replies.

In answer to another question he says that the existence of militant forces in South Africa increases the prospects of a peaceful transition in the country.

'In other words, if you point a gun at a man and say "Hand over your money" and he hands it over, that is a peaceful settlement?'

'No, sir. That is not the analogy. If anyone has pointed a gun in this country the Government has pointed a gun at the non-whites. What I am saying is that if they too have a gun, it increases the likelihood of a settlement by negotiation.'

Rusty is an ideal witness, quiet and unruffled under Yutar's provocative sneers. Many of Yutar's questions are 'double-barrelled' — they are in two parts, and to answer the second part implies a tacit acceptance of what Yutar has stated in the first part. Rusty carefully separates the questions, and answers each portion in turn. It is interesting that Yutar addresses him as 'Mr' Bernstein, a courtesy he does not extend to the black witnesses — they were Sisulu, Kathrada. Yutar's prejudices show even when he is not aware of them.

Finally, Rusty gives evidence about ninety-day detention; how the police had told him they would hold him indefinitely for successive periods of ninety days unless he gave information; one of them said he had twenty-three years to go before retirement, so he had plenty of time to wait; how veiled threats were made; talk of the death sentence for the charges he would face; mention of rewards given to others for pieces of information; suggestions that he could himself name any price he wished.

There is mental torture, Rusty states, in confinement alone within four grey walls with nothing to do, no one to speak to and nothing to read. So much so, that although he disliked talking to policemen, he found interrogation by the police a distinct relief. Detention has given him a violent shake of the hands, impaired his memory and powers of concentration, and led him to states of violent anxiety about trivialities.

When Rusty's evidence is finished a remarkable fact emerges: Yutar has failed to cross-examine him on any of the actual evidence presented against him. He has not asked him a single question about the purpose of the meeting on 11 July, what he was doing there, for what reason it was held, or what was discussed; he has not asked him if it is true he went to Durban as Mtolo suggested, to launch Umkhonto there; he has not asked him if he took part in the erection of the radio masts; he has not mentioned Dirker's evidence about the engine block of the car.

Yutar has been so carried away by his attacks regarding the letter about witnesses, so concentrated on documents and policies concerning the Communist Party, that he has completely forgotten to mention any of the evidence against Rusty. In fact, there is now no evidence against him, and suddenly I am transported on a wave of wild hope. It is ridiculous, really, because I know it is not a question of juggling with legal evidence, that the case is dependent on political conditions in the country; and I know the police are determined to keep him in jail, whatever happens.

One night I go to visit a friend of mine, Gertrude, who is now giving me money every month towards our living expenses. She came from Germany to South Africa many years ago to escape the horrors of racial persecution and fascism, and now it is being re-enacted before her eyes. She finds it very hard to bear.

I tell her, 'Rusty has a chance of getting off.'

She looks at me with an expression of great sadness, perhaps pity. 'How can you say that?'

'There is no evidence against him.'

'But you know it is not a normal situation; it is not a question of evidence.' She takes my hand. 'Don't allow yourself to believe it. You will only suffer the most awful disappointment.'

I look at her sad, kind face. 'Gertrude, I cannot live without hope.'

Her eyes fill with tears, and she says no more.

I cannot live without hope. I have tried every possible way, through sober discussions with defence counsel who express the utmost caution about the possible outcome, through nightly suppression of images of Rusty being home again, through theoretical acceptance of my friends who all say 'They will never let him go', through my own understanding of the whole situation, through my feelings towards the families of the other accused, Winnie, Albertina, Esmé, Caroline — what of *their* lives, what of *their* children? By what right can I long for my own, my personal reprieve?

Nothing works. Hope has come, and cannot be eliminated. From now on I feel myself come alive again. I live with hope.

*   *   *

A key figure in the African National Congress, Govan Mbeki

admits to being a member of the National High Command of Umkhonto; to membership of the African National Congress and the Communist Party. Perhaps 'admits' is not the word; rather he declares proudly that he has played a substantial role in these organizations.

'As you have answered in the affirmative to questions or actions concerning all four counts against you, why did you not plead guilty to the four counts?'

'First, I felt I should come and explain under oath some of the reasons that led me to join these organizations. There was a sense of moral duty attached to it. Secondly, for the simple reason that to plead guilty would to my mind indicate a sense of moral guilt. I do not accept there is moral guilt attached to my actions.'

This tall, attractive man in his fifties, with greying hair and smiling eyes, is probably the best-educated of all the accused. From school he won a bursary which enabled him to obtain a Bachelor of Arts degree, and subsequently he took a degree in Economics, majoring in education and social science. He has behind him a wealth of political experience stretching back to the depression years of the 1930s. His name is a byword in the Eastern Cape, but he has also worked in Natal and the Transvaal. He has been dismissed from two teaching posts because of political activities, and in the 1950s he abandoned teaching to work as Port Elizabeth editor of *New Age*. He was on the national executive of the ANC in 1956, and was named and listed as a communist, although he was not then a member of the Communist Party which he says he joined much later. He is also the author of a book on the peasants of the Transkei, a book largely written in jail and under other difficult conditions.

Govan Mbeki gives a full account of his early involvement in political struggle, dealing particularly with the Transkei. In 1936 General Hertzog stated in Parliament that white supremacy was justified because 'self-preservation is the first law of nature'. Govan goes on to show the forms this 'first law' has taken under successive governments: segregation, trusteeship, baaskap, apartheid, separate development.

The name changed, but not the policy. The position was clearly expressed by the late Prime Minister, J. G. Strijdom '*Die wit man moet altyd baas wees'* (the white man must always remain boss).

Govan describes what has happened to Africans since the present government came to power. 'In the reserves since the early 1950s meetings have been banned ... in the Transkei, Proclamation 400 which was passed four years ago to meet the specific situation has become a permanent feature of the administration. In the urban areas it is virtually impossible to hold political meetings. Chiefs or headmen who do not approve of government policies have been banished. Since 1945 no less than 133 Chiefs have been banished to different areas where they could not make a living.'

He talks of Bantu Education, the attempt to make the African accept inferior status while still in the classroom. And he describes the living conditions of Transkei peasants, in terms of their earnings, the land they work, the taxes they pay.

He gives evidence on political oppression, on social and economic living conditions, health, poverty, taxation, wages, standards of living; he deals with the pass laws. He shows what happened to him personally. He worked in Port Elizabeth for eight years during which time he could never live with his own family; he was not allowed to rent a house because he did not qualify — he had not worked for one employer for ten years; his case was not, of course, unique; many men live in single men's barracks without their families.

Something in Govan's quiet and courteous way of speaking arouses in Yutar a greater antagonism than he has yet displayed to the accused. Pointing a finger at him, Yutar says loudly and angrily: 'I want to remind you that this court is trying issues of sabotage and other offences, and it is not a court of inquiry into grievances of the Bantu, so I hope you will forgive me if I don't even attempt to challenge the correctness of some of your complaints.'

This seems to imply that Yutar is not going to tackle him on the political and social conditions of the people, but this is precisely what he then proceeds to do. Half a million Bantu, he tells Govan, flock to South Africa from other countries because of the good conditions; hospitalization for the 'Bantu' is practically free. There is a St John's eye hospital that gives optical treatment

219

which was not even available to whites. He deals with ritual murders (a form of tribal witchcraft almost unknown now in South Africa).

He attacks Govan for speaking quietly, for being sanctimonious, for appearing to be gentle, and repeats several times that he would 'wipe that sanctimonious smile' off Govan's face.

He returns again and again to questions of identities, places, names, which Govan refuses to answer.

Although Govan's admissions make it unnecessary for Yutar to press his cross-examination of Govan — there is no question of the verdict in his case — he continues to question him for nearly three more days, interspersing questions about documents with the questions that seek information. He is like an angry fly hitting himself again and again against a pane of glass; because the glass is transparent he believes he only has to hit hard enough and he will reach the other side. Govan steadfastly refuses to answer any question which might implicate anyone else.

*   *   *

Denis Goldberg was in many ways the most unfortunate of all the accused. He was arrested at Rivonia by chance, as he had not gone there to attend the meeting. He was, in fact, on his way out of South Africa.

In his evidence he explained that he had come to Johannesburg from Cape Town with the intention of leaving the country after he had reached a stage where he could no longer stand police persecution. Police had followed him wherever he went, driving up and down past his house, hooting and shouting late at night. They had arranged with a neighbour to keep a list of all people who visited him and would afterwards interrogate these people. In December 1962 a bomb had been exploded in his garden and he was fairly certain it had been put there by Security Police. He was disturbed by anonymous phone calls, and one night an obscene slogan was painted on his car.

In May 1963, he left Cape Town secretly, intending to obtain assistance in leaving the country from people in Johannesburg. He had been prevailed on to do some work for Umkhonto before going. As a qualified engineer, he could obtain technical information about the possibility of manufacturing armaments which Umkhonto would then use when weighing up their decision whether to go ahead with the plan for guerrilla warfare.

In the belief that he would soon be far away from South Africa, Denis did not bother to cover his trail very carefully, simply using an assumed name. He also hired post-office boxes in different names and arranged certain cover addresses for himself at which to collect correspondence.

Most of the evidence against him is factual, and most of it is not challenged by the defence. Clearly, he has no chance of being found not guilty. Denis obviously approached his work with professionalism and skill. But it was not a legitimate enterprise, and here his professionalism had failed him. He has left behind him a trail, fully documented, covered by his own and others written records, including his own pocket book found on him at the time of his arrest. The evidence is overwhelming.

The defence team were not certain that he would improve his position at all by going into the box, and felt that his tendency to make jokes, even under the grimmest circumstances, might antagonize the Judge; for Denis has a buoyant and optimistic personality which even his serious position, facing a possible death sentence, cannot quell.

However, Denis felt very keenly that he must give evidence. He wanted to correct those statements made about him, particularly relating to the weekend camp at Mamre, which were not true. But more than that he wanted to state the convictions and beliefs that had motivated his actions. He could not go silently to prison, perhaps even to the gallows, without some affirmation.

And in the box he proves an articulate and logical witness. Warned by the defence lawyers, he suppresses his tendency to joke; remains calm in his straightforward statements of his motives and his beliefs. He is cross-examined by Yutar's assistant, A. B. Krog, who is being given his first opportunity to handle a public portion of the case.

There were actually four people in the prosecution team, but Yutar had in fact monopolised the entire public side of the case. The others operate throughout almost like stenographers, taking notes and passing books and documents to Yutar. Defence thinks Krog, who has a reputation of being a good cross-examiner, may prove to be more destructive to the defendants.

But Krog has been listening for months to Yutar; and abandoning his own methods, he adopts those of Yutar. Lacking the same righteous indignation, he tries sarcasm. 'You have heard defence counsel in this case speak of evidence being tailored to suit requirements. Do you not feel a little over-dressed at the moment?'

He sets out to show that since he used false names and addresses, Denis Goldberg is therefore a man who is naturally deceptive and cannot be believed. It is a tedious performance. When it is finished, Denis has increased in stature. He has dedicated his life to certain ideals; the trial is the climax and certainly for a long time, the end of his efforts. The way he behaves in the witness-box, the things he says, are the summation and in some part the vindication of his life. They may not be part of the orthodox legal process of a normal criminal trial. We understand this, and I share Annie's glow of pride in the sincerity, the integrity and the high courage of her son.

Raymond Mhlaba, perhaps because of his slowness in answering questions — a slowness that is part of his personality — does not appear at his best in the witness-box. This is also due to the fact that he is not prepared to talk about how or why he left the country, except to say that it was a mission for the ANC, from which he had returned shortly before his arrest.

After trying unsuccessfully to get names from Mhlaba, Yutar then states: 'I want to put it to you that in December 1961 you were either in Port Elizabeth or in Leipzig.'

This confirms what defence counsel suspected. The Security Police knew that at the time of the sabotage in Port Elizabeth in 1961, Mhlaba had been outside the country. They know, therefore, as does the prosecutor, that their chief witness against Mhlaba must be lying.

Prodded by Berrangé, the Judge tells Mhlaba that he need not necessarily answer a question that he feels may incriminate him.

Yutar offers complete indemnity, giving the solemn assurance in open court that no prosecution will follow for his leaving the country without a permit. The wording of Yutar's statement confirms beyond doubt that he knows Mhlaba was out of the country during that vital period. Nevertheless, he had led the evidence that incriminated Mhlaba, and was persisting in it.

Had Mhlaba made a better impression in the witness box, had his manner been more convincing or won greater sympathy from the Judge, Mhlaba could only be acquitted. The evidence alone could not sustain a conviction.

Counsel have decided that Elias Motsoaledi and Andrew Mlangeni should not enter the witness box. They had not been at leadership level in Umkhonto and could not really add to the picture of the organisation and its relation to the ANC already given by Walter and Govan. .

Elias has won respect and liking from all involved in the defence through his cheerful and uncomplaining nature. He tells the court about growing up in Sekukuneland reserve, one of a family of ten who lived on four acres of ground. Across the border lay thousands of acres belonging to white farmers — land that was unused. He describes coming to Johannesburg to earn a living, joining the ANC in 1948. Later, when the ANC was outlawed, meetings stopped and newspapers closed down, 'there was nothing else I could do. Any African who thought the way I did about my own life and the life of my people would have done the same. There is nothing else.'

He makes admissions about his activities in Umkhonto, but denies almost all the evidence given against him by people who have been ninety-day detainees. He finishes by saying: 'I did what I did because I wanted to help my people in their struggle for equal rights. When I was asked to join Umkhonto we Sizwe it was at the time when it was clear to me that all our years of peaceful struggle had been of no use. The government would not let us fight peacefully any more and blocked all our legal acts by making them illegal. I thought a great deal about the matter. I could see no other way open to me. What I did brought me no personal gain. What I did, I did for my people. That is all I have to say.'

He put down the notes from which he had been reading and looking at de Wet he said: 'In addition, my Lord, I want to say that I was assaulted by the Security Branch in an attempt to make me make a statement.' He was prepared to give evidence if there was an enquiry. The assault had taken place at Witsdrag Police Station where he was kept in solitary confinement. And even then the police were not satisfied. 'More than three months ago they arrested my wife and detained her under ninety-days. And when she had finished her ninety days she was arrested again. As it is she is still in jail. I consider this disgraceful on the part of the police, my Lord, that a woman with seven children should be punished because of offences committed by me. That is all I have to say.'

Andrew Mlangeni also made a statement from the dock, describing his own life and activity, and joining the ANC in 1954. He refutes much evidence given about him when he was not living in Johannesburg, but admits joining Umkhonto on his return. 'In the ANC I found a political home ... This government and and previous governments have exploited not the earth but the people of those groups who are not white ... I know that you, my Lord, have to administer the law, but when you do so I ask you to remember that we, the Africans and non-white people have to suffer.'

He then goes on to describe assaults on him at Central Barracks in Pretoria, where he was subject to electric shock treatment several times.

When he finishes there is now only argument and judgement.

*　　*　　*

On 20 May, Dr Yutar arrives in court to give the closing speech for the prosecution, the speech which is normally intended to assist the court in summing up and assessing the evidence, relating each piece to the charges specified and the indictment, and attempts to present the entire case clearly. It is unheard of in South African courts that comment, wit or sarcasm at the expense of the accused forms any part of this speech. It should be simply a sound legal analysis of the evidence and the laws bearing on the charge.

But Yutar has his own method of presenting an argument.

His team stagger under a load of thick blue volumes, newly and beautifully bound, with gold lettering. Four volumes to a set. Several sets are handed to the Press. When the turn of defence counsel comes, they are handed one unbound copy of the treatise to serve the whole team of five.

In the few minutes before the Judge appears, defence skims through the document. It proves to be not a legal argument as they understand it, but a summary of all the evidence in sequence, with no attempt at analysis, of its strength or discrepancies. Joel remarks loudly enough for Yutar to hear: 'This is not a closing address. It's a garbled summary.' And Bram later comments: 'His evidence in chief consisted largely of the reading of documents; his cross-examination consisted of reading the documents to the accused. And his closing address consisted of reading the documents to the Judge.'

Yutar hands four volumes to de Wet saying: 'My lord, to assist the court I have had my address typed out and bound up, and I beg leave to hand it in and crave that it may be of some assistance to your lordship.'

He then begins to read from the volumes.

Although the State has charged the accused of sabotage, this is nevertheless a case of high treason par excellence. It is a classic case of the intended overthrow of the government by force and violence with military and other assistance of foreign countries ... Nevertheless, for reasons which I need not here detail, the State has preferred to charge the accused with sabotage.

The reasons which he does not choose to detail are very apparent. In a charge of treason, the law requires a preparatory examination which would have appraised the accused of the evidence against them and enabled them to prepare their defence properly. It also requires that every overt act is attested to by two witnesses. It would have placed the onus on the State to prove the case beyond reasonable doubt, whereas a sabotage charge leaves much of the onus on the defence.

The deceit of the accused is amazing. Although they represented scarcely 1 per cent of the Bantu population they took it upon themselves to tell the world that the Africans in South Africa are suppressed, oppressed and depressed. It is tragic to think that the accused, who between themselves did not have the courage to commit a single act of sabotage should nevertheless have incited their followers to acts of sabotage and guerrilla warfare, armed insurrection and open rebellion and ultimately civil war.

Yet Yutar himself had led evidence to show that Mbeki and Mhlaba had both personally participated in acts of sabotage, and in Mandela's statement he admitted to undergoing military training because if there was to be guerrilla warfare he wanted to be able to stand and fight with his people.

With Justice de Wet listening patiently, apparently undisturbed by the flow of oratory without reference to law, Yutar launches into a sarcastic description of the 'glorious band of brothers' who had gone abroad.

It is a great pity that the rank and file of the Bantu in this country who are peaceful, law abiding, faithful and loyal should have been duped by false promises of free bread, free transport, free medical services and free holidays.' Such policies have never been embodied in the aims of the ANC or related organisations, and there had been no evidence presented to show that they had.

In a dramatic flourish he proclaims: 'The day of the mass uprising in connection with the launching of guerrilla warfare was to have been the 26 May 1963.'

The accused are mystified; they had been arrested six weeks after this date. And the evidence showed that the only armaments they possessed was an air rifle with which Mandela had once tried target practice.

Here de Wet surprisingly intervenes: 'Mr Yutar, you do concede that you failed to prove guerrilla warfare was ever decided upon, do you not?'

The little man is stunned. It is precisely what he has not conceded, he has decided even to fix the exact date. He stammers a submission that preparations were being made. 'Yes I know that,' the Judge says testily, 'the defence concedes that. But they say that prior to their arrest they took no decision to engage in guerrilla warfare. I take it that you have no evidence contradicting that and that you accept it?'

'As your worship pleases.'

Yet he continues to argue as though nothing at all had been said by the Judge. He accuses the ANC and the Communist Party of engineering the shootings at Langa and Sharpeville. There is something ghoulish about such an accusation. Not only did a

226

government-appointed commission find that the Sharpeville tragedy resulted from policemen being unnecessarily fast on the trigger, but to lay the blame for the terrible slaughter at Sharpeville on the ANC is an inhuman inversion of the truth.

Towards the end of his address, Yutar states he has decided to nominate a shadow cabinet for the provisional revolutionary government from among the accused 'for the edification of your lordship'. Perhaps de Wet forgets that his function is to try the accused, not to be edified by Yutar. He remains silent while Yutar proceeds to parcel out cabinet posts to each of the accused to the appreciative titters of the Special Branch. He names Goldberg as Minister of Health because he ran a health camp; Kathrada will be Minister of Indian Affairs, Govan of European Affairs — which he implies would be the reverse of the Ministry of Non-European Affairs which has always existed in South Africa and would be anti-white. Rusty would be Minister of Information ... and so on, naming not only the accused but co-conspirators, selecting Bob Hepple as Minister of Informers. Finally Nelson is to be Minister of Defence and Deputy-Prime Minister, and he then names Albert Luthuli as President. Luthuli, not alleged to be an accomplice nor even an agent or co-conspirator, is being tried in his absence. 'There are not enough portfolios for all the men involved but there would be a lot of internal strife when they came to power, so they would be able to fill the vacancies which would inevitably arise.' Throughout this outrageous and stupid performance, de Wet remains silent.

He finishes his address by saying that the case is not only one of high treason 'par excellence' but also of murder and attempted murder (a charge not in the indictment) and with a final dramatic finger pointed to the ceiling: 'I make bold to say that every particular allegation in the indictment has been proved. There is not a single material allegation in the opening address that has not been proved.'

Customarily the defence reply answers the allegation of the State and deals in some detail with the prosecutor's arguments. But how can counsel deal with this flood of rhetoric? They decide to argue on the issues that had been formulated at the beginning in Bram's opening address.

Arthur Chaskalson rises first to deal with some of the legal questions that have been raised. Speaking fluently and clearly, he brings the atmosphere back to that of a court of law. He refutes the statement that the trial is a trial for murder and attempted murder. He proceeds to demonstrate from the testimony of State witnesses that Umkhonto's clear policy was sabotage in circumstances where there could be no loss of life. The defence concedes that Umkhonto recruited men for military training and that members of Umkhonto committed acts of sabotage. The defence denies, however, that they committed all the acts of sabotage with which they are charged. He mentions the mass of inadmissible evidence that bears no relation to the indictment and quotes legal authorities to show why it is inadmissible.

When he starts to demonstrate from evidence that there were other organizations committing acts of sabotage at the time in question, Justice de Wet tells him there is no need to pursue the argument on that point; he accepts this as a fact.

A substantial part of the State case falls away. They had produced evidence of every act of sabotage of the last three years. In some, such as the removal of a large section of railway line, the acts could have resulted in serious danger to human life. Yet even the State witnesses, Mtolo and Mtembu, had testified that Umkhonto had at all times engaged in acts of sabotage in such a way that there was no danger to human life.

Piece by piece Arthur launches a legal attack which destroys most of the State evidence with regard to acts of sabotage. Of the 193 acts which the State had proved to have happened only about a dozen had been proved legally against Umkhonto and its High Command. Of these, not one involved any danger to human life whatsoever.

The two most serious aspects of the argument are being tackled by Bram Fischer: first, that though guerrilla warfare had at all times been under consideration as a prospect for the future, it had never in fact been decided upon by Umkhonto or the ANC; second, that though the ANC had been aware of, and some of its sections had even cooperated in, the formation of Umkhonto, they were in fact two separate organizations, each independently controlled.

The first point is obviously critical for the fate of the accused themselves; and the second is absolutely critical for the future of every person who has ever been a member of the ANC. On this point will hinge the question in future cases as to whether ANC members will merely be charged with membership of an unlawful organization, carrying a maximum penalty of ten years' imprisonment; or whether, as a member of that organization, they will be charged with complicity in treason or sabotage, with a maximum penalty of death.

Before he can develop his argument on the first point, Justice de Wet cuts him short by saying: 'I thought I made my attitude clear. I accept no decision or date was fixed upon for guerrilla warfare.'

And when Bram starts on his second point, de Wet again interrupts to concede the point by saying it has been clearly established by the evidence that the two organizations were in fact separate, though they overlapped. Bram's weeks and months of intensive preparation come to an abrupt end, before he has said more than a few words. I am almost disappointed that he has not had the chance to develop his arguments; but the defence are naturally jubilant that the Judge has conceded on both points.

Vernon Berrangé rises next, to deal particularly with the case of Rusty, Kathrada and Mhlaba, applying for their discharge on the grounds that the evidence cannot sustain a conviction. Before he starts his argument, he allows himself to express to a certain extent the outrage and disgust that he has felt over Yutar's conduct of the case.

'Dr Yutar delivered himself of what he was pleased to term a number of "observations" concerning the accused, the relevance of which we have found difficult to ascertain.

'We have consulted with our clients about these sarcastic and satirical attacks for the purpose of replying to them. With the dignity that has characterized the accused throughout this trial, they have instructed us to ignore these remarks.'

Vernon is speaking loudly enough for all to hear. The reporters are scribbling busily. Yutar looks hopefully at de Wet, probably expecting him to intervene on his behalf. But at this point de Wet may have realized that Berrangé's icy reproof is directed also at himself for tolerating Yutar's antics; he stays silent.

'It is, however, unusual, and not in the best traditions in which prosecutions are conducted in this country, for a prosecutor to deliver himself in this manner. It will be submitted that Dr Yutar in addressing the court has in instances not set out the facts, and in no instance has he tried to evaluate or analyse the evidence of the witnesses upon whom he relies.'

He deals with the case against Rusty. 'The cross-examination of Bernstein covers 153 pages of transcript. This is not remarkable in itself, but what is remarkable is that in 153 pages there is not one word of cross-examination as to the facts deposed to by Bernstein. The only direct evidence against him related to the erection of the radio masts, and this evidence had been given by a servant at Rivonia who was in police custody under ninety-day detention when he gave it.'

Yutar jumps up. 'That is not so, my Lord. The witness was not in ninety-day detention. He was in protective custody only.'

This is precisely what he had said about the detention of Edith Ngopani, months ago at the beginning of the trial. And the same applies — there is, at this stage, no provision in South African law for this. In addition, Vernon now produces a list of witnesses who were said by Yutar himself to be ninety-day detainees — the list that he had put to Rusty under cross-examination. Included on the list is Joseph Mashifane who had given the evidence about the radio mast.

Yutar colours, and buries his face in his papers as Vernon proceeds to analyse Mashifane's evidence and show it cannot be believed. 'This is the only piece of evidence against Bernstein. And on this basis he is entitled to his discharge.'

With Kathrada it is a different matter. Vernon demonstrates that the main case against him was testified by Essop Suliman, the clown who had been shown to have contradicted himself repeatedly in different trials. The rest of the evidence is that he was arrested at Rivonia, in disguise, had lived there for a while, that he had written a couple of pamphlets and prepared a draft speech for the illegal radio. All this Kathrada does not deny, but it does not prove that he had taken part in Umkhonto or had anything to do with sabotage or the preparations for guerrilla warfare. He had, in fact, had serious doubts about the wisdom of the sabotage campaign, and been very critical of it.

Mhlaba's case is argued with less assurance, not only because of the obvious weaknesses, but also because of the Judge's totally unsympathetic attitude.

There are a few more technical arguments by Arthur, Bram and George, and the defence case is closed.

The prosecution is entitled to reply, but only on questions of law raised by the defence; and this time when Yutar starts once again to recite the evidence against Rusty, de Wet stops him. 'You know, Mr. Yutar, you are only entitled to reply on questions of law.'

The court is adjourned for three weeks while de Wet considers his verdict.

*   *   *

My friends are worried about me; they think I am placing too much hope on the outcome of the case as far as Rusty is concerned. They are afraid of my reaction when the verdict, which they regard as inevitable, is given. They don't say this to me, but I know, for in all sorts of ways they try to prepare me for the worst possible outcome.

But I know — I know I must not think there is any possibility of acquittal. I know it is unreal. Yet there it is. There is a chance, however slender, for Rusty, for Kathy, and also for Raymond. I do not believe for one moment that if one or all of these three are acquitted, they will be released. I know they will be re-arrested, either in court or immediately they get outside. If these charges fall away, there are other charges concerned with contravention of their banning orders for Rusty and Kathy, and leaving the country illegally for Raymond. But these are, in effect, technical charges that cannot carry such heavy penalties, and would bring a term of imprisonment to which there would be a foreseeable end. Three years, five years, even ten years — they can be measured.

For the others there can be no verdict other than guilty; the suspense lies in what sentence they will receive. Although there is still the possibility of the death sentence for some of them — for Nelson, Govan and Walter in particular — I now feel that there will be no death sentences. Not only has the Judge accepted

231

that they had not embarked on guerrilla warfare; but there is also the external world that has brought its influence to bear on the outcome of the trial.

The trial has stirred interest all over the world. The statements and behaviour of the Rivonia men have earned them great respect, and brought tributes from individuals and organizations everywhere, from the World Peace Council that has awarded the Rivonia men a Gold Medal for peace, to students of London University who have elected Mandela as President of their Students' Union. Such indications of understanding and support not only bring pleasure to the Rivonia accused; they also bring doubt and unease to the State and those who support the State. No word or deed from people of other countries has been lost or in vain.

Time — time once rushing past stands still. Like a detainee living in the emptiness of solitary confinement, I try to push time on, and it does not move. The passage of days is immeasurably slow; the clock plays jokes on me. Several hours after each day has begun, I think, 'Well, another morning has gone,' but it has not gone; by noon it is still there. In the afternoon the thought comes a dozen times: the day is almost finished, another day. But it does not finish; supper-time, and it is still there; darkness, and it has not been left behind. Night, and now, I say, the day has really gone, and still it does not go, all night time does not move.

On the evidence, the lawyers say, Rusty must be acquitted, but on the manner in which de Wet conducted the case, they do not know if he will be. If de Wet accepts Rusty's testimony, if he thinks he should be acquitted, then he will acquit — he is not the type of man to decide on a verdict to please the Special Branch or anyone else. But there are indications that in many respects he has not really understood the political intricacies of the case.

In the last few days Nelson Mandela writes final papers for a London University law degree (which he obtains). To write an exam in Pretoria prison is in itself difficult enough, particularly for an African; to concentrate on it while awaiting the verdict of a trial in which he may be sentenced to death reveals once again Nelson's extraordinary calibre.

*   *   *

Thursday, 11 June 1964. It is eleven months, to the day, since the arrests at Rivonia.

The whole process at the opening of the trial is re-enacted — the road blocks, the police massed throughout Pretoria, the packed court, the difficulty in securing admittance, even though we have arrived very early.

At 10 a.m. exactly, Justice de Wet takes his seat, the registrar calls the case of 'The State against Mandela and Others'. The accused stand. Motionless silence. The Judge speaks in his usual, low, rapid way:

'I have recorded the reasons for the conclusions I have come to. I do not propose to read them out.

'Accused number one is found guilty on all four counts. Accused number two is found guilty on all four counts ... accused number three ...'

Kathy is five, Rusty is six. It all depends on what happens to Kathy. If Kathy is found not guilty, then Rusty must be, too.

I have not moved or breathed. It seems even my heart has stopped beating.

'Accused number five is found guilty on count two, and not guilty on counts one, three and four. Accused number six is found not guilty and discharged. Accused number seven ... '

But I don't hear any more. Over and over and over again the few quick words: accused number six is found not guilty and discharged. I am drained of emotion, calm because I feel empty. Annie is clinging to my arm whispering, 'Oh, Hilda, oh, Hilda', but whether with emotion over Denis or for my sake over Rusty, I do not know. I only know I am quite beyond any feeling at all.

As the Judge goes on speaking, I turn just for a moment to glance at Harold and Jean, standing at the back. Harold makes a little sign with his hand, and I know it is true, and he has also heard.

'I do not propose to deal with the question of sentence today,' de Wet is saying. 'The State and the defence will be given opportunities to make any submissions they wish tomorrow morning at ten o'clock.' He rises, court is adjourned.

I know Rusty is fighting with the Special Branch. He is talking in an angry voice as they try to restrain him. I have rushed forward to touch his arm and there is confusion and milling of police all round. They want to hustle him down to the cells again and he refuses to go — he is trying to reach counsels' table.

He is determined that if they are going to re-arrest him after such an acquittal they would have to do it in open court in the eyes of the whole world, not down below in the secret bowels of the court. He brushes off warders and detectives who are trying to restrain him in an attempt to get through to counsels' table. Finally, when restrained by the police, he challenges them loudly to say whether or not they are arresting him. They had obviously hoped to avoid such a scene. Even the Colonel of the jail was pleading with him to come quietly to the cells below where everything would be fixed up.

Everyone is standing. Reporters are pushing forward, the VIP's are standing in the jury box. From the spectators' gallery I hear Ivan's voice call out: 'What's happening?' and I reply loudly, so that the VIPs and Pressmen will hear:

'He's been discharged — but they're arresting him again.'

Hopeless to have believed we could ever get him out from that solid phalanx of Security Police. They are arresting him again. Swanepoel has a hand on his shoulder. They have closed in and sucked him up like one of those jungle plants that captures and enfolds and devours insects … he has been taken down to the cells once more.

Outside the court police form up in a solid phalanx between the African spectators and the court. Albertina Sisulu, wearing tribal dress, leads the crowd in singing 'Nkosi sikelele'. The crowd moves to the back of the Palace of Justice just in time to see the police convoy escorting the accused in their Black Marias from the court to the jail. As the trucks come into view the cry '*Amandla!*' echoes across the square. With hands thrust through the bars, the prisoners have time to respond with the traditional '*Ngawethu!*' before they disappear from sight.

* * *

Around us, the whole world stirs over the Rivonia trial. A night-

234

long vigil at St Paul's, in London. Demonstrations and processions. Discussion at the United Nations.

The court is like a place under siege. Again all roads from Johannesburg have been blocked by police, and road blocks mounted throughout the whole of the Witwatersrand area. There are police check points at railway stations and bus terminals; Africans are stopped, asked for passes, many arrested. Yet despite this people assemble in the Square before eight in the morning. By the time court assembles, in spite of the police and many attempts to prevent people coming to the Square, there are more than two thousand people, mostly Africans, standing silently.

A large group of whites gathers as well, mainly students from Pretoria University, rabid supporters of Afrikaner nationalism, hoping to hear death sentences pronounced on their enemies.

Joel has to intervene to get Elias' mother, Mrs Motsoaledi, into court. Students shout *kaffir boetie* as he takes her arm; eventually he has to go to the Brigadier in charge of security as police continue to debar her.

The courtroom is jammed. The local press, BBC reporters and overseas correspondents are all packed in the well of the court and at the doorways. Police fill almost all the public benches. A policeman who has occupied Joel's chair behind counsels' table refuses to move, until the officer in charge is called to order him to do so.

Last night, Nelson Mandela told defence counsel that whatever sentence he receives, under no circumstances will he appeal. The accused have discussed what they will do if a death sentence is passed, and Nelson says he will make a statement to the court that he is prepared to die for what he believes in, and hopes his death will be an inspiration to his people in their struggle. But he will not appeal. He, Govan and Walter discussed it very carefully and concluded that an appeal might be construed by the authorities as an act of weakness; they want their behaviour to inspire their followers with the belief that no sacrifice is too great in the battle for freedom.

Before de Wet passes sentence, there is to be a plea in mitigation, argued by Advocate Harold Hanson, and with one witness in mitigation — the author, Alan Paton. Paton is a Christian liberal, deeply opposed to sabotage and violence, who has come because he believes the accused men acted from the right motives even if they took actions he himself could not condone. Knowing that their lives are at stake he has agreed to appear for them without hesitation. Witnesses in mitigation are scarcely ever cross-examined. But Paton is subjected to vicious cross-examination by Yutar who attempts to smear him, to hold him responsible for violence, sabotage and subversion. The police snigger and titter. Paton, who has never acted from personal or dishonest motives, becomes angry and disturbed.

Hanson has been asked to use all his eloquence for the purpose of explanation, but not to apologize for what the Rivonia men have done. He has an understanding of politics. His plea is: that the Judge should understand that a nation's grievances cannot be suppressed, and that people find a way to voice those grievances as the African people had found and as the accused had found. His plea is that the Judge remember that his Afrikaner people themselves, in their time of struggle against British imperialism, had conducted armed uprising, rebellion and treason, and appeared before courts for such offences; that the very existence of the Verwoerd Government today arose from these illegal acts of the past by those who were the fathers of the Afrikaner nation. Precedents, he said, exist in South Africa for treason and rebellion to be treated with leniency; not simply because the crime echoes through the history of a country, but because the sentence imposed on those guilty of it will echo down the hall of history for a long time.

Justice de Wet quite clearly has decided on sentence; he is not interested in Hanson's plea and does not even give the appearance of attending to him.

He nods to the accused to rise, and as they stand begins to speak. He says:

I have heard a great deal during the course of this case about the grievances of the non-European population. The accused have told me and their counsel have told me that the accused who were all leaders of the non-European population were motivated entirely by a desire to ameliorate these grievances. I am by no means convinced that the motives of the accused were as altruistic as they wish the court to believe. People who organize a revolution usually

236

take over the Government and personal ambition cannot be excluded as a motive. The function of this court as is the function of the court in any other country is to enforce law and order and to enforce the laws of the State within which it functions. The crime of which the accused have been convicted, that is the main crime, the crime of conspiracy, is in essence one of high treason. The State has decided not to charge the crime in this form. Bearing this in mind and giving the matter very serious consideration I have decided not to impose the supreme penalty which in a case like this would usually be the proper penalty for the crime, but consistent with my duty that is the only leniency which I can show. The sentence in the case of all the accused will be one of life imprisonment. In the case of the accused who have been convicted on more than one count, these counts will be taken together for the purpose of sentence.

It is over. But we have not properly heard! Annie has hardly heard a word, and I have caught some phrases ... 'the function of the court ... not to impose the supreme penalty ...' — we stand together in an agony of uncertainty and indecision, we turn to people around us, we hear someone say 'life', but life for whom?

June, Mlangeni's wife, calls out: 'How long? How long?' And Andrew answers 'Life.'

The men turn for the last time to smile at their wives and relatives but the police are already pushing them down to the cells below. As they move forward Annie cries out in desperation: 'Denis! What is it?' and Denis turns, and spreading both arms in a gesture almost joyful answers loudly: 'Life! Life — to live!'

They are gone. Outside the crowd waits silently until Winnie Mandela walks down the steps and with arm raised in salute calls to them: 'Life!' Then the crowd bursts out singing and unfurls banners which they have been hiding from the police. The banners read: 'You will not serve those sentences as long as we live'; 'Sentence or no sentence we stand by our leaders'; 'We are proud of our leaders'. And Church Square echoes to the slow-moving harmony of 'Nkosi Sikelele'.

The Africans gathered in the square should now feel themselves beaten, leaderless, without hope. Instead, the square is alive with singing, and processions form with flying banners and the illegal ANC's colours fluttering in the wind, moving through Church Square, under the statue of Paul Kruger, saluting those called the enemies of the apartheid State.

We join the crowd at the back of the court, and for an hour or two we wait for the van taking the men from court to prison. We wait for that last glimpse of them through the bars of their van, at least to see someone's face, an upraised arm or fist, to let them hear our last shout of greeting. Africans, Indians, whites, we are packed together in the Pretoria sun, hot in midwinter. There are white hooligans who have tried to start fights in the crowd, smashed a newsman's camera, thrown water and rubbish on the heads of the waiting people; white students and police-men have watched the women in the square form a procession with the ANC colours flying illegally in the wind, and singing, move round the square to wait at the back. Police dogs snap at their heels. Their banners are seized, torn up, thrown into the gutter. And we wait.

Finally the massive gates swing open and the convoy shoots out at high speed, motor-cycles, cars, and at last the van — but instead of turning right as it has done all these months, and passing the massed people, it swings suddenly to the left, so that even at the end we are robbed of the last glimpse of the Rivonia men. But a mighty shout of '*Amandla!* rises from the crowd, and in the distance, some say, there is an arm at the van win-dow held up in salute.

It was Friday. Counsel had obtained from the police and prison authorities an undertaking that all the prisoners would be kept in Pretoria until they have had an opportunity to discuss with them the question of an appeal. On Saturday they wake to read in the newspapers that the black prisoners have all been flown secretly to Robben Island, a thousand miles away from Pretoria. Only Dennis Goldberg is still in Pretoria. Apartheid has reimposed itself, and the consultations, involving a long journey for counsel, must be separated.

Waves of protest run round the world. The life sentences are condemned in many countries.

They are attacked at a Security Council meeting, and a state-ment from Luthuli is read. Demonstrations are held all over Britain, there are marches and vigils with MPs and professors, clerics and writers, trade unions and students. A former Anglican Archbishop of Cape Town flies to New York to present a world petition, signed by representatives of over 160 million people, to U Thant, U.N. Secretary-General, urging the release of the prisoners. More than a hundred policemen stand shoulder to shoulder outside South Africa House overlooking Trafalgar Square in London.

The English Press, from the conservative *Telegraph* to the liberal *Guardian* all express a single thought about the trial: 'South Africa on Trial' is the title of the *Telegraph* editorial. 'South Africa in the Dock', states the *Guardian*. 'The trial itself has been fair,' the *Telegraph* comments:

> but that is not the end, rather the beginning of debate on the larger moral issue. It is the law itself that the South African Government has to justify at the bar of the civilized world.
>
> Whenever and wherever government rests on any other foundation than the general consent of the whole people, the patriotism of those repressed tends to appear in the eyes of the rulers as treason.

'Siege Law' is the heading in *The Times*:

> The sincere, outspoken testimonies against tyranny are proofs that the Government behind the prosecution must share in equity a grave burden of guilt ... Rivonia is a landmark in the course of worsening race relations ... evil laws breed disorder — no severities will in the long run effectively tame a spirited people.

The scale and intensity of overseas reaction to the Rivonia judgement shocks and surprises the South African Press. The Government newspaper, *Die Burger*, describes its impact in a memorable phrase: 'A bloodless Sharpeville', meaning that the harm caused to the South African image is in the nature of that caused by the Sharpeville shootings. And the pro-apartheid Press is querulous and indignant. Was it not a fair trial, they ask? Could men found guilty of what was in effect treason be sentenced to less? What is most incomprehensible to them is that the Rivonia men, found guilty, are regarded as heroes.

They do not grasp that the judicial aspects of the trial are not considered relevant. Only the *Rand Daily Mail* sums up world reaction: 'The case has captured the imagination because it seems to tell a classic, ancient story of the struggle of men for freedom and dignity, with overtones of Grecian tragedy in their failure … Rivonia is a name to remember.'

Through their forthright courage the Rivonia men made the trial their triumph. It may seem a bitter triumph to be sentenced to life imprisonment which in South Africa means the full span of the prisoner's life but they carry with them the conviction that their ideas will inspire other men, and reshape events, and that their vision of a larger humanity will persist and grow, as it has done throughout the ages.

A name to remember. The scholars and lawyers and workers, the teachers and poets and dreamers now splitting stones in the hot sun and sea winds of Robben Island, will yet emerge with all their creative powers to shape the structure of a new society in South Africa. For the time must come when law answers the needs of human relationship, instead of being an instrument of oppression. That day must come.

Rivonia will be remembered as a step towards that time.

* * *

In the corridor of the Supreme Court, just after the verdict was given, and Rusty once more under arrest, Vernon Berrangé ran into Dirker and stopped him to say: 'After that disgraceful exhibition in court, I will expect you people NOT to oppose bail when we apply for it on Bernstein's behalf.' Dirker looked embarrassed and muttering something that sounded like 'All right', walked on.

Rusty was brought to Johannesburg and taken to Marshall Square.

In the evening when I brought food, the young sergeant in charge said, 'But wouldn't you like to see him?' and said I could bring the children as well. Keith and Frances, a little shy after nearly a year, but deeply happy, had two long visits, with the police in charge allowing Rusty to kiss them. There is antagonism between the uniformed force and the Special Branch, and we do not feel these men are so hostile, so much our enemies.

On Saturday morning Toni and Ivan and I go to the

Magistrate's Court where Rusty is to appear and be formally recharged on new charges. The prosecutor says he has had instructions to oppose bail. Vernon tells the magistrate he had been assured by W/O Dirker that bail would not be opposed and he will demand that Dirker come to court to explain why the Special Branch have changed their mind. There is some confusion; it is Saturday, and everyone seems to be off duty and no one can be contacted. Vernon argues, browbeats, gets angry, and at last the prosecutor agrees to bail of R2,000 (£1,000), and in a blaze of publicity, Rusty comes home. We are too happy to care about the new charges which are not yet detailed — breaches of the Unlawful Organizations Act, of the Suppression of Communism Act. We are so happy, we do not care about the pervasive Press and TV men — at this stage, a few more pictures in the paper can't make any difference to the children — and we let them come into the house and take pictures.

Our lawyers drop in during the afternoon and evening, and I love them all very dearly; most of all, Bram, who has worked so unrelentingly, with so much system and direction, so much devotion, so much passion. Reluctantly, pressed by us all, he and Molly have agreed to go to Cape Town for a few days' relaxation, to celebrate their daughter's twenty-first birthday there.

We cannot help thinking about the others; Annie is with us to remind us of how selfish our happiness must be. Yet for one night — and only one night there is so much joy that we seize it as something too momentary to last.

It could not last.

Early the next morning, Sunday, Ivan Schermbrucker walks into our bedroom. We greet him with pleasure, but with surprise to see him so early. He sits down on my bed without a word, and bursts into tears. Between heaving and painful sobs he says: 'Molly Fischer is dead.'

On the way to Cape Town, a motor-cyclist had swerved to avoid an animal in the road, and Bram in turn swerved to avoid the motorcyclist coming straight towards him. The car plunged over a low bridge and came to rest on the edge of a pool of water beneath. Bram and a friend sitting in the front seat scrambled out, but Molly who was sitting in the back, seemed to be unable to move. As they struggled to open the car doors, one on each side, to release her, suddenly the car pitched forward into forty feet of water, with Molly imprisoned inside.

We have to get permission to attend the funeral. A funeral is a gathering within the terms of the Act.

Bram asks me if I will speak in the chapel when Molly is cremated, because they do not want a religious service, and I agree. But later he comes with George Bizos and says I must not speak, because to do so will be a contravention of my banning orders. I argue with them, I do not care about the consequences, but they are gently and firmly adamant. The law deprives me of the right to pay tribute to Molly. Vernon Berrangé reads out what I have prepared, without saying who wrote the words.

About three hundred people, a large number of them Africans and Indians, come to the funeral; a symbol of the great love and respect in which the Fischer family is held. We all disperse quickly after it is over; many of us may not speak to each other, and we know we are watched.

Molly's death is like a terrible symbol of the dark times that now lie ahead.

PART IV
ESCAPE

1

Disintegration

Our lives had begun to disintegrate.

The ninety-day law was a tide that flooded and receded and flooded again. Last year it had swept Rusty away, now once again it was in spate and lapping at the very doors of our home. This time it threatened me.

Last year I had wanted Bram to go away and he had refused, saying he would buy his immunity for the duration of the trial. He felt the Security Police would be reluctant to arrest the leading counsel in the Rivonia trial while the trial lasted. Now he knew his arrest was imminent. He had received warnings in confidence from men who had friends in high places.

In a sense, we had all been aware of a little immunity until the trial was over. The police stated quite openly that they were preparing for a new series of arrests and trials. Until the Rivonia men were disposed of, they were not in a hurry. They had time on their side.

We had no time. We worked against time, time ran out.

Rivonia over, the best-known leaders sentenced to imprisonment for life, the Special Branch was borne on the surge of its almost unchallenged power. To escape the tide meant taking action, action that would finally snap the thread that held us to all those three decades of our life, to our friends, our work, our struggle. How wilfully to break that cord? Easier to remain passive, easier to wait in the uncertain belief that the tide would wash over and away, leaving us where we were.

But where were we? Even though we sat around the fire at night on those chill June evenings, the whole family together, and did word games and the daily puzzle in the newspaper, everything was crumbling, dissolving, perishing. There was really no longer a veneer of ordinary living spread over the holes. We were no longer part of any community, no longer in possession of any pattern for co-operation with others, not even able to maintain a proper way of working for ourselves. We had no more discipline imposed on us by jobs and work; the only regularity was Rusty's daily reporting to the police at Marshall Square, our only discipline the necessity to observe house arrest rules. We had become not only outcasts but a danger to those left, to what we valued most.

We could not even discuss what was in our minds day and night. We were afraid to talk of anything between the walls of our own home, suspecting listening devices. We had to avoid any overt act that might reveal potential action. We were afraid to talk in the car, unconvinced by the opinion someone had given that they cannot bug a motor-car. Sometimes we held a small, whispered conversation standing uneasily next to the empty swimming pool where dead leaves clogged the edges, dried creepers were threaded through the netting of the fence and winter had stripped away the concealing screens of hedge and tree leaving even this centre of our garden exposed and open.

To talk properly we had to go right away from the house, to select some place that we felt could not be overlooked, and from where a conversation could not easily be picked up by one of those powerful little instruments of evil.

On 26 June, Rusty appeared in court for a formal remand; no evidence of any kind was offered, but the case was set down for 9 September, two and a half months ahead; this, one might think, would allow us plenty of time …

*   *   *

What are you going to do now?
Wait and see what the charges look like, we don't even know what they are.
Have you considered leaving?
We haven't discussed it.
Why don't you discuss it?
The case doesn't come up until September. We've plenty of time.

*   *   *

246

But time was running out. A secret informant gave word that the Special Branch were preparing for a big new operation; many more arrests; mass raids; the date was uncertain. The information was passed around the day after Rusty's case was remanded. It was a Saturday. We discussed it, and in the shadow of this new menace I packed a weekend case and decided to spend the weekend alone in a room in Hillbrow. We believed they would not pick Rusty up again for ninety days at this stage — he had been in jail for nearly a year; they would start on a new lot, particularly those who had been out and about during the past year. First I stuffed all my articles and private papers into a briefcase and took them along to some friends to keep for me. When I explained what I was doing they invited me to stay with them instead. Which I did. There were a couple more ninety-day arrests, but no mass raids. I had a restful weekend away from home, and went back on the Monday.

The week passed uneasily. Five more arrests, but no mass action until the next weekend. Friday morning I struggled out of bed when the phone rang at six-thirty. It was Barbara. She said something I couldn't catch, then when I asked her what it was, 'Oh, Hilda, can't you come to me?' I said yes, I'm coming immediately. In ten minutes she was in the car, cried, 'They've taken Geoff,' and burst into tears. Geoff was only one of several journalists who had been detained, and one of hundreds whose homes were raided. The newspapers said it was one of the biggest police swoops on the Reef and Pretoria in recent years. The names of important people, respectable people, non-left, non-radical people whose homes had been raided were spread about. Very few would admit, as did Professor Blacking who held the chair of anthropology at Witwatersrand University, to being among those raided. It would make them suspect, even to their friends; they were terrified and kept quiet.

The names of those detained for ninety days included some of my closest associates. Raids throughout the Cape followed the Transvaal ones.

Our house had not been raided. This was worrying, not reassuring. Rusty said, Go away for a week. I took Keith with me and went by train to Durban to stay with Toni's in-laws. That day Babla Saloojee was detained; two months later he would be flung to death from the seventh-floor window of the Security Police office at The Grays during interrogation.

In Durban I needed the newspapers more than food or drink. *The Star* said: 'The list of people who have been detained under the ninety-day law or who have had their homes searched in dawn swoops has grown steadily in the past three days ...' Vorster was satisfied, and left for a holiday. Official silence descended over the whole question of the raids and arrests. The Press expressed unease — 'One of the great dangers in South Africa today is that the knock on the door at dawn, the sudden disappearance, may come to be regarded as a normal part of the South African way of life'. A report on how a student, de Keller, was arrested at Natal University where he had been attending a conference of the National Union of South African Students (NUSAS): a squad of detectives raided the men's residence at the University at 4 a.m.; one of them told the nightwatchman that he was de Keller's father, and had to see him; a student woke in the early hours to hear de Keller shouting, 'NUSAS, NUSAS, wake up! Wake up! They are taking me away!' He looked out of the window and saw de Keller being ushered into a car by seven men; he was afraid, and went back to bed. Whoever else heard, also cowered in their beds and listened in silence and fear.

Even MPs were worried. The leader of the opposition was worried about the distinguished people whose homes had been raided. The Security Branch behave as though they are operating in a police state, commented a newspaper.

Respectable people, distinguished people — to the end this obstinate refusal to grasp the core. The time they should have protested, the time they should have spoken out, was when the undistinguished, the unrespectable, had been the victims: the reds, the radicals, the extremists who worked over the colour line, the Congress members, the Africans, the disreputable, the unknown, the people whose names counted for nothing. It had all happened before, in other lands. It had begun sixteen years ago in ours. We too had cried: 'Speak out before it is too late.' And the respectable people, the moderates, had turned away because we were red — or because we were black. If you have been a silent witness, it is too late when your turn comes to cry protest.

My hosts, kind but politically obtuse — the deliberate

248

protective coating of 'not knowing' that whites adopted for self-protection — could not feel the week of anxiety through which I passed, eaten with uncertainty about what to do, longing to rejoin Rusty.

By the middle of July the papers reported that at least eighty-two men and women were in solitary confinement under ninety days. The weather in Durban was overcast and heavy. Toni and Ivan motored down at the weekend, and we went down the coast and visited friends, and stood in the surf running over the great curves of beautiful beaches. I looked my last on all things lovely every hour. We drove back to Johannesburg together.

*   *   *

Why don't you leave?
It's not so easy.
Is it any easier to go on like this?
No. And no easier for those in jail.
Are you helping them by staying?
There are still things to do.
How do you think you will do them when you are in prison?
Why don't you go? Why don't you go?

*   *   *

And we had begun to think about it.

Rusty was sorting out books — he never could bear to part with them; we extracted a few, painfully, like pulling teeth, whenever there was a book sale. He stuck coloured tape on the shelves to indicate which books he wanted kept.

We took Toni and Ivan for a picnic to the Wilds, a park full of hills and trees, so that we could discuss it with them. We lay on the dry winter grass and said: 'What would you say if we told you we're thinking of going?'

They said forcefully: 'It's about time! We thought you just wouldn't make up your minds until it was too late'.

We told them they would have to look after the children. 'That's all right, we'll look after them,' they said.

'And if we go, you might be detained for a while — they'd

249

have to release you in the end.' And that's all right, we're pre-pared for it, they told us. So we just said, 'We won't tell you any-thing else so that if you are questioned, you just won't know'.

On Monday Rusty went into town to meet someone he was prohibited from seeing. 'Be careful,' I told him.

In the afternoon a friend came to fetch some books for her children. 'There's a police car outside your gate,' she remarked.

The police van was parked just beyond the gate, behind the hedge. One man in uniform, one in plain clothes, and a police dog. They sat there all afternoon. What were they waiting for? The afternoon ran down. Rusty was late back from town — he had to be home before six-thirty. He did not come. The car stood waiting outside.

After six, the house became silent; the children stopped talk-ing. Toni did not say a word, she looked at me and I avoided her gaze. I went into the kitchen to make supper. I thought, this time I'll die, I'll die, I'll leave the children and drive over a mountain or walk into the sea; this time.

At six-fifteen, gripped by an oppression so strong that it could no longer be borne, I took the car and drove to the corner; behind me, the police started their van and followed. Between the trees, down the darkening street, I saw Rusty coming. I opened the car door as he approached, and tears came. We drove round the block and the van followed us, then drove off. But one more such episode, I felt, and my heart would burst.

We slept uneasily. I woke at dawn, hearing Rusty getting out of bed, seeing him standing and looking out into the street behind the curtain.

'What's happening?'

'Quick,' he said, 'go. They're here.'

I could hear sounds outside. I slipped on a coat, fumbled for shoes. 'I'll stall them as long as I can,' he whispered.

I ran downstairs to the basement. We had planned this much, after we had been arrested during the 1960 emergency. The police had come simultaneously to the front and back doors. But from our basement room a window opened on to a portion of the garden that was concealed from both doors by a jutting wall. There was the possibility of getting out into the back garden and perhaps avoiding them altogether if their attention was concentrated on the house itself. Rusty had cut through the rivets of the metal-bar burglar-proofing so that it looked fixed, but could be pulled inwards if you knew how; the window opened outwards, level with the ground. We had placed a table under this window.

Toni and Ivan were asleep at the other end of the basement room. I climbed on the table and pulled at the bars that rasped stiffly (they said afterwards they were startled awake thinking a burglar was climbing *in*). I did not feel frightened, only strangely short of breath. The window flung wide, I scrambled out. I heard the penetrating ring of our front door bell, and ran down through the wet grass, climbed over the wire fence at the bottom of the garden, thinking really I'm too old now for this sort of thing.

And where next? The nearest friend is probably being raided as well. Push through the bottom of someone else's back garden, hesitate — not that way; it is too visible from our house; another light fence yielded to my impatience and then I found myself out on the street, it was just getting light through the chill grey mist of a winter's morning, standing on the pavement in a nightgown, indecisive, with greying, disordered hair; feeling this is a melodrama without roots in actuality.

I decided on the house of an acquaintance some distance away.

The African maid had only just entered the kitchen. I tapped and tapped on the window until she let me in. The owner of the house whom she called probably thought my suggestion that he should drive me to another house was the easiest way of being rid of me. I lay in the bottom of his car until we reached another suburb, then asked to be dropped on a street corner.

The friends with whom I had stayed before took me in again, lent me clothes, gave me breakfast. Rusty guessed where I had gone and later in the morning contacted me. The police had taken our two typewriters, but nothing else. It had been a cursory visit. Against the advice of our friends, I returned home.

*   *   *

One more day. We discussed possible escape routes and methods, but made no progress.

We could not sleep at night. I would sleep at last, and wake, and listening knew that Rusty was awake and listening too. We were aware of every car coming down the hill, and tensed in the dark to that change of gear when a car turned into our street.

The days were just as oppressive, beset not only with the tension of watching, of being always on the alert, of checking on cars near the house when returning from the shops; but also with the tensions of Johannesburg, always the tensest of cities, now engulfed in the full flood of Special Branch powers; the rumours were whispered around town, the things we knew and could do nothing about, the fear for those suffering physical assault, the fear for those suffering mental torture, the whites' frustrating silence of acceptance, and the Africans' silence of impotence.

The Special Branch had blundered through the years; they still blundered sometimes. They tried to raid the home of a man who had been dead for seven years and raided someone else at an address he had left six years before. But even as they blundered, they had learned from studying the techniques of the political police of other countries; they had used electric shock methods of various kinds; they knew now how to truss a man with hand-cuffs and a pole over and under his limbs, fasten the electrodes, and then make him talk; they attached electrodes to the genitals if he did not yield, the lips and tongue when the victim screamed. Nothing would be left as evidence of such interrogation except two small burn marks where the electrodes were attached, and these would fade and disappear in a few days.

They tried out the Portuguese 'Statue'. They kept detainees standing continuously for days and nights — in one case for five days and nights. Loss of sleep disorientated them. They could no longer control their own minds. The victims would crawl back to their cells with painfully blown-up legs and ankles but in a few days there would be no marks to reveal the ordeal, only the ineradicable scars on the mind for those who broke and gave statements.

Officially there was silence or denial ('The Head of the Security Branch in the West Rand, Captain P. J. Greyling, laughed and shook his head yesterday when it was suggested to him that he had assaulted suspects ... ') but we knew something of what was happening. They had not sound-proofed all the cells. The stories we heard were knives that stabbed our consciences without mercy. 'He moaned all night long in his cell.' 'She refuses all food.' 'They've moved him to another jail ...' How could we leave them? Abandon them all? How could we go? So many have gone, some must stay. And if it means certain imprisonment? What good can people do in prison? Some argued obstinately, even in prison you will mean something, but not if you go; we can't all run away.

I met Ivan Schermbrucker in the evening, in the open. He was not allowed to talk to me, but we met and talked. 'You know you are going to be arrested soon,' I told him. 'It's only a matter of days.' By that time we could see there was a pattern that made his arrest, like mine, inevitable.

He said, 'I know.'

'Then what are you going to do?'

'Nothing.'

'Just sit and wait for them to come?'

He looked at me with infinitely sad eyes. He said, 'Hilda, I *can't* go. How can I go? I can't bloody well go! I can't run away and leave L. and M. and N. stuck in under ninety days. I can't go and leave Helen shut for five years alone in her house. I can't leave Mary sitting in that square mile of Orange Grove. I can't go.'

'Then you're going to jail.'

'Yes.'

I said, 'It might be for a long time, Ivan.'

'I know. I can't go.'

And already there is a rift between us, because I am thinking of going and he is not. Already it is like a barrier dividing us into separate worlds. Already our relationship has changed.

Next morning he came to see me again. We met in the garden, we talked briefly in whispers beneath the fig trees. We said goodbye. He went to work. I took the car and went shopping.

An hour and a half later I drove up under the jacarandas and Toni was sitting on the stoep in the sun waiting for me. She came towards me with that look of anxiety that I now knew only too well.

'Ivan (Schermbrucker) has been arrested.' 'When?' 'Just now, in his office. They brought him home to search.'

This was too close. 'Oh, Toni — I must leave home.'

I went into the house and started putting the shopping away, unwrapping meat, stacking away the groceries.

'Why don't you go then?' she asked with some impatience.

'I will. I must just pack a bag.'

Even then I prevaricated, delayed. Packed a few clothes, went into the kitchen. It seemed I could not summon the actual will to leave the house. I kept finding one more important thing that had to be done first.

'If you're going,' Toni said, 'go. It will be too late soon.'

Without that urging voice, would I ever have left the house?

She took me in the car to a place near the house of my friends. 'Look after the kids,' I said.

My friends were very nice about it all. The room was prepared for me. Their servants were knowledgeable, discreet, trustworthy. I had nothing to do now but to wait.

* * *

I met Rusty secretly for lunch. We discussed plans. I went back to my refuge, the house, large, beautiful and ordered, the garden, full of flowers and beautifully kept. I sat inside with nothing to do but read newspapers. A bomb exploded at Johannesburg station: several people injured.

Later one of them, an elderly lady, died from her injuries. And John Harris, who planted the bomb, would be tried and sentenced to death and executed.

John Harris was a young school-teacher who joined the Liberal Party and became active in a committee to promote non-racial sport, the South African Non-Racial Olympics Committee (SAN-ROC). He was banned, he had his passport taken away, he saw the deterioration of conditions in South Africa; the Secretary of SANROC was arrested, and shot at while trying to escape, and jailed.

Later he joined ARM, African Resistance Movement. Its object was to commit sabotage to force the Government to reconsider its policy. Then there were many arrests of ARM members, and some fled the country. In Johannesburg only John Harris and his friend John Lloyd were left. They left dynamite with Harris. He felt he was one individual left with some form of power — the dynamite — and he had to do something. He thought of putting a bomb in the station, then phoning a warning to the police. He thought the public address system would be used to clear the concourse. He had not intended anyone to be injured.

He took the bomb in a suitcase and sat on a bench in the concourse. He was aware of all around him — 'I was part of the world. The world and I are one.' He had the sensation of sitting in a glass ball.

He left the bomb on the seat and phoned the railway police. He said, 'This is the African Resistance Movement. There is a bomb in the centre of the concourse timed to go off at four-thirty-three. Please clear the concourse.' It was then four-twenty.

He phoned a newspaper, and another. He drove away. He felt happy, 'like a centaur'. He thought the station would be cleared; it seemed so organized, so cut and dried, so beautiful, such a beautiful plan'. Police and Press went to the concourse, but it was not cleared. The bomb went off, injuring many people, one fatally.

John Harris went home, went to bed, and in the night was found there and taken by the police. He was beaten up, his jaw was broken in two places.

At his trial, John Harris made a full confession, his counsel pleaded insanity, but he was found guilty, sentenced to death, executed. He walked to the scaffold at Pretoria Central Prison singing the American freedom riders' song, 'We Shall Overcome' — 'oh, deep in my heart, I do believe, we shall overcome some day.' Many Africans would be executed for sabotage, but John Harris was the first white man so to die.

The Johannesburg station bomb acted as a catalyst, liberating the Nationalists from their few remaining inhibitions, giving them a pretext for openly declaring their full identification with what Esmond Romilly once described as 'that mixture of profit-seeking, self-interest, cheap emotion and organized brutality that is called fascism'. They could now use the bomb to justify what was truly unjustifiable. They used it to whip indifferent and uncommitted whites into line behind them. They used it like a miniature Reichstag fire.

Respectable citizens and the Press rushed in to condemn what

255

they called a callous and politically meaningless act of terrorism
The Press published blown-up pictures of a badly injured baby
This one terrorist act became the excuse for all the brutality and
terror of the past and present, for all the repression and terror of
the future. But the African people in the townships, so my
friends told me, were saying it was a good thing — 'let some of
the whites be killed the way they are killing our people'.

In a fury at the injury to whites, Security policemen dragged
three of the people from their ninety-days cells to the scene of
disaster at the station concourse to witness the mess. Astonished
Press colleagues glimpsed them before they were taken away
again. All had been visibly assaulted.

Over the weekend someone took me out discreetly and I visited some friends. These few I felt I had to see; whatever happened I would not see them again for a long time. I did not tell
them this,; I said goodbye to them only in my heart, and hoped
that later they would understand.

Monday, and our plans had still not become definite. Monday
was the last day of the winter holidays and I had promised Keith
that whatever happened I would come back to see him off to
school on Tuesday. So that night, after it was dark, I left my
refuge and walked through the streets to my home. Keith
remained aloof and rather cold until I went with him to his
room; then he cried and said, 'But I wanted you to be here
tomorrow, when I go off to school.' So I promised him I would
come back in the morning.

I got up early and walked home by a devious route. I kept my
promise to Keith, he went off happily to school. I prepared
some food for the evening meal, and went back to my refuge.

A day ebbed by very slowly.

Mid-morning when a sense of quiet had fallen in house and
town, I left my friend's house once again and walked along suburban streets towards my home. From the road that skirts the
Children's Home and runs along the top of the hill facing Regent
Street, I could stand and look distantly at the forbidden territory
of my own house and front garden.

I was like a ghost, invisible and lonely, but still drawn irre-
sistibly to the world of life, to the house that had been the very
centre and heartbeat of my daily existence, the shell surrounding

256

that living organism, my family. And seeing it, I knew the reality of that isolation through the very clichés with which it spoke to me — the smoke rising from the chimney (Claud in the kitchen stoking the stove), a dog running across the lawn, the movement of curtain through the open window where stands the desk at which I always worked.

And this feeling of isolation became even more acute because of the lack of any physical signs of danger, or even the certain knowledge of its presence; if, for instance, the path had been mined, to step down on to it would have been deliberately to invite reprisals of a known, measurable kind: death or mutilation. So you could have weighed such probable consequences against the need to take the risk.

But what was the barrier that stood now between me and my normal life? It was not measurable, the results unknown, the consequences of moving forward and down there, and stepping along the path to the front door, could not be assessed.

The compulsion to step out of my twilight world of being and not being, of seeing but not being seen, became formidably strong. I could not tolerate any longer this hovering in half-life. No one can live indefinitely on the edge of disaster. Our ability to survive all these years of abnormality had been due precisely to our ability to bring an everyday normality into our lives. Except for the recurring crisis periods, the times of mass raids and arrests, the weeks before the treason trial arrests, the days leading up to the emergency in 1960, the times when a special threat blew up, we had conquered the tensions of our tight-rope existence.

Visitors from abroad, when confronted with some sharp aspect of the police vigilance under which we lived, had sometimes asked: 'How can you stand it?' And we always found it hard to explain that we could stand it because for a large portion of the time we could successfully ignore it. Our escapes had been splendidly effective; the trips to the Game Reserve, camping excursions, holidays by the sea, Sundays around our swimming pool for every week of those gloriously long summers; the hospitality of the open door and of the friendly traffic that passed through it so constantly; work; domesticity.

And it was only when we could no longer leave the taut

confines of Johannesburg, when holidays were reduced to coloured slides and animated remembered times, when visitors came at their peril and ours, and Sundays were quiet and the door closed all day and the windows curtained every night, only then that we reached a point where it was no longer easy to confront the abnormality of our lives.

Only a few people I knew have been able to turn their backs on the responsibilities and emotional ties of family life and unburden themselves of possessions and all but the most elementary needs. My most important possessions, the children, were at that stage still too strongly tied to every cell of my physical and mental being, and I could not find the will to set them on one side and live without them. They — and the need to bring so intolerable a situation to some sort of resolution, drove me back to that dangerous house. Not foolhardiness, not a longing for martyrdom. The ending of uncertainty, even when that end is prison, can be a relief, as I and others had found in 1960. We did not go to jail with pleasure, but the breaking of the enormous tensions that had gripped us in the days before our arrest at least brought back a tolerable situation.

Standing on the hill above my home, I was compelled to take some step to force the crisis which had so far only been sidestepped. I went back to my refuge, packed my case, and told my friends I was returning home.

Rusty was irritable and apprehensive. 'What's the point of it?' he asked.

And the children also wanted answers. 'Have you come home to stay this time?'

'Perhaps. For a while. We'll see I don't know.'

So I came to spend the last night of all in my home in Regent Street.

*   *   *

We could not relax and we had forgotten how to sleep in peace. We lay and listened for cars and footsteps and heard each other's wakeful breathing and listening. At half-past six it was a relief to see the winter light and welcome the end of such a night. I said, 'Well, we survived that one,' and began the

258

Saturday stripping of beds and sorting of washing. I put soup in the pressure cooker and began cooking food for the weekend. The telephone rang.

A falsely urbane voice with a veneer of upper-class English accent asked for me and announced itself as Mike Bain.

'Mike Bain?'

'Yes, Mrs Bernstein, you don't know me, but I know friends of yours in Durban, and I have a message for you from them.'

'What is the message?'

'Oh, I'd prefer not to give it on the phone.'

The voice was coy and fruity; and phony. These few words had revealed it.

Everybody knew that our phone was tapped, so many things were not said on the phone. But no one with a message from friends in Durban which could not be given over the phone would then phone me and tell me so. I was not, in any case, expecting any messages from anyone in Durban; and I didn't know anyone called Mike Bain.

I suspected it was the Special Branch, but did not know what sort of game it was nor what they wanted. They still had not learned that we could be forewarned by their silly telephone calls, designed to save them the tedium of coming out to see for themselves whether their victim was at home.

I had a conversation with Mike Bain. He said he would come and see me; I asked him if he knew how to get to the house; he pretended he did not know, I began to give directions. We had one of those peculiar conversations when you know the other person is evading the truth, and each plays a game of acceptance with the other.

I told Mike Bain I would be in all day, and he said he would call after lunch.

I put down the phone and said to Rusty, 'That was a fishy phone call.' I had heard the office sounds in the background. He was obviously consulting someone else, because the office sounds blacked out as he put his hand over the mouthpiece for a few seconds.

Neither Rusty nor I mentioned 'Special Branch'. Rusty said, 'Let's get out of the house — take the kids somewhere.'

I said, 'I'll just finish the washing, and we'll go.'

He went into the front room and stood at the window looking out into the street; watchful, tense, smoking one cigarette after another without taking his gaze off the street.

In fifteen minutes time I heard him call, 'Aren't you ready yet?'

'Nearly — just a few minutes,' I answered. 'I'm just putting in the last load of washing.'

Two minutes later he called again, this time compelling urgency in his voice: 'Hilda — where are you?'

'Here — in the kitchen.'

'Get out — quickly; the back way.'

And I am at the end of the garden among the trees, as they arrive at both the front and back doors, in less than thirty seconds.

Somewhere behind me in a kitchen never to be entered again, the washing machine is going into its rinsing cycle, the pressure cooker sends out its puffs of steam, the children are unaware that I have gone. The bright winter sun illuminates the normality of Saturday morning in a Johannesburg suburb.

2

Hiding

My mind is split in two contending parts.

One compels me to find a place to hide, to get off the streets, the streets are dangerous.

The other watches a car turn the corner with acceptance; let it be them, let them come now and pick me up.

They contend, but spring from the same source. I want to be with the others, the ones I worked with, the ones I care about; I want to share whatever they must endure. But we were united in a long battle and will not voluntarily surrender; our object is to preserve freedom of action as long as possible.

The car drives past — not theirs. But they are, at this moment, circling the block looking for me. What unexplained accident of movement prevents our weaving paths from coinciding in both place and time?

Which direction shall I take and where shall I go? Oh, let them come, I hope they will come.

July mornings in Johannesburg are cold. I am wearing only a blouse and skirt. How foolish to be walking aimlessly along this street without even a jersey or a jacket. I have in my skirt pocket a piece of paper with the words of a song. Every day now for a long time I have been memorizing words of poems and songs; this is my private preparation for ninety days. When I was in jail before, poetry had been important to me; every poem remembered was like a gift; I know it will be even more so under ninety days. In solitary confinement remembered things are the link with life, the only conqueror of the emptiness of time, the weights that hold the balance of sanity.

The crumpled paper reminds me that I know what to expect; I am ready.

I keep it in my hand as I take a decision and walk to a house belonging to people I know. This will not be a place where I can stay, but perhaps they will take me somewhere else.

No one at home except an African servant. Shall I wait or go somewhere else? And where? I ask the servant to go to my house and discreetly find out what is happening. In a little while he comes back with a message from Rusty: They are driving around looking for you; don't go out on the street again.

I go into a bedroom; the sun makes a bright patch on the floor. I lie on the floor in the warmth of the sun and wait.

At lunchtime my friends come; once more I lie in the back of a car, covered with a blanket, and they drive to a quiet suburban street with trees and big gardens and no one about; there I transfer to the floor of another car; watch, under the seat where I crouch, a man's foot on the accelerator pedal. How stupidly melodramatic this is! But it is real.

The house to which I am taken is also not safe; none of the homes of friends are safe for me. All afternoon we sit, peering at occasional cars down the street from behind curtains. Then in the evening my friend goes out and visits a woman she knows, Eva. She comes back and says: 'It is all fixed. I simply asked her — Will you let someone who is in hiding from the police come and stay with you for a night or two? She didn't hesitate or even ask me who it was. She simply said— Of course.'

So I go to Eva, whom I have not met before, who has had no part in politics, but is not afraid to do what she thinks is right. She lives alone, and tells me, 'Stay as long as you need.' She thinks up ways of keeping her friends from visiting her for a few days. 'When I'm not well, they know I like to be left alone. I shall simply say I'm not well for a while.' She runs a hot bath for me and mixes a drink. She makes up a camp stretcher, but insists that I sleep on her wide and comfortable bed while she, not young, not light, creaks all night on the narrow stretcher near the floor. 'You'll need your strength more than I will.'

In this refuge I must learn to be patient, to sit and wait. 'When a man is happy he can be idle,' wrote Ilya Ehrenburg, 'but in misfortune action, however futile, is a necessity.' But I must not act.

Even Rusty does not know where I am staying. A message has been sent to him, saying I am safe. We devise a way of communicating: Toni takes a note to College when she goes there on Monday. She leaves the note and some clothes for me in the cloakroom. She does not speak openly to the person who will pick them up; she simply murmurs to her as they pass in a corridor: 'There is a bag for you in the cloakroom.' The bag is collected and taken to someone else's home. In the evening it is passed on to Eva. Eva brings it to me. So, with notes passing through many hands, we make our decisions.

Rusty writes: 'They came back for you on Saturday night and again on Sunday morning. I am trying to find a way'.

I write: 'If they come again and don't find me, they may take you — if we go, it must be soon'.

Be patient! We both know now the time has come for us to go. A note says: 'Be ready on Wednesday night'. Be patient ... a quiet day. Eva is at work. Slightly clouded sky. I read, try to change my face with make-up, make coffee, wash underclothes, and long to be gone. For a whole year now, it seems, I have been waiting, waiting for time to pass. I want to go back to an existence where you live with time, and regret its going. I am entirely cut off from the very roots of my existence, my home, my children, my husband, my friends, my work. My work: it is so sadly incomplete; it is too late to think of things undone.

I watch traffic through a window up a distant hill, and wait.

* * *

Tonight Eva has another note. Rusty says I must not go without first seeing the children and explaining to them. Eva is strongly opposed to this unnecessarily dangerous enterprise.

She says, 'Can't you go without seeing them?'

'No, I can't. I must see them.'

She says, 'But if you have to choose — to see them now, and through doing that imperil your hopes of ever seeing them again; or to go without seeing them, knowing you will then have a better chance to be re-united in the future? If you think about it that way, can't you go without seeing them?'

After a while, when I can control my voice, I say, yes, I can go without seeing them.

But Rusty insists. So on Wednesday afternoon I leave my refuge and Eva. I kiss her goodbye, a woman I did not know a few days ago but who I now know so well; shut in together we

263

have talked and talked, she has told me of her childhood, and shown who she is. May we meet again one day.

The place of assignment is a public park, and there I go disguised and in borrowed clothes. Keith laughs at my make-up. Frances runs, runs to meet me from over a hill. Patrick is away at boarding school; we will have to write to him as soon as we can.

I tell them we have decided to go away. We cannot go on living like this. 'We are going to try and get to a safe place, and then we will send for you. Toni will look after you.' Frances understands, and just for a moment her eyes redden, then she controls herself. Keith asks, 'How long before you send for us?'

'We don't know. Not too long. As soon as we can.'

'A week?'

'Maybe two or even three. But as quickly as we can.'

A blue van stands on the road at the top of the hill, just outside the park. I noticed it in another place when I was coming. I am uneasy, it is time to go.

Toni looks at me with dark eyes. 'Are you frightened?'

'Terrified!' But I smile to pretend to her that I am not serious. She is not deceived.

I walk away, turning to wave, to take a last look. Toni has her arms around Keith. If we are caught it will be years and years before we see them again. They will be grown, and strange.

3
How Far is Lobatsi?

The border between Bechuanaland Protectorate (now Botswana) and South Africa runs for hundreds of miles with only a barbed-wire fence to divide the two countries. There are police posts and patrols where the few roads cross the border; and farms on both sides of the border whose white owners will hand us over immediately to the South African police if they find us on their land.

Bechuanaland is a great, arid, undeveloped country; much of it is desert; there are few towns, small and far apart; peasants' kraals, scattered over great distances. The towns — villages, really, lie along the border close to South Africa. Most of the interior is blank on the map.

In this year, 1964, the countries surrounding Bechuanaland are hostile to refugees; South-West Africa (Namibia) to the west, South Africa and Southern Rhodesia (now Zimbabwe) to the east and south. In the north lies the Caprivi Strip, part of South-West Africa which is occupied by and under the control of South Africa. It is a narrow tongue all along the top. Between Caprivi and Southern Rhodesia there is a three-mile gap where Bechuanaland has a common frontier with Northern Rhodesia (now Zambia). The way to it is across uninhabited bush, leopard and elephant country, with sandy tracks, but this is the only way out. This is the escape route.

The newspapers write about underground routes through which refugees are 'piped' across the border. There is no mapped route, no safe way out. Refugees must cross the border at night and avoid armed police and dogs. Refugees need guides to show them where they can cross or they will land in the arms of white farmers or be lost in the bush. The first destination of every refugee is Lobatsi, only three miles across the South African border, 240 miles from Johannesburg. We must reach Lobatsi if we can before morning.

I am to meet Rusty and the unknown car that will take us to the border at 7 p.m. on a road next to the Planetarium behind the Witwatersrand University.

A car driven by an African takes me to the Planetarium and drops me there at seven. He has not been told who I am, nor where I am going, but when he leaves me he says, 'Go safely. Good luck.'

In the shadows of tall wattle trees I stand and wait. Across the road is the Exhibition Ground. There seems to be a lot of activity there, with big men who look like SBs hanging around. Supposing the driver of the car has betrayed us, and they are just waiting for Rusty to come? Rusty is late, there is no sign of him or the car. Perhaps he has already been picked up by the police. What will I do if he doesn't come? I walk farther into the darkness of the trees, holding my bag with clothes which have been given me for the journey. An occasional car drives up the street, swishing past without turning in to the avenue of trees. The leaves mask the street lights; from the darkness I see men hanging around the turnstile across the wide road; I look at my watch; I strain to see him come …

He is here at last, but the car has not come. Who is it? What sort of car? Rusty does not know. The arrangements were all made through a series of contacts, Rusty spoke to A. who carried a message to B. who went to C., and C. arranged the car and driver. Wait here, Rusty says, and I stay concealed in the shadows while he walks down the road …

Some time later a car turns, drives slowly among the trees. I step out, it stops, Rusty opens the door for me. This is the one.

This. The escape car, the high-powered machine that must rush us to the border, dodging police and possible road blocks. It is a shabby, rattling old sedan, a model produced just after the end of the war, driven by a tall bearded African with a youth beside him on the front seat. The kind of car and driver that will inevitably draw the attention of the police, who stop such cars and search them for *dagga* (Indian hemp), illicit liquor, or stolen goods. If they stop this car they will find two whites sitting in the back; without doubt they will hold us to investigate what we are doing in such a car. It could not be more dangerous.

Rusty has blackened his bleached eyebrows and fair hair, and

266

wears an unfamiliar hat. He pulls it over his face and sits well back. I put a thin black scarf over my face. 'Who is he?' I whisper.

'I don't know. He calls himself McClipper.'

'But who — ?'

'He has taken people before. He does it for money.'

'How much?'

'Seventy-five pounds. For what he's risking, it's not so much.'

I ask McClipper which way we are going.

'I usually go through Zeerust,' he replies, 'but this time I think we will go through Lichtenburg.' 'Why?' He says he thinks he has been through Zeerust too often. Lichtenburg might be safer. Road blocks?

Sometimes on one road, sometimes on another, sometimes none. It's a matter of luck.

From the moment I get in, I am afraid.

That cliché about the icy hand of fear — fear is not an icy hand, it is a burning acid that flows through every vein.

I have never in my life known such agonizing fear, a fear that does not decrease but eats into me hour after hour. Why such fear? There is now too much to lose. Rusty has broken his house-arrest order by leaving home after 6.30 p.m., and the banning order that confines him to Johannesburg; two more charges to add to those they have framed already. His bail will certainly be cancelled. I have not been charged. For me first ninety days, then charges, then a trial. We have staked too much.

All these years we have known fear, all that long time of trouble and tension, of meeting people you could not meet and doing things you were prohibited from doing; the years of raids, of listening for cars at night, anticipating arrests; the time of the emergency with one awful week of mounting tension and crisis; the years of concealed discussions, of watching who may be following, of calculated risks. Fear, yes, but not this kind of fear. Fear when you are in control of yourself and of a situation, when you act deliberately and for a positive purpose. A constructive fear, not this crawling, miserable fear that turns my insides to liquid — the fear of someone who is running away. To be caught doing something worthwhile is one thing, and you have pride and self-respect, and defend your actions, like the Rivonia men. But to be caught for nothing, for running away —

I am completely and totally the victim of this abject, nightmare fear.

We have left the lights of Johannesburg and are out on the dark road. It is not so bad when there is no other traffic, but each time we see the headlights of a car far away coming towards us, or even worse, overtaking us from behind, each time the acid fear; I cringe, I close my eyes.

Yet we are not stopped. The car lights appear behind, come nearer and brighter, glare into our car, swerve out and pass, and the rear lights glow red and small in the distance. We go on and on, passing small towns.

At about 10 o'clock we approach the small diamond-mining town of Lichtenburg. McClipper breaks a long silence to say: 'I hate this town. They're always stopping you and searching you. The police, ahhh, they're too active here.' His car, with its Johannesburg 'TJ' number-plate marks it as 'foreign' to the town. At that time of night police are always curious to know what 'foreign' cars driven by Africans are doing. Whites can drive anywhere at night with impunity, but Africans are perpetually suspect and liable to be stopped.

As we enter Lichtenburg we see two police cars parked in the road ahead of us; we drive straight towards them. To avoid suspicion, McClipper cuts his speed and drives slowly. The police are standing and talking; they do not stop us, and they do not follow us. We are stopped twice in the town by traffic lights. But when we leave Lichtenburg, the road to Mafeking — the last town before we approach the border — lies ahead, and we travel for long stretches without passing, or being passed by cars. It is late, we are farther and farther from Johannesburg, the miles pile steadily on. The car, in spite of its age, is now as McClipper puts it, 'ready to go'.

'We will not drive through Mafeking,' he tells us. 'That is where there might be a road block. We will slice off along the road to the township — first the African township, then across the Coloured township.' from Ramosadi we connect with the main road for Pitsani, and somewhere along that road we will leave the car to walk to the border.

With the lights of Mafeking in sight, we veer off the main road, and soon we are driving in a crazy fashion across the veld, through the black shapes of sprawling township homes where there is no light to be seen. McClipper seems to know every ditch, corner and tree, every obstacle and hole, in this wild ride. There is no road, no track even, but ditches eroded in the hard soil over which we bump like animated puppets and dodge first this way, then that. How many times has McClipper driven this way to avoid Mafeking? And for what purpose?

Mafeking's few street lights recede, string out, become isolated white circles glowing coldly in the distance. Our car lights must be visible for miles, conspicuous across the black veld and sleeping townships. Surely the police will see them, investigate them. On the horizon behind us one of the lights appears to be moving. It is following. Rusty says no, it is our movement that gives the appearance of motion to the light. I am not convinced, I see it moving, coming towards us. No, no, he says, look, it is still as far as it was — farther.

And now we hit the road again. Our headlights steady, cease shooting up and down cutting the night at odd angles. The lights behind us have all disappeared. We are the only ones awake in this dark corner. We are nearly at the place where we will leave the road and start walking.

McClipper is driving slowly, looking carefully along the side of the road. He has driven a stake into the soil just off the road to mark the place. In this thick darkness it is difficult to see, but he knows more or less how far down the road it is; and finds it.

As I get out of the car, the tide of corroding fear subsides although I cannot wait to get away from the road and into the concealing bush.

'Now we must walk,' says McClipper. He leaves the boy, his nephew, to sleep in the car. 'The time is right,' he says. Midnight. About seven miles to the border, at least two hours of walking. We will reach the border between two and four. And when we have crossed, how far to Lobatsi? McClipper is vague. 'Oh, three, four miles, a little more. You have a long hard walk ahead.'

He adds: 'I will go half-way to the border with you, then you will go on without me. I can't walk as far as the border and all the way back to the car. Arthritis. My legs.' He pulls up his trousers to show us bandages on his legs.

In spite of the arthritis, he sets off with a long stride and light step. I walk behind him with two water bottles slung across my shoulders, and behind me walks Rusty with two canvas airline bags containing a few clothes. In the car I had changed into slacks and walking shoes, and had abandoned high-heeled shoes and some food Rusty had packed.

It is a night of absolute darkness, completely without sound: no moon, and few stars. We walk in this blackness and silence over level ground, through rough grass and among the small twisted trees of the northern Transvaal. McClipper walks easily but I must hurry to keep up with him — his stride is much longer than mine. I do not mind, I am released at last from that cringing terror. I feel in command of myself again and a return to my private belief, temporarily lost, that I can face up to any situation. I am in control.

From time to time we appear to be on some kind of track that deteriorates from hard earth to thick dry sand. It holds the feet, you must work at walking. Sometimes McClipper stops dead, holds up a hand for us to stop, and listens, listens. We listen too, straining to hear what holds him. There is no sound in this life-less country. It is strange, there are no sounds of insects. The veld at night is always alive, there are always the clicks and rus-tles of birds or tiny creatures. Not here. No life, even in the trees, even in the grass. I have never known such a completely silent, dead and black countryside.

Then a dog begins barking; we must be near an African vil-lage, but we can see nothing. He barks and barks, and as we walk silently by, lunges at us with ferocious teeth. Fear of the dog, but a greater fear that his bark will wake someone. We have been warned: don't talk, sound carries far at night in the countryside; don't strike a light, it can be seen for miles, police patrols watch out for lights; don't go near villages, some of the Africans are not to be trusted, they are in the pay of the police; the border patrols use dogs and binoculars; be over the border while it is still dark.

After an hour of steady walking, McClipper says we have reached the point where he will turn back. Whispering, he shows us the general direction we must take to reach the border fence, about another hour's walking away. As we stand with him, far and faint a cock crows in the darkness, then another. McClipper says solemnly, 'You hear that cockcrow over there?' 'Yes.' 'And that one over there?' 'Yes.' 'If you follow a line that runs between those two cockcrows, you will be going the right way.'

How do you walk between the remembered sound of cockcrows? We have tried to take some sort of sighting of the general direction on a few stars that are now visible, all that can be seen in the intensely black night. There is no more track; nothing is visible in this difficult country in such complete darkness. Sometimes it is heavy sand that drags at our feet, pulling us down at each step; then fields of ploughed earth, waves of churned-up, broken ground over which we climb and stumble, rise and sink. The bushes with their long stiletto thorns are a constant hazard; they are dark patches that cannot be identified until you have walked into them, then they stab at hands and legs, pierce clothes, entangle everything. You must tear yourself out of these thorn traps, they are like hooks that try to hold you. The ground falls away into holes, ankle-twisting pits into which we fall.

The time for reaching the border has passed. The fence is a mirage, a ghost that leaps into sight always a little ahead, then dissolves into nothing as we approach. How many times I have seen that fence, and each time a few more steps and it becomes a bush, an entanglement of thorns, a twisted tree. We change course, thinking that perhaps we are walking parallel to the border. When the ground clears of scrub, against the stars there is a distant hill made visible by the faint glow of reflected light in the sky beyond it. Surely that is Lobatsi — there is no other town anywhere near. So we walk towards the glow in the sky, hour after hour we see it beyond a hill. The hill dissolves, becomes another one, remote and unreachable; the glow remains beyond us, and there is no border.

Suddenly Rusty says: 'A glow like that in the sky, visible from such a distance — Lobatsi is too small. It must be Mafeking.' Have we really been walking for hours in the wrong direction, *back* towards Mafeking? We change direction again, turn away from the trap of the light reflected in the sky.

What time is it? It is too dark to see a watch. We are exhausted and stop to drink water and rest. I thought I could walk any distance, but my limbs are not prepared to take me. One leg has become painful and very stiff; it does not respond properly. The ground is very cold and after we have rested I have the greatest difficulty in walking again. Still the darkness and silence, intense and complete.

We light a small torch only once, to hold it to a compass, and from this we try to assess the direction we must take. Although we try to conceal the light, we are afraid to light it again; even a small glow is visible from afar.

We are without direction, floundering hopelessly in this hostile, stony country where night is a silent curtain. Perhaps we have walked in a circle. The stars have moved down the sky, we have abandoned them for they did not lead us to the border. When it gets light, Rusty says ... what point in carrying on? Shall we wait until dawn? Barren, cold ground with no insect-life, where only the sour wind and sharp dry grass survives. I can't rest, I must keep on walking, for if we stop for long I will not be able to stand up again.

I have fallen more than once. The ground falls away into holes again. Rusty stumbles into one like a pit, up to his waist. We'll break a leg or ankle, he says, this is useless. For the third time we try to stop and rest, for the third time I know that rest is fatal. It is hopeless to continue, but impossible to stop. Surely it must be time for dawn to come. Long night that never ends. Miserable country of holes and dagger-thorns.

At last there is an awareness of change; not so much that the sky lightens, as that darkness has diminished. Then an end to stars, and greyness spreads over the sky to reveal a desolate flat plain, a vast and empty expanse of land, deathly grey and dry after three years of continuous drought. No border fence; no huts, paths, people, nor any sign of life; nothing but straggling dead bushes, their thorns long and bleached; and the cold persistent wind that has blown across thousands of miles of desert to this bleak place.

And we know now that we are hopelessly lost; we have walked through the night and do not know where we are, nor in what direction to reset our course. Somewhere out of sight are men with Alsatians, standing where the land is higher, and scanning the countryside through binoculars. I am not afraid any more, only miserable beyond words at risking so much and coming so far to end up in this wind-scourged, drought-bitter land.

Light, but no sun. We go on walking and after a while find a sandy track, which must lead somewhere; walk along it for a while until Rusty says — look — tyre-marks; this must be a patrol road. In a panic, we quickly walk away from it, look for cover, but find nothing; humps in the ground flatten as we approach, what appear to be bushes dissolve into a thin tracery of twigs. As we search for a place to hide, we see some huts on the horizon. They appear to be part of a farm, which is probably white-owned; the buildings seem more substantial that those of a kraal, so we skirt around them and away. Farther on is an African kraal. No sign of life. We sit down and wait. After some time a man emerges and Rusty approaches him. They walk back towards me. He says he will show us the way to the border; it is not far, he says, the fence is over there. He is surly, unfriendly. Can we trust him? We walk quickly for about ten minutes, the land dips, and there, clearly visible, almost beyond belief, is the border fence, a double line of barbed wire with a strip of no man's land in between, at the base of two small hills. So we were less than a mile away. We almost run the last few hundred yards; we have thanked our taciturn guide and given him some money. Then we are over the first fence, and over the second and in Bechuanaland.

* * *

We had asked our guide the way to Lobatsi. He had waved a vague hand beyond the wire in the direction of a hill. 'Over there.'

'Is it far to Lobatsi?'

'Far,' he had answered, 'very far.'

For a short while we walk directly away from the border fence. When it is out of sight I have expended my final reserves. My muscles will no longer obey, they will not respond as they should; when I force them they painfully protest and impede each step.

273

So Rusty leaves me with the bags, huddled against a thorn tree in a useless attempt to obtain protection from the burning sun now high in the sky, and from the freezing, incessant wind.

In a moment he has gone beyond the sloping land and I am alone; lean back against the tree and fall into a doze. In a half world between waking and sleeping I am possessed by an uneasy dream of home. The hostile wind, the bare and empty land, combine to produce a sense of menace. *Home no longer a refuge but a place of danger — leave, leave. But I cannot leave, they need me, I have too many things to do. 'I cannot let thee go, I hold thee by too many bands ...'*

The staccato barking of a dog, half-heard, penetrates and pulls me back into the present. He stands some distance away from me, I am the intruder, he has revealed me and announces this with quick, sharp barks. Over the hill behind him a woman comes, walking with a curious lift of the leg and rolling of the body caused by some deformity of the hip. Rusty is with her. She comes to me, takes the bags, and leads me to her kraal over the hill. My pain and fatigue are visible to her; she encourages me, 'It is not far to go.'

The kraal is two reed-roofed mud huts in a courtyard of beige-coloured dust, ringed by a fence of twisted branches. There is one thorn tree, and nothing else. Nothing at all growing in a countryside unbelievably dry, barren and desolate. In this lonely and empty land that has long forgotten the feel of rain, the people have become dry and barren too, life has drained out of them, they are as grey as the wind-blown earth.

Because she once worked in Johannesburg for a while, the woman speaks some English. The men who sit around a small fire on the ground cannot communicate with us. A little girl, about eight years old, with trachoma-clouded eyes, stands in front of us and three times speaks to us in Sechuana. When we can only reply in English, she becomes impatient of our obtuseness and walks away to play with sticks in the sand.

The woman brings two small, crudely made chairs for us to sit on. My leg and knee are so painful and stiff, I am so tired, I can scarcely perch on the small chair. She observes, and limps into her hut, to come out again bearing a kaross and blankets. These she spreads on the ground, and motions us to lie on them. She brings a jug of water and apologizes because she has neither tea nor food. There is nothing except the hard mealie porridge the men are cooking in a pot over the fire.

'Where is Lobatsi?'

'It is far, too far.'

'If we start walking now, when will we be in Lobatsi?'

'If you start now, you will walk all day, and when night comes you will still not be in Lobatsi.'

Rusty and I discuss possibilities. We have friends in Lobatsi. If we can reach them by phone they might be able to arrange for a car to fetch us.

'Where is the nearest store?'

'It is far, very far.'

'Is there a telephone there?'

'No.'

'Where is the nearest telephone?'

'It is at Ramabatlana' — the border post, patrolled by the South African police.

'Isn't there a school anywhere here?'

'There is a school, but it is far.'

'Is there a telephone at the school?'

'No.'

No telephone, no store, no village, no method of communication. 'Can we hire donkeys?'

One of the men has two donkeys harnessed to a wooden sledge, which is loaded with brushwood for burning. She laughs, no, no, you cannot ride donkeys. Why not? No, no, no one rides donkeys.

'Are there horses?'

She thinks; she says there are some horses, but she does not know if we can get them.

She limps to join the men around the fire. She talks and talks, and they sit and argue with her. Eventually one of the men — her husband, we think — takes the donkey sleigh and goes to look for the man who has the horses. We lie in the sun and shade, and wait.

After a long time he returns to say that the horses are out in the fields and cannot be fetched.

The woman again joins the men around the fire, harangues

and harangues them. After a while one of them rises, fetches a bicycle from outside the hut, and goes in search of a man at a place called Good Hope, a man who, she thinks, may have a car.

Another hour passes. The man on the bicycle returns to say that the man with the car is not there.

Again, the rapid argument around the fire. The men scarcely move. She worries them, she beats them with words, she pours out torrents of words on their apathetic shoulders. They resist her, they do not want to move from the fire, they have no desire to do anything any more; they are not interested in us. The drought has destroyed what work there was in the fields; three years of drought, three years of insufficient food, and the will to assert themselves in any way has gone.

Only the woman swings and limps around the kraal, bullies the men, tries to organize some form of transport for us. We, who are unknown to her. The woman must move, think, organize, survive, because there is a child playing in the dust; she cannot join the living dead around the fire.

She sends the man away on the bicycle to go and look for another man who is known to have horses. Then she takes a bucket on her head and walks three miles to fetch water. The water is thick, greenish-yellow, the colour and appearance of motor oil. She heats it on the fire, pours it into a basin and mixes in some salts. She puts a chair at the basin behind a screen of branches, makes me take off my slacks and put my feet in the water. Then with firm, strong hands she massages my swollen feet and legs, exclaiming with pity over the dried blood of the thorn scratches.

Midday comes and passes. We had wanted to be in Lobatsi before two o'clock on the afternoon of this day, because when Rusty fails to report to the police by two, they will know he has gone. It would be better for Toni if she could show the police a telegram from us. If she does not hear from us, she will not be able to tell them anything — where we have gone or anything else. She will not know that we have got through.

However, the country pace cannot be accelerated. The man on the bicycle returns to say that the man says his horses are sick and cannot be used. Blank country, blank life.

But the woman does not flag. The day moves on, too hot in

the sun, too cold in the shade. The men sit round the fire, the woman drives and drives them with her tongue.

In the late afternoon I hear the sound of something approaching — a sound like a cart. We look over the kraal fence, we see it, to our joy. Two horses and a parody of a cart, a few planks on wheels. This cart, the woman tells us, will take us to a village where we should find a man who has a car who may be going to Lobatsi.

Before we leave, one of the men who had been sent to the store hours earlier, arrives with tea, which she makes for us.

We drink the tea, we thank her, we give her some money which she did not ask for — and we say good-bye. She does not ask us any questions. She has not cared about payment. And I do not even know her name.

*　*　*

There is just enough room for me on the narrow seat beside the man driving the cart. Rusty must cling precariously to the back, sitting on the edge and hanging on with both hands. The driver whips his horses and sets off along a bumpy track, sometimes deviating to drive straight across country. We are flung around, I have to warn Rusty ahead of big bumps or he will be thrown off. This is a hair-raising ride, but I am so grateful not to be walking that I don't really care how uncomfortable it is. We stop at kraals here and there, where people gaze at us with friendly curiosity; our driver talks to them; he does not speak any English, and we cannot talk to him.

We finally approach a cluster of huts and we see that this is a small village with a girls' school. The girls wear the navy blue pleated serge gymslips and white blouses which were the standard uniform of English girls' schools in another decade. Our driver takes his cart to one of the huts, puts us and our baggage down, and drives off.

We have no idea where we are. If we are close to the border, meeting up with the wrong person could be dangerous, even fatal.

Outside the hut is a motor-car. Rusty says, 'There's a white man in the hut ...' We hesitate, but it is too late to back out. In any case, he has seen us, so we risk it and walk into the hut.

An African and a white man sit together at a table counting out a pile of money. There is a high iron bed with a pink taffeta cover on it, and sitting on the cover, a plump brown hen. Pinned round the wall are religious prints from some Victorian Bible — Nebuchadnezzar on hands and knees, naked but with a long grey beard, eating grass; a chocolate-box Christ, soft and characterless, with a shiny bright halo, his hand raised in blessing over small children; coloured photographs of the royal family.

The African rises as we enter, shakes hands, and introduces himself and the white man, a strange reversal of South African codes which do not permit a black man to speak first before a white. He offers us chairs. We say we have been told that here we might be able to get a lift to Lobatsi.

The white man says, 'I am going to Lobatsi in about twenty minutes. If you don't mind waiting, you may come with me.'

The two men finish counting out the money, put it into paper bags and conclude their discussion. As though to signal the end of their business, the hen cackles and hops off the bed, fluffing and fussing, and leaving a large brown egg on the pink coverlet.

We go outside to the car. The African shakes our hands again, and mentions casually the name of a South African political refugee who has crossed the border some weeks before — his way of telling us that he understands how two white people, dusty and unwashed, arrive off main traffic routes at this isolated village where only Africans live.

The white man — an agricultural officer employed by the British authorities — is equally discreet. We discuss the drought, the crop failure, the difficulties of agricultural development in a place where there is no irrigation, the erosion of the sparse grass because Africans keep too many donkeys. We drive first along a dusty track, then later join a wider road, and in about an hour we are in Lobatsi. At our request, he drops us at the post office. He has asked no questions, and does not even know who we are. The car journey has been about forty miles.

McClipper, did you know? Perhaps not. Probably you yourself had only the vaguest idea, when you warned me to be ready for a long, hard night's walk, and directed us to follow a trail that ran between the memory of the sound of two cock-calls, of how far it really was to Lobatsi.

4
Blowing in the Wind

Lobatsi is two streets that meet to form a T. At their junction is the railway station. If you follow the top arm of the T to the right beyond the station in two minutes you are outside the town and on the road back to South Africa. If you turn left just beyond the station and cross the railway lines, you pass the dusty compound of the police post with its Union Jack flying from a pole in the centre where the single-storey, corrugated-iron roofed buildings stand; officers in khaki shorts and bush jackets look like a caricature of some outpost of Empire; beyond in a permanent cloud of orange dust you approach the scattered shacks and houses where the people live.

If you follow the left arm of the top bar of the T, there are a few shops, and the town ends.

On the upright leg of the T, the general stores on each corner, the fly-ridden cafe with its cracked cups and tables awash with spilled mineral water, cold tea, vinegar from the chips; the hairdresser; the liquor store; a newly-opened bookshop with a very limited selection of paperbacks, a few educational and religious books; the Lobatsi Hotel; and a little farther down, but out of the centre of the town itself, a cluster of new buildings, a garage, a new post office, a chemist's shop.

Then the road snakes out of Lobatsi, past the abattoirs (this country has only one export apart from men — cattle) and a couple of miles farther on is the new Cumberland Hotel; another small location; dusty, scrubby bush; and the road runs north into Africa. There is only one road into Lobatsi, the road from South Africa that joins the top of the T; only one road out — the road to the north.

When you walk down the main street, everyone in the town knows you have passed by, who you were with, where you came from and where you are going.

This is not simply the idle curiosity of a small country town.

Everyone *is* spying on everyone else. Lobatsi is the gateway into and out of South Africa for all the 'politicals'. Organizations that are banned in South Africa have public representatives in Lobatsi. Refugees constantly cross the border, and all must come to Lobatsi to report to the police before going further. Possibly an African refugee might stay in the territory for a while without his presence being reported to the authorities, but any white who enters Bechuanaland cannot be concealed.

The bar of the Lobatsi Hotel is the centre of gossip among the local whites, almost all South Africans, upholders of apartheid. Don't stay at the Lobatsi Hotel, we are advised; it's not safe for you. The town, after all, is only three miles from the South African border. It is indeed a frontier town, like something out of a Western: crooked pavements with steps going up and down at different levels, and unpainted verandas; the stores mainly owned by Indians, some white-owned — have shapeless floral dresses hung on racks among the farm implements, bales of cloth, sweets, cottons, tinned foods and bags of mealie-meal, and a procession of spiky-legged African children present their tickies (threepenny pieces) for a twist of mealie-meal or salt or sugar.

Dust dominates the town; grey dust among the shops and pavements, orange-red dust along the road, rising in clouds all round the location, coating the dried bushes and small trees.

The police know everything that goes on: the South African police move freely backwards and forwards across the border and have nearly all the whites in the country ready to do unofficially what might be tricky for them to do themselves; the Protectorate police in Bechuanaland, under the authority of Britain, only want to avoid trouble. Refugees are potential trouble, therefore the sooner they move on and out the better.

You cannot expect co-operation from people who don't know who you are. We want to find an Indian shopkeeper, Azad, who will put us in touch with our friend Maulvi Cachalia. Azad owns a store in Lobatsi. We walk into the first Indian store we see and ask which is Azad's shop, but are met with evasion.

'Not here.'

'But which shop is his?'

'Don't know.' Heads shaking, glances at each other.

'Where can we find him?'

Silence. They turn away and pretend to be busy behind the counter.

We walk down the street and try in a shop further along. Eventually a youngster, less suspicious than the others, shows us the shop.

Azad says it is too far to walk to Maulvi's house, and lends us a truck and driver who takes us through the location and down a lonely track to a white house standing in a dusty yard, where a dog on a long chain refuses to bark at intruders.

The house is the centre to which refugees come. Maulvi Cachalia and Dan Tloome, who crossed the border together a few months ago, live here.

It is a bachelor establishment; a big, awkward, silent Bechuana girl is supposed to be looking after the house and cooking meals. Dan's wife is in Swaziland, where she works as a nurse and where his sons are at school. Family life for this small, quiet man fell to pieces two or three years ago under the impact of political pressures, government bans and economic difficulties arising from them. Maulvi's family is still in Johannesburg where for so many years he has been a familiar figure — one-time president of the Transvaal Indian Congress.

If we were destitute, as so many refugees are, we could stay here, but we are not. There is danger of kidnapping and as we are white, they think it better for us to go to the Cumberland Hotel. Maulvi and Dan take us to find Fish Keitsing, the ANC representative in Lobatsi, who will take us to report to the Bechuanaland authorities.

We are happy to see Fish, tough, wiry, smiling, unchanged, as full of vitality and talkative as ever. Fish. He hates the name and tells us solemnly he has adopted a new one: Ntwaitsili. 'Fish' carries with it suggestions of inferiority, 'Jim Fish' is slang and a derogatory South African term for 'African'. We want to please Fish and try to remember to use his new name; but it is long and complicated after the simple one-syllable word, and in any case he has been 'Fish' to us for so many years, it just slips out.

Fish was the eldest son in a Bechuana family of six children born in a little village, Khane, in the interior. His father was a peasant. When he was a young man, Fish enlisted with the Native Recruiting Organization as an indentured labourer on the

South African mines, and worked for years as a miner. This is the only way out of a primitive, dull, slow, unrewarding existence in the undeveloped, unproductive, under-populated places of Southern and Central Africa — the only way to earn cash for tools, cattle, taxes.

He went down the mine at 2 a.m. every day and emerged at 10 a.m., for which he earned 1s. 8d. a day, plus the usual concrete bunk in a mine compound, food, and medical attention. When his contracts ended he left the mines, went to live in Newclare (an African suburb of Johannesburg, with Sophiatown, now eradicated), and joined the African National Congress. With ANC volunteers Fish defied unjust laws in the Defiance Campaign of 1952 and served thirty-five days' sentence at a notorious and dreaded prison, Leeukop Farm Jail. When he came out he became very active in Congress work.

One night there was one of those pre-dawn pass and permit raids in the Western Areas, when the police behave like an army of occupation, bash down doors, drag people shivering out of their beds, and load them into the *kwela-kwela*, the pickup van, off to jail. One police team had netted about thirty victims who were huddled together, handcuffed, on a street corner, waiting for the *kwela-kwela*. Out of the dark came Fish Keitsing who calmly ordered the African policemen in charge of the victims to release them. A crowd of onlookers backed him up. Astounded, the police obeyed. As they retreated in the direction of the nearest telephone, they allege they saw Fish Keitsing reading out the names of the jubilant victims, one by one, to hand them back their pass books and their freedom.

This was the exploit that earned Fish the name of 'Robin Hood' of Newclare. He was inevitably arrested, charged with assisting prisoners to escape from custody, and sentenced to a year's imprisonment. While he was still serving the sentence he was charged with treason, and brought to court to join the other men and women so charged. The treason trialists were soon out on bail, went home each night to their own families if they lived in Johannesburg, or to the families with whom they were boarding. Only Fish came to court each day in custody from the Johannesburg Fort, and went back to his cell each night until his sentence was finished.

The story of Newclare's Robin Hood was presented by the State as evidence in the trial. Defence counsel, unmoved by its romantic features, challenged the admissibility of the evidence; the prosecutor solemnly explained that the campaign against pass laws was carried out by members of the liberation movement in furtherance of the treason plot.

Fish returned to Bechuanaland at the end of the treason trial and now organizes the onward route for refugees. He is on the friendliest terms with everyone — even first-name terms with the Chief of the local police — and everyone shouts greetings to him when he drives by. A few days before we arrived, the ANC van that he drives had been blown up in his front yard by saboteurs. He is a target for enemies as well as a rallying point for friends.

In a borrowed truck, Fish picks us up in the morning and takes us to the Bechuanaland Police offices just beyond the railway station.

The politest policeman we have ever met in our lives interviews us. We are fingerprinted, photographed against the wall of his office in the brilliant sunshine, questioned, and given three months' asylum as political refugees.

Tall and smoothfaced, the Lobatsi Security Chief, Sheppard, asks questions but never comments. His questions appear to be routine, on a form, but experience makes us evasive. We do not believe the senior security men in Lobatsi pass information on to the South African Special Branch but we know what everyone in South Africa knows. Somehow, by someone, the information given to the authorities in Bechuanaland, as in the other Protectorates, ends up in the files of the Special Branch in South Africa.

We are prepared only to give harmless information. What organizations did we belong to? We tell him, but only of the time when they were legal and we were permitted to belong to them. After we were banned, we are not prepared to say. What political activity were we engaged in? Why did we have to leave illegally? What made us decide to go? How did we reach the frontier? Where did we cross the border? Who guided us? Who did we speak to? ... our answers are vague and evasive. There are long periods of silence when we say no more and Sheppard does not press a question. His chief comment is 'Good-oh'.

As we leave his office, a Malay, unshaven, untidy, sitting on a chair outside, greets us by name; but we do not know him. He looks utterly exhausted, near collapse.

* * *

We have been in Lobatsi for a week, and the prospect of moving on seems farther away than when we arrived.

How does the refugee from South Africa move on from here? A railway runs along the eastern border, from Lobatsi through Francistown. But it starts from South Africa, and after leaving Francistown enters Rhodesia; and is under South African management. Only recently the Rhodesian authorities took a group of African refugees off a train and sent them back to South Africa. A South African Indian refugee who boarded the train at Lobatsi was dragged off farther up the line and beaten up by whites.

There are no regular plane flights, only a private air charter company — South African owned — with an office in Lobatsi.

No, only one way — the road, the long, difficult road to the north; through bush, jungle, desert; 600 miles from Lobatsi to Kasani, the last police post at the border into Northern Rhodesia; 300 miles from Kasani to Lusaka, capital of Northern Rhodesia (Zambia). These are only the first stages of the journey.

Refugees travel without documents or papers. They have no passports, and are identifiable only by their own word, or that of people who may know them. When they have crossed one border illegally they must then be legally admitted across new borders and obtain a transit permit to cross Northern Rhodesia. Who are they? They say they are refugees from political persecution in South Africa, and there have been hundreds of these, whites and blacks. But there have also been South African Government agents and spies claiming to be refugees. What did you do in South Africa? Why did you have to leave? What organizations did you belong to? Sheppard is not the only one who wants answers to these questions.

The African National Congress of South Africa had its external headquarters in Dar-es-Salaam (now in Lusaka), and has offices in other African countries. Its representatives are known and respected; if the ANC says: we know this man or woman, we worked with them in South Africa, the refugee is likely to get entry permits, transit permits; even so, organizing the way out is difficult. And who wants you if you are not known?

We are fortunate in having the friendship and assistance of the ANC. Even so, we come up against difficulties in organizing our journey on.

We have the right to stay for only three months in Lobatsi; we do not, in any case, have enough money to live in an hotel for three months.

There is a refugee camp in Francistown and with other refugees we are waiting until overland transport can be arranged. One truck has been ready for some time, but a second truck is being repaired. It should be ready in a few days, Fish says. For the journey north, after Francistown, trucks must travel in twos — the journey is too dangerous, the country too isolated for one.

Meanwhile Fish, Dan and Maulvi agree that it would be unwise for us to go to Francistown and wait there. Francistown is too close to the South African border; it is surrounded by farms owned by whites who are openly hostile. They have just burned down a new building put up to house refugees. Conditions in the camp itself are difficult enough without us.

Francistown has an airfield, but it is owned by the Witwatersrand Native Labour Association. The WNLA recruits men for work on the gold mines of the Witwatersrand; for this profitable traffic, this most valuable of the country's exports, they have constructed their own private airfield to fly the men down to the mines in the south and back again when their contracts are finished. They allow chartered planes to use their field, but are difficult about refugee planes. It was on their Francistown airfield that the plane sent to fetch Goldreich and Wolpe was blown to pieces.

So stay in Lobatsi, they tell us.

Almost every day for a week we have walked into town to find out how the repairs to the truck are progressing. Each day a new difficulty. It will be ready in three or four days; the garage says they need a spare part and must send to Mafeking; the spare part cannot arrive until next week; Mafeking cannot supply the spare part, they are sending to Johannesburg; it should be put on tomorrow's train; the spare part does not arrive; the garage has found something else wrong with the truck as well. Maulvi mutters, 'That garage — they're not repairing the truck, they're sabotaging it.' He may be right.

The day after we arrived, walking into town from the hotel, we passed a garage. Rusty said, 'Let's see if they have a map of this place. I want to try and find out where we were last night.'

An Indian came up to us and we asked him if we could buy a road map.

'I haven't one,' he said.

'Don't you keep any maps here?'

'No, none at all.' He looked at us. 'But wait a minute. I have a map of my own at home. I will get it for you. It will only take a moment.'

'What about the other garages? Don't they have maps?'

'No, no, there are no maps. But I have a map. You can have my map.

We thanked him but said it did not matter. He insisted.

'No, you must have it. I'll get it. You'll need it.' And then, putting a finger to his lips: 'Don't worry! I know everything!'

In this town everyone knows everything.

Every day during the week — sometimes more than once a day — Sheppard or his assistant Higgins, or both, come to visit us to find how we have progressed with our plans to leave. They are polite, they are oblique, they never say very much, but they are anxious for us to be gone. It is their district. Trouble for us, in their district, will be trouble for them.

There have been too many unpleasant incidents involving refugees in the Protectorates — assaults, kidnapping over the South African border. The results are always a nuisance, questions asked in Parliament in London, someone kicking up a fuss, the British High Commissioner having to make investigations. We know there is a very secret squad of the South African police which specializes in these incidents. It is generally believed that they organize the kidnapping, not in uniform, but ostensibly as ordinary white civilians; always the deed is done in such a way that the police must have had a hand in it. Anderson Ganyile was kidnapped from Basutoland by South African police and smuggled secretly to a jail in the Transkei. It took months for this to emerge and an international scandal before he could regain his freedom. Dr Abrahams was kidnapped from South-West Africa and brought to South Africa. Rosemary Wentzel was kidnapped from Swaziland and taken to solitary confinement in a Pretoria jail. There were protests, but the British authorities delayed, and she finally bought her release by becoming a State witness against her former colleagues. It is difficult to keep kidnapping quiet; but once it has been done, it can be too late to set it right again.

Sheppard keeps a careful check on us so that he knows what is happening, but we would be foolish to think we are getting any real protection from the Bechuanaland authorities.

Most days we walk from the hotel to Lobatsi; sometimes Fish borrows a truck and comes to pick us up. If we walk, we go to the general store owned by Azad, where we drink boiled-milk tea and talk to Youssef Omar, who is helping in the shop as he waits for his future to be settled.

Youssef Omar is the unshaven Malay who was outside Sheppard's office the morning after our arrival. He had crossed the border the same night as we did, only he had walked eight nights to get there from Johannesburg — eight nights, sleeping in holes in the ground away from the road during the day. Omar had belonged to an underground group, the African Resistance Movement, ARM, every one of whose members is now in jail or out of the country. He knew the police were looking for him and decided to leave. Youssef had already served a year's sentence on a political charge; in jail, he had been in solitary, beaten and tortured by electric shocks. He could not be sure he would stand up to it again. 'I would talk, man, I couldn't stand it again.'

Like us, he is hoping to be able to join the overland transport. Every day we expect a departure date.

Nobody takes any notice of us, and we feel safely anonymous. Even so — a sense of unease. One afternoon I go to the hairdresser. Rusty says he will meet me in town in an hour. He does not arrive on time. Suddenly I panic. I go out into the street, straining to see if he is coming; run back into the shop and phone the hotel. They say he has gone out some time ago. I run up the street in a fever of anxiety — I should not have left him to walk in alone; it is a quiet country road, therefore it is dangerous. A car with local whites in it could drive past, see him walking by himself — they could kidnap him, assault him, even kill him; there would be no witnesses. Past experience has shown that those responsible for such acts are never named, tracked down, or brought to court. Rusty has to walk, because there is no public transport in Lobatsi, and no taxis or private cars that can be hired.

At last, there he is in the distance walking along the road towards me. I cannot let him out of my sight again; I must stay close to his side; we must be together all the time. Whatever happens must happen to both of us together.

Three days after our arrival, at Dan and Maulvi's house, Saturday, lunchtime, Dan switched on the radio to listen to the news broadcast from Johannesburg: 'Lionel Bernstein, the Johannesburg architect recently acquitted in the Rivonia trial, has arrived in Lobatsi with his wife Hilda … ' The lull was over. Dan says, 'Now you will have to be careful.'

We had arranged that afternoon to meet two white friends of ours, Jim and Riva, former South Africans who were living in Lobatsi. They were so afraid of being seen in our company that they would not come to the Cumberland Hotel, but asked us to walk along the road beyond the hotel; they would pick us up in their car. We drove with them through the swirling dust, the colourless and distressed countryside, until we found a place to pull off the road. There we sat beneath shrivelled trees, drinking coffee out of a thermos, while they told us of the empty and sterile life they led, the vicious hatred of the Lobatsi whites towards deviants like ourselves, their fear and dislike of the blacks.

Being away from the hotel that afternoon was a stroke of luck. After the broadcast, the Press descended; we were newsworthy, they wanted stories. The hotel had been besieged with phone calls all afternoon.

At dinner, in the hotel dining-room, a man sitting at the next table said in a loud clear voice: 'Have you heard that fellow Bernstein is here in Lobatsi? It was on the lunchtime news.' We concentrated on our food. So far they had not identified us. But our invisibility was wearing off.

As it was Saturday, a film was being shown in a hall next to the hotel. The film: *The Guns of Navarone*. Hard-seated chairs in a cold and draughty hall; the hotel manager sitting at a table at the door collecting the money. I could not concentrate on the film; the danger and suspense made me uneasy. I did not want the tensions of the story; there is enough suspense in real life.

Half-way through the film the manager came up and whispered to Rusty that there were two men outside who wanted to see him. Sheppard and Higgins. Have you made any further plans? We had not.

Sheppard asked, 'Have you inquired about a flight north at the local plane company?'

'No.'

'You didn't approach those people?'

'Do you think I should?' Rusty asked.

Sheppard never gave a direct answer. 'I don't think I could advise you. But there has been some talk around town. You know how it is.'

'What sort of talk?'

'Well, they were talking about bombing the airstrip ...'

We again assured him that we had not approached the local company, and did not intend to do so. Sheppard managed to convey to us that we should act carefully. It might just be a lot of bar-talk, but ...

'There is too much loose talk around town,' he said, and told us he would come and see us in the morning.

I was pleased to abandon *The Guns of Navarone*. We locked our bedroom door that night, and the door leading out on to the balcony. They were back again on Sunday morning, and we had another vague interview which did not seem to take us anywhere except to give us the feeling we were definitely not safe. And when they had left there was a hoarse hurried phone call from Riva: 'Are you all right? Listen, don't go out today. Stay in the hotel. Keep in your room ...' She had heard something in the Lobatsi Hotel bar.

We did. The tedium of doing nothing in an hotel bedroom cannot be compared with the tedium of jail; we did not complain.

In the afternoon Sunday newspapers from Johannesburg, we read an embroidered story of our flight across the border, admiring the front-page pictures of our children: Headline: 'The family the fugitives left.' The report quoted Ivan as saying, 'Overnight I have become the owner of a house, a car and three children.'

From our balcony we could see the Sunday life of the little location across a field in the distance, at the foot of some hills. The deep brown shadows on the red-brown pondokkies; a dog barking distantly; someone shouting, a gramophone playing, the wind whirling the red dust. But no singing. In Johannesburg, on a Sunday, a location would be full of the sound of singing. And there would be parades of women in their colourful blue and white church uniforms, chanting and carrying a banner. Bechuanaland lacks song, it has a listless air.

* * *

Monday. The most dangerous time, the weekend, has passed. We must find out what is happening about the road transport.

First we go to the garage where we find Fish, and receive the inevitable news of further delays. Fish says the truck cannot possibly be ready before the end of another week.

When we come out of the garage there is a big yellow Ford Galaxie outside, with three hefty-looking whites in it. It has an SAS numberplate (South African Railways).

Refugees must report on Monday mornings to the police. We walk over to the police compound and check in with Sheppard. When we leave, the Galaxie is parked just outside the compound. We walk down the road to Azad's shop and stop to have tea and talk to Omar. When we leave, the Galaxie is waiting outside the shop, starts up, and follows us down the street.

A little later we are at the chemist's shop to buy a few toilet articles. When we come out the Galaxie has gone, but now there is a red Volkswagen with a South African number-plate from Cape Town; we had noticed it in town earlier.

We walk down to the station. Toni has packed a suitcase with some clothes for us, and railed it from Johannesburg to Lobatsi. We want to see if it has arrived. For once, the wind has stopped blowing and the winter sun is hot. We do not hurry, but attract unwanted attention. The stationmaster and some other white railway employees gather in a group and watch us, then follow us out of the station; they stand and watch us walk down the street. The red Volkswagen is there.

Back at the hotel the Press have been phoning repeatedly. They all want to know our plans; when are we leaving, and how? We also have a call from Rhodesian Television in Bulawayo. On a poor line, with both of us shouting at each other, some man says he wants to charter a plane and interview us when we arrive at Francistown, because it is too far to come to Lobatsi. He says, 'Will you phone me when you are leaving, and let me know if you will be in Francistown, or where you are going?' I say yes to end the discussion, but will not do so. It would be crazy to announce our plans over the phone to Rhodesian Television or anyone else.

On the way down to dinner in the evening a smiling African intercepts us; a thin, well-spoken, greying man with an unfamiliar face. He shakes hands and says he has been asked by one of the South African newspapers to find out the latest news of our plans. We have nothing to say to him, but we talk for a few minutes; and ask him a couple of questions. Then he tells us he actually works for the Bechuanaland Information Department, and getting news is a sideline. We are coming to know a little about the devious ways of Sheppard. This man may actually be sending news to South Africa; but on the other hand, it may be one of Sheppard's ways of crosschecking on our plans.

The only books left in the bookshop that I have not read are those I don't want to read. Oh, Lobatsi! The next morning, we are in town once again seeking news of the truck repair. We go down to the refugee house and find it is being stripped, scrubbed and transformed. Furniture stands outside, floors are being washed, windows are wide open. Three women refugees have arrived and they are hard at work making the house more livable.

They are Duma Nokwe's wife, Tiny, Alfred Nzo's wife, Regina, and Tandi, a shy, silent woman from Port Elizabeth who has succeeded in her second attempt at crossing the border. The first time she was arrested at the border and taken off to jail for ninety days.

Even the helpless Bechuana girl is working. The kitchen drawers are being emptied of their stale ends of bread, dirty cutlery and paper bags.

'That car yesterday,' says Maulvi, 'you remember that car that was following you around?'

'The yellow Ford?'

'No, the Volkswagen. You know what happened? It's not a good idea to walk around.' He stutters a bit when he gets excited. 'N-n-nno. Better try and arrange to get out; no, you can't wait for the truck.'

'It's not advisable to wait for the truck. It's going to take too long,' Dan says.

'No, they can't go by road, in any case; it will be too dangerous for them.'

'And it will draw attention to the whole convoy.'

'What happened to the Volkswagen?' we want to know.

'Well, Tiny and Regina went to the police compound yesterday afternoon to report their arrival. While they were there the Bech. police brought in the red Volkswagen with its driver. The police then searched the car, and took a shotgun out of it.'

'How do they know?'

'They saw it — here, ask them. They saw the police confiscate the gun.'

Tiny comes and says, 'They sent the car and driver back over the border to South Africa.'

One man who was trailing us with a gun has gone. But how many more are there?

Lobatsi is not safe.

* * *

We have agreed with Maulvi, Dan and Fish, that we cannot go on the overland transport. If we did, the departure would be splashed in the Press and the whole operation under public scrutiny. Anywhere on the road, the long empty road between Francistown and Kasani, something could happen to the trucks. We have become a danger to the others. 'Even if the truck were ready,' Dan says, 'you couldn't go on it now. If it had left immediately, before the publicity ... And we don't think you should

292

hang around Lobatsi in any case, waiting for it. It will take too long.'

A week after our arrival in Lobatsi, we try to make other arrangements to leave. We phone air charter companies in Northern and Southern Rhodesia. We don't want to do it from the hotel; too many people could listen to our plans. Each call takes a long time to come through; half an hour, an hour. Rusty has phoned a company at Livingstone. They were very vague about the possibility of chartering a plane and said he should phone back later. He phoned Lusaka, too. A company there advertises itself as running a charter plane service. But they were also vague. They don't know if a plane is available to fly to Bechuanaland, and cannot give any idea of what the cost would be.

We put through calls to Salisbury. We are not happy at the idea of chartering a plane from Southern Rhodesia, but the company does have planes that fly down as far as Cape Town. At Salisbury they seem unable to say whether or not they have a plane to come to Bechuanaland; they tell us to phone the company headquarters at Livingstone.

Eventually we get through to Livingstone, the same office we first phoned. We are told they do not have a plane available for charter. Yes, they are a charter company; yes, they do have charter planes. But at the moment they haven't a plane that we can charter. When will one be available? They don't know. Another call to Lusaka draws another blank.

All this takes two full days. We are gradually driven to believe that the various companies in the phone books are either all one company with different names, or else operate together. And that as far as we are concerned, refugees from South Africa with considerable notoriety, there will be no charter planes available.

The Press phones the hotel incessantly.

Everybody in Lobatsi knows who we are and likes or loathes us accordingly. There is a British Parliamentary delegation representing Conservative, Liberal and Labour Parties at present in the town; they have been touring the Protectorates. They know who we are, but scrupulously avoid greeting us; except for the two Labour Party members who come to talk to us one night in the privacy of our room.

293

A big, overweight, rugby-type South African sits in a corner of the dining-room eating enormous quantities of meat. He glances at us, and away, and I think he would cheerfully stick a knife in our backs; but early next morning he comes to our room, introduces himself. He is going back to Johannesburg, asks if we would like anything done such as messages delivered to the children, and wishes us luck.

A waiter passes and murmurs friendly remarks or drops words of advice. 'Be careful,' he mutters one morning as he passes our table, 'there are two *dogs* outside. They are — excuse me,' he says, '*dirty pigs*.'

In the bar one evening Fish, Dan, Regina, Tiny and another ANC man, Joe, come over for a drink and a talk, bringing with them a little man with greying hair and prominent teeth. He is introduced to us as a local chief who is in town to meet the British Parliamentary delegation. We sit and drink together. The chief has a splendid flow of English and a roguish sense of humour. There is much talk and laughter, and soon the African barman is enjoying it almost as much as we are. He stands grinning from ear to ear, enchanted, his eyes following whoever is speaking; he laughs when we laugh. There are no legal barriers to prevent social mixing of black and white in Bechuanaland, as there are in South Africa. But economic differences and social status constitute their own barriers. Africans scarcely enter a place like the Cumberland Hotel, except as servants, waiters, cleaners, delivery men. The barman has probably never seen white guests at the hotel drinking together on terms of social equality with Africans.

* * *

This morning it is cold outside. An icy wind is blowing once more, the wind that rarely seems to die down in Bechuanaland. The location is enveloped in clouds of dust; funnels of dust swirl and dance across the veld. All over this huge country the wind pesters the arid earth — where has all the topsoil gone? It's blowing in the wind, the persistent, uneasy wind.

Meanwhile, on the advice of our ANC friends here, we have sent a telegram to Tom Nkobi who runs the ANC office in

Lusaka. We don't know his phone number, so we have wired him to ask him to phone us at the hotel.

We sit in the sun, out of the wind, on the hotel veranda, reading and waiting for phone calls. It is a morning of furious activity in the hotel, with preparations for the luncheon, local VIPs arriving, cars driving up with guests; and we too have visitors. Dan comes with another ANC man to chew over the problem of getting away. Small, quiet, restrained — in another country Dan would have been a scholar, perhaps a research worker, or a professor teaching a new generation. His personality does not seem right for the type of life he has had to lead.

Higgins also visits us this morning, and a little later Sheppard, who is polite and cagey as usual. We sometimes feel that Sheppard, cast in the role of a Security man, is determined to act absolutely true to type. He has never made a direct suggestion of any kind to us; but has ways of talking round a subject. He rather likes plotting. He certainly keeps himself informed of every single thing that happens. When we reported to him the two cars that had followed us, he took down all details, made no comment, but we knew that he had already dealt with the Volkswagen.

At this time, two months before Northern Rhodesia is due to become independent Zambia, we must get permission from the authorities there for transit through to Tanganyika. The ANC's Lusaka office is trying to do this for us.

Sheppard visits us twice. The morning visit is routine, then in the afternoon he says he must speak to us privately in our room. He has some highly confidential information. He has just heard through Government channels that the Northern Rhodesian authorities have given us a transit permit.

Half an hour after Sheppard has gone Fish comes breezing in to show us a telegram from Lusaka, which says that the ANC has obtained clearance for us to pass through Northern Rhodesia on our journey out.

Tom Nkobi phones us. We explain our predicament and he says he will see what can be done.

In the evening, for a couple of hours, we forget the truck, the spare parts that never arrive, the refugees waiting in boredom in Francistown, the men in cars, the threats. Tiny and Regina and

Tandi cook supper for us all at the refugee house, Dan makes a blazing wood fire so big that we roast and can barely see each other through the smoke. We recall the days when we could, and did, work together — the big conferences and demonstrations; the mass meetings on Sunday mornings in Number Two Square, Alexandra Township, or Freedom Square, Fordsburg; the great mine strike of 1946, the squatters movement when 'the people overflowed' and set up their shacks and shanties on the veld; the bus boycotts, the women's anti-pass demonstrations; packed rallies on the City Hall steps; the Defiance Campaign, and the fight to prevent the destruction of the Western Areas and Sophiatown, with its bounding vitality; the endless situations involving outwitting the police, the armed men invading meetings; Ida Mntwana leading the triumphant singing of freedom songs in a joyous surge of the assertion of power, while the police fumbled nervously through handbags and pockets. Meetings in locations, meetings in tiny candle-lit rooms, meetings in halls and houses, meetings in cars, meetings in the bushes, on the veld. Loud voices and easy laughter of South Africans. Optimism, confidence, the unquenchable vitality of South Africans. Where have all our comrades gone? They're in prison or exile, every one. Comradeship, hope, purpose. We are leaving it all. That, too, is blowing in the wind.

5

The Road to Palapye

Tom Nkobi phones again from Lusaka. He has chartered a plane to fly to Palapye on Monday morning and pick us up; we must be at Palapye fairly early and wait for the plane.

Palapye is a village with a landing strip, to the north of Lobatsi and on the road to Francistown.

At the house we discuss how to get to Palapye. 'If I had a truck I would drive you there,' says Fish. The only other way is to board the train which comes from Mafeking and reaches Lobatsi every night at half-past eleven. It arrives in Palapye at four in the morning. Go to the station without booking tickets beforehand; once on the train there should be no dangers or difficulties; get off at Palapye in the early hours of the morning; the plane should come and pick us up before anyone even realizes we are there.

It seems reasonable enough. Rusty thinks it will be all right. Perhaps it is just the tension of the past few weeks that makes my mind shy off the thought of that train journey.

From the house we walk back to town through the dusty location. We pass the house close to the location houses, where a white man lives and keeps leopards in cages. The cages are big wire-netting constructions in the open under scattered trees. There are several leopards stretched lean and long and graceful as though growing out of the branches; but it is very hot, the smell is appallingly strong. Leopards are dangerous in the bush, but why keep them in stinking cages?

Even when we pass groups of children, this place lacks the noise and life of the townships 'over there' — across the border. There is malnutrition in every South African location, and often severe, as the children lying with kwashiokor in hospitals prove; but still there is life in the South African locations that springs around you in the streets. The children will run after you shouting, 'Ullo, seester!' with good-natured grins. Perhaps the last three years of drought, of uncultivated land, of no crops, have brought these people too close to starvation; a rapid dwindling of life.

A van passes bearing a loudspeaker and decorated with the emblems of the Bechuanaland People's Party. Elections will take place soon, the first step towards independence. What immense changes are needed, how much building-up from almost nothing, how many schools and hospitals, how many industries must develop, before the people of the new Botswana can themselves be free. Can people made listless by insufficient food and indifferent by the grey hopelessness of their lives inject the necessary effort into it?

When we pass the station, Rusty pauses to have a look at the timetable. There is a train every night of the week except Sunday. This means we will have to leave on the Saturday night train and spend another day and night in Palapye.

So on Saturday we prepare to go. We have told Sheppard our plans. We have gone to town in the morning to meet our friends in one of those typical vague Lobatsi arrangements of unspecified time and place. We have sat for a while in the greasy and fly-spotted tearoom, watching the procession of shabby Africans and ragged thin children buying cigarettes and chips. We have discussed the final arrangements and gone back to the hotel and packed our cases. We will have supper at the hotel and sign out without prior notice. Fish will borrow a truck again and pick us up after supper. He will take us down to the refugee house, where we will stay until it is time to go to the station.

I am increasingly apprehensive.

We wait with our cases at the side of the hotel, in the dark. Fish arrives at a quarter to nine, cheerful as always, and drives us down to the house; the room is cold and filled with wood smoke. I did not want to leave the hotel. While we were at the hotel, I felt, they would be reluctant to do anything to us. We could retire at night and lock the door of our room. I am reluctant to creep out of this hole and face new difficulties and unknown dangers.

Lobatsi, with its secretive and menacing atmosphere, its rumours and whispers, and men standing on street corners. Today South African Security Police crossed the border and came to Lobatsi. They were from Johannesburg, and brought along Youssef Omar's brother-in-law with a message. We want you, Omar, to return to Johannesburg with us. You will just have to answer a few questions, and we will give you indemnity from arrest; we guarantee your safety. But if you refuse, we will arrest your wife and hold her indefinitely. Sergeant Dirker is now sitting in your home, awaiting our instructions.

Omar's brother-in-law said: 'They simply brought me along to tell you this. I can't advise you — you know best what to do.'

'Does your wife know anything at all?' we ask Youssef.

'Nothing, nothing. She has never been involved.' He cannot bear to think of her becoming a hostage.

But what value can be put on the promise of indemnity of the Special Branch? They do not have the slightest intention of keeping any 'honourable' promises if it does not suit them. They obviously want him as a witness against others. If Omar does not give satisfactory evidence or answer questions satisfactorily, what good will a verbal promise do him in Johannesburg? He will end up in jail. If his wife knows nothing, they may arrest her, but they cannot hold her indefinitely. If they are going to arrest her, they will do so regardless of Omar.

Everyone agrees that Omar's return would be fatal. Colonel Klindt himself has come with the posse as far as Mafeking and stayed there, while the others under a Colonel Britz continued to Lobatsi. They are returning tonight; he must make up his mind.

At half past ten Fish comes to take us to the station. Maulvi is coming to see us on to the train.

Outside the house the location lies in darkness. As we drive over the sandy, bumpy tracks, dust rises in great clouds and spins away into the night behind us. Fish drops us some distance from the station, on the far side of the railway line. It is a good night for him, moonless and misty; he has an assignment to meet some more refugees at the border.

Darkness and silence. And I am afraid. A single platform serves trains from both directions; at one end is a small square building, the ticket office, and outside this building a single electric light bulb burns in a halo of mist. The platform is completely deserted. No porters, guards or other passengers. We are the only ones who have come for the train — who takes a train from Lobatsi to anywhere? Nobody.

We three, Rusty, Maulvi and I, cross the tracks, our footsteps crunch on the loose grey stones over which the rails are laid, a penetrating sound in the silence. We approach the platform from the end furthest away from the office — and the light. We climb up, stand in the shadows of a group of tall wattle trees, put down our bags and wait; Maulvi walks up the platform towards the office to get tickets for us.

No sound of the train yet. It is probably leaving Mafeking. Behind the wattle trees there is an open station yard, beyond the yard the main street of the town. It is all asleep and silent. No lights, no people, no cars, no sound or movement; only the small upright back of Maulvi retreating from us towards the light.

At that moment — perhaps for a second I thought it was the sound of the train, but it was not — as though from nowhere, beams of lights like searchlights sweep across the platform. A car, a Land-Rover, drives at speed into the station yard, stops with a squeal of brakes; the lights switch off. Immediately behind, another car drives into the station area. The doors open, men get out of the two cars.

These are not passengers for our train, and we know it. We strain to see who it is, standing partially concealed by the trunks of the wattles. 'What are they, whites or Africans?' Rusty says, 'Whites.'

They are big men, at least six of them, and in the cold quiet air of the night their voices carry — we do not know what they are saying, but the language is distinguishable as Afrikaans. In size and shape and manner they are unmistakably the Special Branch.

They walk on to the platform and stand together next to the ticket office. One of them, a big man with his overcoat collar turned up round his head, starts pacing slowly up the platform towards us.

The single light burns, the train does not come, the men move and talk beneath the light, their breath misty — it is one of those films of mist and darkness when you do not know exactly what is happening. Now I am involved in this film, not as a spectator but as an unwilling participant. I do not know my part; I do not know what I must do next. When we were young and went to

300

the cinema we grabbed each other with fearful delight and terror; our hearts beat faster at such moments.

I might cry out like de Keller, 'Lobatsi, Lobatsi, wake up, wake up! They are taking us away!' But who is there to hear? Where are Sheppard's men — Sheppard, who has seen us every single day in Lobatsi, sometimes twice a day, who knows the South African Security men are here — and knows we are going to board the train. We peer backwards and forwards in the darkness, but there is no one else anywhere in sight, only the men on the platform.

Come, train!

One man, Colonel Britz, paces slowly down the platform; each step is sharp and clear and slow; paces slowly, deliberately, passes the trees into whose shadows I wish hopelessly to dissolve, continues to the end of the platform, turns on his heel, paces as slowly back again. He does not look at us as he passes, but there is the slightest movement of his head — he is aware of us.

In five minutes the train will arrive.

Then Maulvi comes hurrying back down the platform towards us. 'I didn't get your tickets. It's the Special Branch. You mustn't get on the train … '

It seems to me the train will be escape. If they don't do anything to us before it arrives, we can get away on the train.

'If we don't get on the train, what are we to do? How can we get away from them? We must get on the train,' I insist.

'No, no, you can't get on the train. They will get you. If not here, then further down the line. It happened to M. They pulled him off the train somewhere down the line and beat him up. They phone through to their friends.'

Maulvi tells us what has happened at the ticket office. When he saw the cars coming, he stopped to see who they were. He saw the men get out, then a minute or two later he heard someone call him softly, ssss-sssss, from the side of the office. A man, standing in the shadows — someone Maulvi knew, who said: 'They are the Special Branch. They heard the Bernsteins are leaving tonight. That's why they are here. You had better warn them.'

In the distance we hear at last the sound of the train. When it comes into the station, we will run away.

301

'In a moment,' says Maulvi, 'jump off the platform — down there — ' with a great noise and bright lights the train pulls in to Lobatsi station — 'now!'

And we jump off the high platform into the sandy yard, behind the wattle trees, we run past the police cars and out of the yard; across the street; push open a gate and into the back-yard of a house.

Have they seen us? Once off the platform it is almost completely dark. The train lights illuminate the area, but we were behind the curtain of the trees. And what, in any case, would they have done? Would they have prevented us boarding the train; or would they, as Maulvi thought, simply have made sure we were on it, so that they could plan some action further down the line? The staff on the trains is all South African; the men who work for the railways are all upholders of apartheid.

Lobatsi might be too public a place; but where the train goes anything could be done; nobody would know. No evidence, no witnesses.

Huddled on the stoep of someone's house in the dark, we hear the preliminary sounds of the train's departure; the doors slam, the whistle blows; then the first slow statement of engine and wheels, mounting rhythm and gathering speed.

The train is a thin snake of light in the unbounded blackness of the continent. We hear it accelerating away from Lobatsi, we hear it hooting and calling in the distance as it goes, as though to exorcise ghosts, as though to announce itself, as though to give itself courage to face that lonely dark journey into Africa.

* * *

Back at Azad's house, we sit on the cold slippery plastic chairs, with Omar, smoking endless foul-tasting cigarettes.

Omar is still upset and shaken at the blackmail threat to his wife, and talks without conviction about going back to South Africa. Maulvi has suggested we walk back through the location to the refugee house, and spend the rest of the night there. But I am terrified at the thought of that long walk through the pitch-dark location. Maulvi says he is going outside to 'scout around'.

All these years I have known him, and never thought of him

as a particularly brave man. His manner of speech would give the impression that he is a nervous sort of person. True, he participated in the big passive resistance and defiance campaigns in the past, and also deliberately courted imprisonment in protest against unjust laws. But that was with others. We were all bold when we drew strength from the whole group, we were all fearless when we were united and together. Tonight Maulvi is by himself, and courageous by himself, he walks calmly out into the unlit streets of Lobatsi to see if it safe for us, and to find a place where we can spend what is left of this ruined night.

As he turns the corner he hears a car coming up behind him — a car at this time of night in Lobatsi can only mean some sort of trouble. 'Maulvi, Maulvi!' It is Sheppard. What is Sheppard doing there in the early hours of Sunday morning? 'Do you happen to know where the Bernsteins are?' he asks. Sheppard evidently has information that we did not board the train.

Maulvi tells Sheppard that we are still in Lobatsi; he says he wants a report from us in the morning. Maulvi has also found a room for us in an Indian house next to the Lobatsi Hotel. We take a few blankets out of Azad's shop, and spend the rest of the night huddled on divans, fully dressed under the blankets.

* * *

The problem, next day, is: how to get to Palapye in time to catch the plane. We have no way to cancel the plane. It is Sunday, the ANC office in Lusaka will be closed, but in any case they have no telephone and we do not even know their address, only a post office box number. There is no way of communicating with them to get them to postpone its departure.

In all Lobatsi there is no car or truck for hire; the truck Fish has borrowed from time to time is not capable of a journey of more than a few miles. There are private individuals with cars and trucks — Azad's truck is a new one — but everyone is afraid of the consequences if they help us to get out of Bechuanaland. When we have gone, they must stay, three miles from the Republic of South Africa, entirely dependent upon it for everything, their trade, their occupations, their supplies, needing too to cross the border from time to time to Mafeking or

303

Johannesburg. They would like to help us, but are afraid. Isn't it possible for us to get a lift in one of the Bechuana police vans, we ask Sheppard. No, it is not possible. Through Maulvi, we have approached all the Indians in Lobatsi who might help.

There is, for example, Haffajee. He is light-complexioned, with a boyish face and a slight stutter. 'I would take you, indeed it would be a pleasure, but you see, my clutch, something is wrong with the clutch of my car ...'

'It's a new car,' Maulvi intervenes sternly.

'Yes, but just the same the clutch is slipping. You know what the road is like, there is so much sand on the road. If there wasn't so much sand, if the road wasn't so bad, or if I could rely on my clutch — otherwise I'd take you, with pleasure, it would be a pleasure ... but I can't risk it on that road when the clutch ... '

We spend Sunday in the house where we lodged for part of the night. Our Indian hosts feed us and with great courtesy provide us with towels to wash and chairs to sit on the veranda in the sun. Their silent, sullen women serve the meals that we eat with the men, clear the tables, disappear into kitchens and back rooms. They disapprove of us — why shouldn't they? — they know that we can only bring trouble.

A long morning of fruitless discussion and waiting. At lunchtime, as we sit down to eat, a tall young white man walks into the house; he wears overalls and asks: 'Who wants a lift to Palapye?' We eye him suspiciously. He has a strong South African accent.

'Why do you want to know?'

'I have a truck,' he explains. 'I can take you to Palapye.'

We dare not accept this offer. He talks to us for a while, tells us he also hopped over the border to avoid arrest. We are suspicious for this is a typical Afrikaner, the man-in-the-street kind: solidly, one hundred per cent, behind the apartheid State. We question him, probing. The story that comes out is plausible enough, and probably true. He had an affair with a 'Coloured' girl — a breach of the Immorality Act — was wanted by the police, fled, returned later to South Africa to be arrested and sentenced to four months' imprisonment. He came back to Bechuanaland on his release, legally with a passport, to marry his girl and settle here.

304

Perhaps it is true — perhaps a trick. We simply cannot afford to take a chance, so we turn his offer down.

In the late afternoon, when there is not a single possibility that remains, I suddenly make up my mind. 'I am going to ask Azad to lend us his truck.' Azad is a friend; he has been kind and hospitable to us and to Omar, but he has not offered us his truck. Every single item that he sells in his shop comes from South Africa. He has helped other refugees; we are different. The notoriety of the Rivonia trial and the association with Nelson Mandela has placed us in a special category. I hate to force him into a position where he must refuse — which he will not like — or agree which will do him no good; but we are desperate.

We walk down to Azad's place and standing in the yard I ask him, 'Will you lend us your truck to go to Palapye?' He turns to Maulvi, discusses it with him for a moment, then he agrees.

We now make our final arrangements. Fish will come with us to drive the truck back. If there is an extra seat in the plane, Omar will fly out with us. Fish is also arranging additional men to travel with us as bodyguards. We will leave at about eleven at night.

Once more we go down to the refugee house, where it is quiet. The women are out walking, and we lie down and try to rest for a while. I feel almost joyful. With Fish and his friends, fear is dispelled, confidence returns.

Later in the evening Omar brings Azad's truck, and some time after eleven we say goodbye to Dan and Maulvi and the women and leave, armed with crowbars.

We drive on through the night. There are no lights behind us, no other traffic on the road. Dust, clouds of red dust. Twisted white thorn bushes and distorted dead trees illuminated by the headlights of the truck on either side of the road. Hour after hour these shapes like apparitions appear against the deep black darkness, writhe towards us and vanish again, to be replaced with more, and more and more. This empty world, devoid of life, just dust, semi-desert, the white-lit bushes, and darkness again.

The road is rough, but not too rough, in a better condition than we expected. Rusty, Omar and Fish take turns to drive. In the front we sing; we sing for miles and miles, for hours.

Sometimes we sing freedom songs, and sometimes I sing endless verses of English folk songs. Songs and dust in the night on the road to Palapye.

At half-past three in the morning we stop. We have made good time — too good; we don't want to arrive in Palapye before dawn. We gather dry wood from the road verge and light a fire, a great red blaze in the heart of Bechuanaland. It is like being alone on a planet in space, suspended in a dark universe without beginning or end. The fire is our signature of identity, while we feed it with dead wood, while it crackles and flares, we exist. We exist only within the circle of its light; beyond that, there is nothing.

We drive on. I am sleepy, but doze only briefly, jerking up again and again to watch the unfolding road. It is like so many long car trips in the past, when we drove through the night from Johannesburg to the Cape, singing, and counting the brilliant falling stars, and getting sleepy, and watching the never-ending road.

The sky reddens and lightens. At about six in the morning we approach Palapye. Mud huts with thatch roofs set within circles of twisted branches of thorn trees, protection against leopards or lions. The village is just waking, letting the cattle out of kraals in what must be the very centre of Palapye.

An outpost of the Empire. We drive to the dusty compound where the Union Jack flies from the single-storey buildings; the police station. Early morning sweepers are at work in the station compound. They are dressed in khaki uniforms, wearing broad-brimmed hats turned up at one side. They tow two dry branches along and, walking up and down the compound, draw the branches behind them, leaving straight trails in the thick red sand: lines drawn in the dust every morning before the white man arrives. The wind of Bechuanaland, the ubiquitous never-ceasing wind, obliterates the twig-trails before the sweepers have cleared the last corner of the compound.

We have to report to the officer in charge, a man named Dennis who is unpleasantly abrupt. At least Sheppard was invariably polite, even though his 'Good-oh' didn't do us much good. Dennis has been expecting us, he knows about the plane, but as yet he has no news of it.

306

We must wait.

This dusty space with a few one-storey brick and *pise-de-terre* buildings with corrugated-iron roofs, a thin tree or two, people standing in groups waiting around or squatting beneath the dried and leafless branches; this area without pattern or order or design, without defined roads or pavements, is in effect the town centre of Palapye.

Now the sun is high. The wind still blows, swirling the ochre dust, but the sun is hot. Fish has taken the truck to go and find some friends of his. We move around, finding places out of the wind, in the sun. Later, when Fish brings the truck back, I sit in front and try to read, while Omar and Rusty sleep at the back. We have had nothing but water to drink and no rest for two nights, but I cannot sleep. I am too tired to sleep.

Dennis has been told that the plane is on its way, and should be arriving later on in the morning. I sit listening, listening, trying to hear the sound of a plane, dreaming and waiting for the sound of a plane, but it does not come. The hours drift slowly by. We wait. The wind blows and blows.

Then it is long past midday. Dennis says there is no further news of the plane, but he thinks we should drive out to the airport and wait there.

Dennis believes in the plane, Rusty and Omar and Fish believe in the plane, but I do not believe in its existence. I do not tell them this, but there is no plane; it is a fantasy, an illusion. The sky will remain pale and empty, the air will be disturbed only by the unending wind, the plane will not come. I am heavy and sullen and still with this special knowledge.

But we drive out to what Dennis calls the airport. It is an empty field with a windsock, and to get there Fish cheerfully drives us through dongas and across the veld, brushing between cattle and breaking through bushes. Dennis arrives in a car by a more circular, but better, route, and there is a truck with African police.

They all listen for the plane. We stand in our separate groups, Dennis with his companion; the Bechuana police in another group; Rusty with Fish and his companions. The Bechuana police watch us as though mesmerized. There is no motive behind this regard, it is the reaction of Africans accustomed only to patronage or paternalism from the white man, seeing for the first time a friendly and equal relationship.

But I go back to the cab of the truck, to get out of the insistent and tiring wind, and to avoid the compulsion of listening for the nonexistent plane.

So another hour passes as though in a dream. The wind blows, the sun shines hotly, there is nothing to be seen, blank open sky, blank open earth, a pale, wind-driven empty world; until at last there is a change of posture in the men standing in the field — I cannot hear what they are saying, but even from their backs I can see they are listening intently. I climb down from the truck and I, too, hear the suggestion of a distant hum which fades and recedes, and at the moment it seems like imagination, reappears more steadily, more clearly. Small high, far off, it is less a metallic challenge to space than an acceptance; it appears almost to twirl and drift, like a leaf.

It is a tiny red and white plane that circles the airfield to come downwind; a fair-haired boy, looking about nineteen, steps out and walks towards us.

This, then, is the last link in that chain — the pipeline? — or underground route? This youth, who does not even know the names of the passengers he has come to collect, is also a part of it. Behind him stands the woman in the lonely kraal, limping across the sharp dead land to fetch water to bathe my feet, haranguing and haranguing the indifferent men into action. Eva, creaking on her camp-bed and bringing me bitter lemon to drink in the bath; McClipper driving along dangerous roads; the friends who concealed me and transported me; Dan and Maulvi, Omar and Fish; the ones who carried messages and notes; all who helped, whatever their motive; it is as though we have been passed from hand to hand, strangers and friends. All, all were links without whom the chain would have broken.

Now I see why I did not, in the end, believe in the existence of the plane. The plane is their success, it is our failure. The plane breaks the last contact and withdraws us finally from that world of endeavour which henceforth we will touch only peripherally.

There is no room for Omar. He will go back to Lobatsi and

come later, and by another route. We thank them for all they have done, we say goodbye and climb into the plane.

As we bump across the field, they raise their fists and cry, '*Amandla! Amandla!*' and we too raise arms and shout, '*Ngawethu! Afrika — Mayibuye!*'

Our voices are subjugated by the noise of the plane, dispersed by the force of the wind. We see them standing there with upraised arms, diminishing in size as we rise higher and higher, as our plane trembles against the wind and space; until they are scarcely marks on that boundless land, and we are alone with the never-ceasing wind and the white-hot blaze of the African sky.